Reaching for the Sky

Reaching for the Sky

Empowering Girls
through Education

Urvashi Sahni

BROOKINGS INSTITUTION PRESS
Washington, D.C.

The Brookings Institution is a private nonprofit organization devoted to research, education, and publication on important issues of domestic and foreign policy. Its principal purpose is to bring the highest quality independent research and analysis to bear on current and emerging policy problems. Interpretations or conclusions in Brookings publications should be understood to be solely those of the authors.

Library of Congress Cataloging-in-Publication data are available.
ISBN 9-780-8157-3038-5 (pbk : alk. paper)
ISBN 9-780-8157-3039-2 (ebook)

9 8 7 6 5 4 3 2 1

Typeset in Garamond

Composition by Westchester Publishing Services

To the struggles and smiles of daughters everywhere in the world

Contents

Foreword

Joyce Banda
Former President of the Republic of Malawi

It was in 1987 that I first started advocating for women's empowerment and rights. This was after I had walked out of an abusive marriage. At a time when women did not and could not walk out of an abusive situation, I had found the courage to do so. When I rebuilt my life and confidence, when I had my own business and financial security, and a meaningful life for myself and my children, I looked back and wondered about those women who didn't have the courage to do what I did. It was then that I started the National Association of Business Women to promote women's economic independence and equality in the household.

Urvashi, like me, also started her work as a women's rights activist in the late eighties in India, driven to action following her cousin's death. As a young woman, she had tried to fight and negotiate the gendered cultural limitations forced upon her. Later in life, however, she came to her much-valued realization that being a woman was about "being an equal person, [and] having equal rights in society." Many years later, as an educator, Urvashi now teaches this important lesson to her students at the Prerna School, which she established for the empowerment of the poorest and most vulnerable girls who are denied education and wholesome childhoods due to poverty, abuse, and neglect.

This mission is one I deeply admire as it highlights our shared belief in the value of holistic and rights-centered education of the girl child. In 1997, after receiving the Africa Prize for Leadership for Sustainable End of Hunger, I decided to leverage that recognition to improve girls' education in my country by establishing two primary schools and one secondary school. Rights education is the binding principle of the schools' curricula: teach the girl child, so that she is aware of her rights from an early age. Not only does this benefit her academically, but also empowers her later in life.

Urvashi takes the idea of rights education still further in her practice at the Prerna School and advocates for a Critical Feminist Education for girls early on, so that the girls reflect on their circumstances, understand the social and political structures that frame their lives, and learn to resist those structures. She demonstrates how a school can construct all teaching and learning efforts to ensure that when a girl finishes school, she has "a perception of herself as an equal autonomous person deserving respect and having equal rights"—which is one of the key objectives of the Prerna School.

This book's unique strength lies in the way Urvashi unpacks the problem of girls' education and rights, by integrating the voices of the girls and teachers with her own voice. As the girls narrate their stories, we learn about their everyday struggles of living in extreme poverty in a gendered world, and we are reminded of the many obstacles they face as they try to survive their realities. The book then leads us to see a hopeful solution in the education model of Prerna: reflections from teacher, girls, and their parents shed light on the tools and interventions that have empowered many girls to rewrite their life narratives.

Affirming the complexity in providing a meaningful education to girls in poor and patriarchal societies, this book recognizes that schools and teachers need to do many things to succeed: paramount is taking a whole-of-girlhood approach. This means looking at girls' lives as a whole, and responding holistically to their many needs—be they social, emotional, or physical. A school must not only build up her aspirations, but also provide her with the tools and necessary skills to fulfill them.

One lesson that I never fail to teach girls in my school is to have a mission in life and to state it at a young age. Prerna School offers guidance on how such practices ought to be formalized in schools: the girl child states her aspirations, and it filters through her parents, as they engage with her stories from school about having a mission in life. Such dissemination of ideas toward parents is critical for building vested interest in their girl child's education. This is what I call building the demand side of girls' education and empowerment.

We need to mobilize families and communities to promote mindset and behavioral changes toward girls and women. Here, schools and teachers have a meaningful opportunity to be a driving force for change at the household level because they are respected by the community. If, for instance, teachers assume leadership and work with mothers and women in the community to form strong networks to support women, the ultimate benefit will be to girls. In this framing, Urvashi also draws our attention to how empowered girls themselves go on to advocate for their mothers and other women in their communities.

For a daunting and complex task, Prerna shows it is possible and doable. Girls' education lives up to its full promise only when schools, educators, and communities aim to truly transform girls' lives by empowering them with voice, agency, and a recognition of their own worth as equal persons.

I do believe, truly, that our continents and countries, are going to change for the better if we, who come from these societies, take the lead and inspire the global community toward action. Urvashi is setting a brilliant and ambitious example, and it is my honor to write this foreword as a testament and ode of inspiration.

Preface

This book tells the story of how one small school in India kept girls in school and made sure they graduated. The students faced all the challenges that poor girls face in any country, with conditions and compulsions at home that were not supportive of learning, thus putting them at great risk of being pulled out of school. If their mothers' lives and the condition of their own lives at home were any indication, one could not have predicted the trajectory their life journeys would ultimately take. It also tells the story of how this happened from the perspective of the girls and their teachers. Books or discussions about education are seldom told from this important perspective.

In the pages that follow, I look at the school, Prerna, closely, at the key actors—the teachers, the students, their parents—and present their perspectives, along with mine as founder of the school. Most important, I describe the school from the lens of the students, especially six girls—Laxmi, Aarti, Khushboo, Sunita, Kunti, and Preeti—who studied in Prerna for over six years and graduated a few years ago, focusing on what the school and the education, the teaching and learning in the school, meant to them and why. Though ideally schools should be for students, their lives and their voices are often invisible and inaudible components of discussions about schools and education. In such discussions, goals, processes, pedagogies, curricula, achievement scores, assessments, attendance, retention, and various policies are all described in detail, but we never hear from the students about what this means to them and does or does not do for them or for their lives. We seldom get a sense of their lives at home, the challenges presented by their lives, the specific needs that arise, or whether the education they get meets their needs.

In this book, the students tell us ways in which they felt supported by the school to make their lives better, and how the school worked with them so they stayed in school and completed their education. How did their education enable and empower them to change their lives? How did they experience school? How did the school impact them? What was the curriculum like? What was the pedagogy like? What were their teachers like? What role did they play? How did the teachers perceive their own roles? How was the school structured? What ideologies and philosophies undergird and define teaching and learning in the school? This book also looks at the parents, especially the mothers, and brings in their voices and concerns as we listen to the challenges they face in their communities regarding their daughters and the place of education in their lives, and how the school helped them educate their daughters.

Most of the discourse and research about girls' education, its challenges and solutions, is done from a 1000-miles-in-the-air perspective. Most such discussions, viewed from a societal, country level, or the global macro perspective of policymakers, researchers, and academics, are reduced to enrollment, retention, dropout, and completion numbers. The challenges are restricted to "societal factors" and "school factors." The tone and substance of the conversation is abstract, distant, and impersonal. While the macro perspective provides useful information, locating problems and solutions in larger social and economic structures, showing also the magnitude of the problem, pointing out the crying need for redress and solutions, such discussions are inadequate. They are not peopled by girls' lives or their voices speaking of the conditions at home, in society, and in school, telling us what they need, what helps them, and what makes their lives better. Girls' lives are lost in this discourse, even though the discussions are supposedly about them. The discussions take an instrumental approach, describing the effect of girls' education on the country's progress, on economic and social development, on maternal mortality, on the education of their children. It is not apparent from these discussions that there is a concern for a girl's right to her own life, to a full human existence, and a willingness to see education as a pathway to that goal.[1]

This study offers a close look at girls' lives as described by the girls themselves. Girls call attention to their lives—at home, in society, and in school. They speak to us of their struggles, tell us what they need to make their lives better, tell us what a particular kind of education has meant to them, how it changed their lives, what worked for them in their education and what didn't. I hope their voices will enliven the discussions and debates around girls' education and take them in useful directions.

Though this is one case, illustrated by a relatively small number of girls, their experience counts. Their lives are uniquely their own, situated in a particular set of circumstances and in a particular geography. Far from trying to resurrect the "racialized, classed and geographically specific trope of the 'Third World girl,'"[2] this book attempts to situate the discussion on girls' education in these girls' lives, which, though unique, share many elements with the lives of girls in other countries where patriarchal structures and norms prevail. Kunti, one of the focal students, said, when I asked her why she was willing to share her personal story:

> People should know about all the things that are happening in our society, how we deal with them. Our learnings, whatever we have learned here, should go to others also.

Her friend Khushboo added:

> So like, I am empowered, I want that [for other girls]. However far my voice can go, if there is any girl, anywhere, who wants to speak up, raise her voice, by hearing my story she can learn that she can also change her life, like I did, and go forward.

The students featured in this book want the audience to read their stories as triumphant tales of resistance, resilience, and empowerment, which might inspire other girls like them. Aarti expressed her hope that:

> Others learn from our stories, they can be inspired—that "even after going through so much this girl is still standing, she has overcome, because of her education. If she can fight her circumstances, then why can't I?"

The story of Prerna School demonstrates a serious and clear possibility of how a school can change girls' lives. The stories in this book give detailed descriptions of the complex, multiple ways in which teaching and learning are played out in the ground reality of classrooms. It shows both the complexity and the simplicity of the task ahead, by weaving together the lives and voices of girls, their teachers, and their parents and situating these in the context of the intricate social political processes of a school space.

Girls' education has received a great deal of attention from the global development and academic communities, with the spotlight on programs that work.[3] Even so, still there is not enough research giving a close ethnographic description and analysis of education—and more particularly, schooling as it is practiced in the daily reality of classroom life—revealing its in-process, inter-personal, inter-contextual, inter-structural complexity, to deepen our understanding of school success and failure. What is the role of the school in the girls' lives? That is, what is its structure—its social and political ideology, curriculum, pedagogical processes? What is the culture of the school, its ethic and practice? And most important, how do the girls experience school? This book attempts to fill this gap.

Education, especially for girls living in poverty in countries like India, is an extremely complex undertaking; it requires a multi-perspective approach to be understood and addressed effectively. Macro and micro perspectives both are necessary, especially of those who are most affected by the issues and problems. Large social problems are played out in the mundaneness of daily life. Political and social structures, the explicit and implicit ideology that governs them, impact people as they live their daily lives. As we get closer to real lives, we better understand complex concepts of power, hegemony, difference, and equality. Structural understandings must emerge from within structures, by understanding people as they grapple with structures, as we all—myself, teachers, and students—did, and learn how to make sense of them and how to act within and upon them. The problems of gender equality and girls' education as a pathway are enormous, and their enormity tends to overwhelm, leaving many of us feeling helpless. Perhaps looking closely at a specific example and real lives might show helpful directions and solutions with greater implications.

Putting the Story Together

In putting this story together, I have distilled the struggles and experience of our 14-year work with Prerna, the lessons learned and the ones we are still learning. In collecting data and constructing this story, which also can be considered a case study, I have adopted a mixed-methods and multi-perspective approach. My goal is to illustrate how the multiple actors in the school understand, define, and implement an education for empowerment, what learning and life outcomes are enabled by the school, and what directions and insights can be derived from Prerna's experience.

My research assistants and I collected quantitative and qualitative data over 12 months. The qualitative data include a retrospective account of the history, vision, and theoretical underpinnings of the school from my reflections as the founder-director and those of the principal and some of the teachers who have been there since the inception. The goal was to describe how the school defines learning and determines its educational goals, along with the justification based on the theory of change. I have constructed the perspectives of all the stakeholders—the teachers, parents, and students, some current but mostly alumnae—from semi-structured interviews, focus group discussions (FGD), and questionnaires.[4] The quotations of students and teachers throughout the book came from these interviews, focus sessions, and questionnaires. I hope this story will resonate as much with their voices as mine. I have used the data from teacher and principal interviews to understand how they perceive their students and their relationships with them and how they define their own roles and responsibilities in the classroom.

I interviewed six focal students intensively and had many focus group discussions with larger groups, including some girls we did not succeed in keeping in school but who returned later, all of whom participated enthusiastically. There were many more girls I could have chosen, and they were willing to tell their stories, but I chose Laxmi and the other five girls because they were among the first students to join the school and because they are articulate about their experiences. I chose them also because their lives were among the more seriously challenged, though Rakhee, the principal, said to me: "There are so many Laxmis in the school." The narrative is populated by the voices of many other students as well, thus widening the student perspective.[5]

I have tried to weave all those narratives together, borrowing theoretical frameworks and ideas from thinkers and scholars like bell hooks, Paulo Freire, Gerda Lerner, Kamla Bhasin, Ritu Menon, Vina Mazumdar, Nivedita Menon, Nelly Stromquist, Nel Noddings, Audre Lorde, Arjun Appadurai, Edward Bond, John Dewey, Charles Taylor, Kathleen Gallagher, Anne Dyson, Glynda Hull, and many others. I was inspired by these thinkers, as was the approach Prerna continues to iterate, but my interpretation of their theories and feminist practices was ultimately grounded in and shaped by the local cultural and political realities in which my students and I are embedded. There is room for critique of the assemblage of concepts presented in this book, but I, and Prerna, are guided by the proximities of practice and, thus, see theory as useful insofar as it can help inform this practice.

I am conscious that my combined position as the director of the school and researcher for this book, further complicated by my caste and class position relative to the students, carries risks: first, of influencing the interviewee responses, given my position of power relative to the students, and also of influencing the objectivity of the narrative, and second, of my being interested in presenting the school in a positive light. I recognize these biases as well as my influence as the participant researcher, teacher, and director. However, the participatory nature of the research also included the students and teachers, allowing all of us at Prerna to see this book as an opportunity for a self-reflective, critical examination of our school, which we all still see as a work in progress. As for the interview responses, the teachers, students, and I have worked together for several years, in some cases more than a decade. There is a fair degree of mutual comfort arrived at over a long period of working together, which I hope has diffused much of the power distance created by my official position. These interviews are not the only time we have had conversations about our lives, Prerna, its goals, and our practices. Our interviews often turned into critical dialogues as we began discussing the issues that arose. Even for the purpose of this book, the interviews spanned several conversations, formal and informal, making it possible to cross-check the responses for accuracy and to look for the subtext and hidden responses.

Taken together, it is my hope that the voices of the girls and others associated with Prerna will support a central argument that education, to be truly transformative, must be grounded in the reality of students' lives and must respond to their special needs and challenges with respect and care.

Acknowledgments

There are many people who have made this book possible, and I would like to thank them all. First, I am immensely grateful to my students and teachers at Prerna, for trusting me with their stories, for reflecting on their lives with me—even if that meant reliving the painful experiences of the past—and for having the courage to share their stories with the world. This book would not have been possible without the trust, willing cooperation, and work of the Prerna staff, students, alumnae, and their parents, especially their mothers, and I thank them all for their participation and for lending me their voices.

I would like to thank my research assistants, Anshu Jain and Samarth Shukla, for their tireless efforts in helping me throughout the journey of this book. When I was flagging toward the end, Anshu kept soldiering on, giving a close reading to the manuscript several times, making sure I did not miss important details, for which I am very grateful. Their assistance has been invaluable. I thank Moni Kannaujiya and Anand Chitravanshi for the photographs and the videos included in the book.

I thank Echidna Giving and the Center for Universal Education at Brookings Institution for awarding me the Echidna Global Scholars Fellowship in 2012. This gave me the time and space to write the book's first draft, in the form of the research paper, while I was at Brookings.

I am grateful to Rebecca Winthrop, particularly for her faith in my work and her encouragement to share it widely. I want to particularly thank

Christina Kwauk for her patient reading and re-reading of the manuscript and her help in shaping the book with valuable suggestions and edits. I am grateful to John Felton and Janet Walker from the Brookings Institution Press, whose editing made the book much more readable. I am also thankful to my peer reviewers for their critical feedback, which helped reinforce the arguments I present. And there were many anonymous friends and family who helped me by reading chapters and giving valuable feedback, which has certainly strengthened the book. I thank them all.

I would be remiss if I failed to thank the Rockefeller Foundation for awarding me the residency at their Bellagio Center in May 2015. It gave me the time and space to begin writing the book in dead earnest. In addition, I gratefully acknowledge the support provided by the John D. and Catherine T. MacArthur Foundation and the government of Norway, without which the publication of this book would not have been possible.

Finally, I thank the Brookings Institution Press on behalf of the Prerna family for helping to share our work with a wide audience by making this book a reality.

Reaching for the Sky

1

Letting Girls Learn

I come to school to learn, so that my life gets better!

—Laxmi, a Prerna alumna

Laxmi, a young Dalit woman, was born in Lucknow in 1992.[1] She lives, along with her father and four younger siblings, in a one-room house, a half-constructed, abandoned dwelling they moved into 15 years ago, when her mother was still alive.[2]

Laxmi is the third child in her family, although the first to survive. Her eldest brother, at 15 months, drowned in a pond at the construction site where her mother was working. A sister died at birth. Though Laxmi's father is a commercial painter, for several years he has worked only intermittently. Her late mother had been a construction worker, carrying bricks up steep scaffoldings on her head as part of her work. She was married at age 12 and gave birth to seven children in 23 years, dying at the age of 35 in 2005. Laxmi's father was 14 when he was married and did not attend school after fifth grade because he was required to graze his family's goats. Laxmi is now the eldest of five siblings, with one younger brother and three younger sisters. She was enrolled in a local school, which she attended irregularly, and dropped out after two to three years because her mother was sick and needed care, as did a baby sister, and because they were poor and had no money to pay her fees.

> My sister, Lalita, was born and then my mother had TB. She used to cough a lot in the night, and there was no one to take care of her. I would

Laxmi

wake up at night, massage her, put oil on her body; still she didn't recover. She was sick for months. I had to take care of her, and Radha was very small, so I stayed at home.

Laxmi had been working as a domestic helper since the age of seven, earning 1000 rupees per month (about $15), which went toward food for the family when her mother was not working. Laxmi's mother had a "uterus surgery" (likely, a hysterectomy) after her seventh child, but was compelled to go back to work at the construction site only three weeks later. The stitches ruptured, and 13-year-old Laxmi took her to the hospital, making several trips back and forth for the next few months.

I used to stay and take care of her, clean her. She vomited a lot and her back used to hurt unbearably. The doctor scolded me for not getting her treatment in time. Father wasn't bothered. He was drunk most of the time. Then we brought her home, but she started to get worse. Her breathing became very difficult. I got very scared and called all the neighbors. Mother's sister came and gave some leaves, saying she might get better. But nothing like that happened; she was taking her last breaths. I didn't know what to do, but I got an auto rickshaw and put her in it. I wanted to take her back to the hospital. But she died right there in my arms in the auto. I couldn't do anything. Then we were alone. There was no one who could take care of us. So I started working in more homes [seven in all]. Neighbors helped with food and milk for the baby. Lalita [eight-year-old sister] also started working in three homes. Father did nothing. In fact, he sold off the gas cylinder and everything we had for his drinks. He drank all the time and couldn't take care of us.

One year before her mother's death, Laxmi found out about Prerna from a friend who was enrolled there.

It had just opened, just one month before I heard about it. My friend told me about it. She told me that the fee is only 10 rupees per month and it is in the afternoon. So I thought, I can pay the fee and if it is in the afternoon, then I can finish my work in the morning, and go to study in the afternoon. It would get over by 5:30, so then I could go back to work in the evening again. So it was perfect. So I joined the school and then my education started again.

She described her day:

In the morning, I made breakfast at home and then left for work at 6. I would go at 6 and come back around noon. Then after bathing, would come to school at 1 o'clock. Then I would study and after that would go to work again from there at 6. It would be 9 to 9:30 by the time I would finish work there. And then I would cook. It would be 11 by the time I would sleep.

She and her younger sister Lalita, nine years old at the time, both enrolled in Prerna, while Radha, the five-year-old, cooked the afternoon meal and took care of the baby at home.

Laxmi is an alumna of Prerna, a school I founded in 2003 for girls with lives like hers, prompted by the belief that all girls should be given access to education. Today, Laxmi has finished her bachelor's degree.[3] She is working at a call center providing services to banks, where she has been recently promoted to head sales manager. She is currently earning 25,000 rupees ($374) per month. Her employers have also offered to pay for her MBA, and she has enrolled.

Her three sisters are enrolled in Prerna. Through all these years, she has never given up on her father, despite his neglect and abuse. With her encouragement, he has had some success in overcoming his drinking habit.

Laxmi feels strong. She says:

> My life is different from my mother's. I have controlled my life a lot, taken care of myself, wasn't married off. Now I might even go to Chennai for a job.

She attributes this change in her life to her education at Prerna, which she says enabled her "to make my life better." This book tells the story of Prerna, describing how it provided a safe and supportive environment so girls like Laxmi could stay, learn, grow, and become empowered to make their lives better.

Being a Girl

Laxmi's story, and those of her friends, presents a stark yet vivid picture of what it means to be poor and a girl in India. It also lends a face, flesh and blood, to the statistics about the condition of the lives of millions of girls globally, and particularly in India. According to a survey conducted in 2007, when Indian girls from all castes and social classes were asked if they liked being girls, 48.4 percent said they didn't want to be girls.[4] As we look at Laxmi and her mother's lives, it is not difficult to see why. India's daughters, like millions of girls around the world, rich or poor, Dalit or Savarna, are unwanted, unequal, and unsafe at home and on the street.[5] According to some estimates, approximately 25 million girls worldwide and one million girls in India are killed before birth as a result of sex selective abortions.[6] Furthermore in India girls between one and five years of age are more likely to die than boys the same age because of poor nutrition, female infanticide, and sheer neglect.[7] Plan International's urban program found that, in Delhi, 96 percent of adolescent girls do not feel safe in the city.[8] Crime reports say that, nationally, 848 women are sexually harassed, raped, or killed every day.[9]

Laxmi and her mother's story corroborate the shameful statistics reported in every account on the status of girls and women around the world. Unvalued, uncared for, victims of neglect and violence, girls and their mothers have lives that are precarious, circumscribed, unfree, and hard. Fathers and husbands exercise enormous, almost absolute, control over the minds and bodies of these girls and women. Laxmi's mother had no control over the number of children she produced. Despite the fact that her husband defaulted on his responsibility as provider for the family, his traditional role in a patriarchal family which meant she and seven-year-old Laxmi had to take on that responsibility, she continued to suffer his abusive, drunken behavior. According to her world view, she belonged to her husband and he had every right to do what he wished with her. This is a story many of our students tell of their families and homes.

Whereas the intention is not to demonize male figures, fathers, and husbands in Indian society, I do not attempt to hide the truth as told by the girls. The statistics relating to gender-based violence—both domestic and street violence in India—support the girls' testimony. This book takes a clear look at gender relations and reveals the shameful legacies of patriarchy.

Barriers to Education

Girls in India and everywhere, especially when they are poor, face several societal and school-specific barriers to education just because they are girls.

Child Marriage, Girl Slavery

Early marriage contributes significantly to the curtailment of Indian girls' lives. Laxmi's mother was married at 12; her friend Preeti's mother was married at 13, Sunita's mother at 13, and Kunti's at 15. Laxmi's father and family were ready to marry her off at 14, when she was in grade 8.

> He had started from grade 8 only, forcing me because I was growing up, so people who live around [were pressuring him]. Basically it's society only which forces us to get married [by commenting that] the girl is getting mature, she should be married, she might go wrong. So he would listen to others and tell me to stop studying and get married. That's what people would say at home; don't study and get married.

Of the 15 million child brides in the world, more than one-third are in India.[10] Child marriage rates in India are the second highest in the world, with Bangladesh topping the list. Of Indian women aged 20 to 24, 47.5 percent were married by age 18, and of these 16 percent start bearing children soon after marriage.[11] Given that child marriages are arranged by parents without the consent of the children—in effect, girls are given into physical, economic, psychological, and sexual bondage—it would be more appropriate to describe child brides as *girl slaves* and child marriage as *girl slavery* rather than dignifying their status with the term *brides*. Statistics report that child brides (that is, girl slaves) are more likely to be abused sexually and physically than unmarried girls. For most girls the world over, child marriage means the end of education and the beginning of childbearing. "There is no more abrupt end to childhood than marriage or becoming a mother."[12]

Poverty and Gender
Laxmi's story illustrates how education for daughters is low on the value scale for poor families. Her mother, like 60 percent of the mothers in our school, was illiterate. As with Laxmi, many of the girls enrolled in primary schools are pulled out as soon as a need arises, for all the reasons that research tells us girls in poverty are pulled out: family health issues, burden of domestic work, sibling care, and working outside the home to supplement the family income. Laxmi and her friends Preeti and Khushboo were pulled out to take care of younger siblings because their mothers needed help and were themselves suffering ill health due to repeated pregnancies and overwork at home and outside. The burden of housework and childcare is firmly and squarely laid on the shoulders of girls as young as five years of age, like Laxmi's younger sister Radha, and girls begin to work outside the home to help their mothers sustain their families as early as seven years of age, as did Laxmi and her sister Lalita. No money could be spared for their education, nor could the family find the time, or perceive the need, to send them to school. Laxmi was enrolled in school, but it does not seem her previous school did anything to stop her from being pulled out. It is likely that, in Laxmi's case, the school pushed her out because she could not pay the tuition fee. So though Laxmi was enrolled and would count as "enrolled" in a survey meant to determine girls' enrollment in primary school, the fact that she was pulled out before she completed grade 3 would negate the enrollment, lending weight to the Plan International argument that "enrollment is an inherently flawed measure of access."[13]

The stories of Laxmi and her friends in the pages to follow give a closer look at their lives and clearly show the barriers to education for girls from poor families in India and elsewhere. Girls live their lives in a grim, complex context where gender, poverty, and caste intersect.[14] The consequences of patriarchy are evident. The girls and their mothers regularly face violence at home. Girls are prey to forced marriages at very young ages because families can see no other way to secure their livelihoods; also, marriage presents a means to maintain girls' chastity and caste purity. Many of the girls are inducted into child labor in their family's struggle against poverty.

Drop Out or Push Out

Laxmi and several of her friends tell us that until they came to Prerna, their previous schools did nothing to keep them in. The schools not only took no measures to stop them from being pulled out, they often actively pushed them out with their insensitivity to the students' circumstances. Schools push girls out when girls experience the school environment as unsafe and unfriendly and when they fail to provide the support that first-generation learners need. Often teachers convey their own low expectations and low value of education for girls, because they, too, believe the destiny of girls, especially poor girls, involves marriage, motherhood, and domestic or physical labor.

Laxmi and her friends illustrate the concern in India and worldwide that even when girls come to school, many of them don't stay very long and, therefore, don't learn very much.[15] They exemplify what global discourse is beginning to realize: providing access to education to girls isn't good enough. As a result of a concerted effort by national governments, international agencies, nongovernmental organizations (NGO), and other community and institutional actors, great strides have been made in granting girls access to primary education. The number of girls not attending primary school has been cut almost in half, though even today 62 million girls worldwide do not attend primary and lower-secondary school.[16] The focus has now shifted to retention, completion of secondary education, and quality learning. So, not only should girls come to school; they must stay and complete, and they must learn.

As Gene Sperling, Rebecca Winthrop, and Christina Kwauk write: "The story of girls' education in 2015 . . . is still a story of both immense progress and a still-devastating crisis."[17] They make the important point that though great strides have been made in primary school enrollment of girls, a major challenge in girls' education is "ensuring that they complete school."[18] In the future, these authors say, "the goal for girls' education can be nothing less than a high-quality secondary education."[19]

The Promise of Girls' Education

The discourse around girls' education is especially charged at this moment, globally and in India. The world has finally come to the conclusion that developmental promise cannot be fulfilled unless gender equality is focused upon seriously. Schooling for girls, especially completion of a high-quality secondary education, is now touted by experts as imperative and central to national development. Girls' education is considered a magic bullet for combating many of the most profound challenges to human development, promising many social and economic benefits.[20] However, the discourse around girls' education is still driven largely by the "efficiency" argument rather than a rights-based one. In other words, success in girls' education is measured in terms of gains for societies, families, and gross domestic product, and its value in training the world's future mothers rather than its intrinsic benefits for the girls themselves.

There are voices—for example, Malala Yousufzai, Graça Machel, and Julia Gillard—that counter the efficiency argument and reinforce the central contention of this book, that educating girls is important for the simple reason that it is a girl's right to be educated. Girls have the right to a fully human experience, and education is an important endowment that helps them achieve that. If educating girls resulted in nothing more than that, it would still be important because it is their right. Girls' rights are human rights! And girls have the right to a fully human life of their own choosing.

To bring this argument down to the case of a single person: Laxmi, of course, will make a better mother if she gets to complete her education. But what is more important is that she should have an education because she has a right to be educated so that *her own* life gets better, so that she achieves the full developmental potential of *her* life. Her life will get better if she is empowered by her education to recognize her rights as an equal person with human dignity, and if she is equipped by her education to fight for her rights when they are thwarted, if her education teaches her to recognize that she has a claim to a life of her own choosing, which includes being able to choose when or if she wants to marry and to choose to become a mother or not.

Education, Empowerment, and Gender Equality

A term used widely in recent international development discourse in close conjunction with girls' education and gender equality is *women's empowerment*. Education and empowerment are equated in the international development discourse as though they are necessarily related, leading to greater agency of women and, with that, an improvement in their own well-being and that of their children and society.[21] The development discourse also suggests that the promotion of gender equality and empowerment of women will result from the removal of gender disparity in primary and secondary education.[22] In 1986 the "National Policy on Education"—an important policy document for education in India—took a more enlightened view and brought the issue of gender and girls' education center stage.[23] While it linked education of women and girls to their empowerment, it went a step further and defined the goal of education broadly, stating that "education should be a transformative force, build women's self-confidence, improve their position in society and challenge inequalities."[24] This statement can be read as not taking for granted that education is necessarily a transformative force leading to women's empowerment; instead, it recommends that education should be such. This is a welcome and well-intentioned move, but it needs elaboration. It needed to go a step further and describe what such an empowerment-focused education would look like and recommend relevant changes in curricular content, pedagogical practices, institutionalized processes, and organizational structures.[25]

What Is Empowerment?

Empowerment is a much used, overused, misused, theorized, and re-theorized term.[26] In the 1970s the Women in Development movement associated empowerment with getting girls into school and giving them economic independence. From a gender and development perspective in the 1990s, empowerment includes recognizing and challenging gendered structures of inequality.[27] The World Bank defines empowerment in its broadest sense, as the "expansion of freedom of choice and action."[28] Asserting that gender empowerment is a process toward greater equality, or freedom of choice and action, Naila Kabeer defines empowerment as "the expansion in people's ability to make strategic life choices in a context where this ability was previously denied to them."[29] The idea of *agency* is an important element of becoming empowered, as people must be significant actors in the process of becoming empowered, not mere beneficiaries. Karen Oppenheim adds that women's empowerment involves knowledge of their rights to exercise choice and capabilities.[30] Arjun Appadurai defines empowerment in terms of developing a voice and a capacity to aspire.[31] Jo Rowlands's definition encompasses all of that, adding two more critical dimensions: a belief in self-worth, self-respect, and self-acceptance, which she calls "power within," and the ability to act with others to challenge discriminatory structures, which she calls "power with."[32] Yogendra B. Shakya and Katharine N. Rankin call this *subversive agency*, which is the capacity of resisting dominant structures and ideologies.[33] In India, the women's movement helped shape the definition of empowerment, defining it as being essentially about recognizing systemic and structural sexist oppression and then acting to change existing power relations.[34]

These definitions of empowerment all refer to adult women and their lived worlds, and have been criticized as distorting "girls' needs, circumstances and capabilities."[35] However, these concepts can be used along with the work of the few scholars and programs that have studied girls as subjects specifically and developed into a framework that addresses girls as well as adults.[36] Focusing specifically on schools' potential for enabling the empowerment of girls, I define empowerment as a process of developing a feminist consciousness, which involves gaining a critical understanding of one's social and political reality.[37] That means:

> ✧ Recognizing one's subordination and the underlying structural causes of it

> ✧ Recognizing oneself as an equal person deserving respect, with choice and agency

> ✧ Perceiving oneself as having the right to access the capabilities or skills needed to exercise choice and agency and act to overcome one's subordination and marginalization

If Laxmi and her friends are to have better lives, and if they are counting on an education, then it must empower them in these ways.

Empowerment and Education: Necessary Correlation?
I lend my voice to scholars who have questioned a necessary correlation between women's empowerment and education.[38] They point out that there is insufficient empirical analysis, particularly qualitative in nature, that supports this view. The *World Development Report 2012: Gender Equality and Development* cites evidence from around the world and reports that, despite narrowing of gender gaps in physical assets and human capital, when it comes to access to education, there still remain significant differences in the agency of boys and girls—and men and women—which results in differing life outcomes for men and women.[39]

Plan International cites the cases of both Latin America and the Middle East, where increased levels in female education have not led to corresponding equality in the workplace or at home. Girls and young women emerge from school still struggling with the idea that they are second-class citizens. The organization's 2012 *Because I Am a Girl* report states:

If girls are to play an equal part in society, once they finish their education, that education must be truly empowering and equip them with the capacity and determination to challenge the discrimination they will inevitably face.[40]

Thus, education does not necessarily lead to empowerment or gender equity—unless there is a focus on process, content, and curricula that critically addresses inequitable social norms and structures. In 2010 the United Nations Girls' Education Initiative, meeting in Dakar, emphasized the urgency of putting a "rights-based empowerment framework" at the center of all educational effort and making gender equity the "centre of transformative, quality education, supported by gender-responsive curricula and teacher training."[41]

An Empowering Education: Transforming Girls' Lives

Laxmi speaks of how education transformed her life:

And then I found Prerna; my first stage of change came from Prerna only. Because if Prerna wasn't there, I would not have been like this. Probably, I might also have got married early; just raised kids, like Mother, three to four kids and with a husband who drinks and beats me, gives no money. I don't know if I would have been alive or not.

Laxmi and her friends—Sunita, Aarti, Preeti, Khushboo, and Kunti—found Prerna. They returned to school because they discovered a school that was so inexpensive they could afford it and also because it was possible to fit it into the extremely demanding schedules of their difficult daily lives. The school welcomed them, even though they had been out of school for some years, or had never been schooled, and helped them make up for the time they had lost. Not just that; the school looked at their lives closely, tried to understand the many challenges they faced every day, and fought hard for them and alongside them to resist pressures to pull them out of school. As Laxmi said:

Like in Prerna, they don't focus on studies first; first they focus on children. Like, where have they come from, who are they, what kind of children are they, so what kind of education should they be given. It's not about just coming to school, studying, and going home like in other schools. But here, apart from studying . . . they ask what are our problems; they understand.

Everything about their education in Prerna—their teachers, the curriculum, the culture of the school, and the way it was organized and structured—was focused on helping them construct a sense of themselves as equal persons worthy of being respected by themselves, their communities, and others. Education enabled the girls to build a capacity to aspire, to take charge of their lives, and to flourish. Today, they are strong, empowered women, with a fair degree of control over their lives. They have been able to resist early marriage, are earning a living and supporting themselves and their families, hoping and planning to buy homes for themselves, and charting a path for their lives. Their school fought to keep them in and made sure they stayed and learned to read, write, and recognize themselves as equal persons with a right to determine the course of their own lives.

It seems that not only must girls come to school, stay, and complete educational studies, school must also help empower them with the knowledge that they have the right to use this education for their own purposes, that they are equal persons with choice and agency, aspirations, and a voice to speak up against discriminatory practices and social structures. This is the key lesson I learned from my ongoing work with Prerna and is the central argument I make in this book.

2

The Girls' Own Stories

We needed food, clothes, and Mother was neither educated nor did she have any money. There was no way of earning money in the village. I remember having only one dress, which I wore for months, wearing nothing when I washed it. My mother still wanted to send me to school.

—Sunita, a Prerna alumna

In this chapter I present the stories of Laxmi's friends: Aarti, Sunita, Khushboo, Preeti, and Kunti. Though the girls' stories are different in their details, they are similar in that they, along with their families, are all subject to the structural violence inherent in caste, poverty, and patriarchy. All are impacted by patriarchal misogyny, like millions of girls in India and elsewhere.

Much changed for the better in the girls' lives over the years in school, and they all have come a long way. Today they are all well on their way to becoming empowered women although still struggling with an overwhelmingly unequal power structure and social norms that disenfranchise and marginalize girls. They are, however, aware of the discrimination they face and are struggling consciously, with the will to succeed. The girls all attribute this change to their school education. In interviews and personal communications with me, they spoke fondly of Prerna, which they call the place that enabled them to change their lives.

Aarti

Aarti is an alumna of Prerna. She joined school in the sixth grade and graduated from high school in 2009. She is the first girl in her family and neighborhood to earn a bachelor's degree. Today she is studying for both a B.Ed. and a master's degree in public administration. She has resisted early marriage, has recently moved to a full-time position as a teacher at Prerna, and is working hard to build a career. Aarti has bought a small plot of land and is planning to secure a loan to start building. She talks about how her education has changed her:

> I used to think—that, so what if I study, I will still just be married off. Because eventually everyone just gets married off. Then here, I learned that marriage is not everything, that I can have a life of my own. I can become anything I want.

Savarna by birth, Aarti was born in a village in Bahraich in 1991. Her mother, married at 16, is illiterate and her father was schooled until the tenth grade. The eldest of five children, Aarti has two sisters and two brothers. Aarti's mother lived in a village with her children, and her father, living away in Lucknow, would come to visit from time to time. Her mother enrolled Aarti in the local village school where the teachers came on an irregular schedule. Aarti, however, attended regularly and finished fifth grade. There was no upper primary school in the village, and most girls stopped studying because they were not allowed to travel alone to the nearest upper primary school. It wasn't safe. She says:

> I started crying that I want to study more, so everyone said that no girl from our village goes out of the village to study. How will you go? So I couldn't go. My one year was wasted like this. Father used to live in Lucknow and then there were a lot of problems in the village, because Father wasn't around; nobody was there, no one was supporting us. Food was a problem; three to four days would pass and we wouldn't get any food. Mother was not allowed to go outside, would just stay under the purdah [the veil]. She wasn't even allowed to stand near the door. So, in this situation, when Father wasn't around, there would be wheat lying around, but unless someone took it for grinding, how would we eat?

Aarti

One day her mother fainted with hunger and illness. She told her husband it was impossible to live in the village like this. She would either go back to her parents or move to Lucknow with him. The father then took the family to Lucknow, where he worked with a doctor as a compounder. But housing for seven people was a problem. They found an abandoned room where they were allowed to stay during the day, having to move to the hospital at night, occupying any bed that was empty, sometimes even sleeping in the operation theater. "It was so scary," Aarti says.

It was under these circumstances that Aarti joined a low-end private school in grade 6. She found that she had not learned much in her village school, as she was way behind the class. The teachers did not help her catch up and would regularly beat her when she did poorly on tests. She was miserable and failed the first year. Humiliated and scolded at home for wasting scarce resources, she was pulled out. When friends told her about Prerna, her only question was, "Do they beat you in Prerna?" On being reassured that no one ever beats children there, she joined the school. She was admitted to sixth grade, helped to catch up, and promoted to seventh grade in just six months.

Aarti described the education in the schools she had attended before coming to Prerna:

We didn't even know how to take an exam. In fifth, we came to know that we would have an external board exam, so we were clueless. We didn't know. So they gave us answer sheets, made us sit inside the room, closed the doors, and gave us the guidebooks—and we didn't even know where the answers were, so we would go to teacher to ask them what the answer was. So they would tick the answer in the guidebook, tell us to copy from here to there, and we would write it. It was the same in Prasad school in Lucknow.

Meanwhile, her father had started drinking and beating the children and their mother regularly. She doesn't know why he changed from being a distant but fairly caring person to an abusive one, although she does blame alcohol and "bad company of other men" for it.

At times, he would smash her to the wall, holding her neck, and Mother wouldn't say anything. We were so small; we didn't know what to do. When we would hear his voice, we would hide under the bed. We were so scared of him.

Driven to despair by the repeated beatings and an insecure housing situation, which continued for nearly two years, her mother once threatened to poison all her children and herself so that it would end all their problems. It was under these circumstances that Aarti continued to come to Prerna and brought her two sisters with her. She remembers how she felt about her school:

In Prerna I felt like I belonged, like is it even possible that teachers can talk so nicely to students, care about them? I hadn't seen that in any other school, that you can go to your teacher and talk to them about your personal problems. It will be just about studies, but here discussing our lives was part of being in school.

Despite the grim conditions of her home life, Aarti stayed and completed. She feels she has changed because of her education:

First, the fear has gone. I think I am really smart [laughs self-consciously]. I think I can face any problem in the future. I can't stay silent if I feel something is wrong. I want to learn and grow. I can't stay at home now and do nothing. I want a career, a government job. I am preparing for that. . . . Like teachers used to say—girls should have an identity of their own, not only be someone's wife, daughter, or sister. So I learned to think like that about myself.

Sunita

Sunita graduated from Prerna in 2012, got her bachelor's degree in 2016, and is working for a master's degree. Today she feels unafraid and fully able to face the future. She says:

I still have to work very hard and learn a lot. But I know I will be able to do whatever I want. I can face all problems. I am not afraid now.

Sunita is a Savarna by birth, born in 1993 in a tribal region in Chhattisgarh. Sunita's mother is illiterate. Her father, a farmer with minimal schooling, married her mother when she was only 13. After Sunita and her sister Manisha were born, he abandoned them, leaving them defenseless in the village. Sunita finds it hard to remember his face. She remembers her parents fighting and her mother getting beaten. She also remembers living in extreme poverty:

We needed food, clothes, and Mother was neither educated nor did she have any money. There was no way of earning money. Mother used to labor in our family's fields, she would sell wood, cow-dung cakes, or just hire herself out as daily labor, but no one gave her any money. They would give us rice in return. Some of which we ate, and the rest we sold to buy other things. It was horrible! At times we had no food for days. I remember having only one dress, which I wore for months, wearing nothing when I washed it. My mother still wanted to send me to school, but what happens in that village is that they don't admit girls in school. So I never went to school there.

It became impossible to eke out a living in the village in Chhattisgarh. Her mother, guided by her older sister who lived in Lucknow, took the plunge, borrowed money at high interest for train tickets, and came with her two daughters to Lucknow in 2000 in search of a livelihood. Sunita was then just six and Manisha was one. Asked if her mother was scared, Sunita replied:

Sunita

She must have been but she never said so. But what was there to be afraid of? There was so much bad happening already, so how could things get worse?

Helped by her sister, Sunita's mother found work at construction sites, carrying bricks on her head all day long, up steep scaffoldings on high-rise buildings. When she found work she got paid around 100 rupees ($1.50) a day. They lived in a temporary shelter at the construction site, life got a little better, and they had food in their bellies. But Sunita still did not go to school:

So, Manisha was small. Mummy never thought about sending me to school because when she was out for work, I would take care of Manisha.

After a while Sunita started working part-time as domestic help in a home nearby to supplement their meager income.

The lady [her employer, an old lady who lived alone] there started to teach me to read. I liked studying. She told me about Prerna. She had seen girls [in school uniform] coming from a building nearby. She asked me to go and look for the school and find out more about it. So I went and that's how I found Prerna. It was in 2004. I was 10 years old. So, I asked for admission there. I met Rakhee Aunty.[1] She said you come and study. See how much you can grasp. So I got admission in class 2. So, I started studying. After some time I brought Manisha also. Manisha has also finished class 12 now and wants to do a bachelor's in fine arts.

She described her daily routine cheerfully:

After waking up in the morning, I would go for work. I would do whatever work was there in that house. Then I would go back to my house and do some work there too. And then have a bath and come to school. Then after school, I would eat something. Then go to work again for a few hours. Then I would return at night, do my homework by the streetlight, since we had no electricity and the candlelight wasn't enough. Then sleep.

Sunita speaks of her mother's support:

Mother supported me a lot. She used to say, "I don't want to see you doing the kind of work that I am doing. And I don't want you to get married the way I got married. You should know everything, be more aware and then you should marry." And that's why she encouraged me to study more and more. She never said no to education. She is so happy that I and my sister are studying so much.

Sunita has been working as a teacher's aide in the special needs division of Study Hall School and wanted to become a trained teacher. However, she has changed her plans and is currently enrolled in a master's in social work degree program at Lucknow University, which is also my alma mater. She said with a firm, determined voice:

I want to become something and show my dad. If I were a boy, he probably would not have left me like this. He never cared to enquire about us—nothing! I feel very ashamed to say "papa"—I never use this word. My mother keeps telling me that I must respect him because he is my "father." But I don't agree. He has never come to see us ever. I don't remember what he looks like. But I am going to show him one day that we did fine without him. I am determined to get my share of our land from him. He is not going to give it to his children from the other woman. It is my right and I am going to have it.[2]

Sunita attributes her fearlessness, strength, and confidence in the face of problems to her education at Prerna.

> I felt very good after coming here. . . . Like there was nothing to be afraid of, from anyone. We would tell my teachers everything, all our daily problems. And they would help us by explaining very nicely. Even our studies, they explained so well we understood. We were never afraid. I began to feel very strong.

Khushboo

Khushboo completed her school education despite violent opposition from her father, who turned her out of his house because she insisted on continuing her education after the tenth grade. Her grandmother took her in and supported her, and she finished her bachelor's degree and is pursuing a master's degree in women's studies from Lucknow University. The first person in her family to graduate from school and get a college education, she works part-time and supports her grandmother and herself.

Khushboo was born in 1993 to a Dalit family in Lucknow. Her mother was illiterate, married at 18, and passed away at 22 while giving birth to a son, who died with her. Khushboo was only three. Her father, a plumber, schooled only until the second grade, married twice after her mother died. The second wife, after two children, died trying to end an unwanted pregnancy, her third in three years. Khushboo thinks of her kindly:

> She was illiterate but had an educated mind. She was very kind to me and even sent me to the local village school for a year. . . . She had a girl and then a boy and then was pregnant again very soon. Then she said she didn't want more children, because they were all small. There was hardly any gap between the children. She wanted an abortion. My father wouldn't let her. So she went ahead and took some medication. And then she was sick. She was admitted in the hospital. I saw her body; it was all blue. She died the same day.

Left behind were a one-year-old girl, a six-month-old boy, and Khushboo, then age five, who was pulled out of school to take care of her siblings and do the housework. Her father married a third time, to an illiterate woman who was not so kind to the three stepchildren, perhaps because she had to

Khushboo

leave her own two-year-old daughter, from a previous marriage, with her mother. She had six daughters from her marriage with Khushboo's father and is pregnant a seventh time, determined to have a son. During this time Khushboo was expected to stay home and help, therefore was never sent to school.

Khushboo learned of Prerna—that it was in the afternoon and was nearly free—from her friend Laxmi. Her paternal grandmother, or *daadi*, who in her words was her "real mother," stepped in and took her to school. Her father objected. Her grandmother offered to take care of Khushboo's two siblings and argued that since the school was in the afternoon, Khushboo could be spared for a few hours after she had finished the housework in the morning and could do more in the evening after school.

Her father finally agreed and even enrolled the other girls in the household in the school. He paid the minimal fees for Khushboo till she reached seventh grade and then stopped, saying he could not afford the cost and Khushboo had had enough schooling anyway. Her grandmother then stepped in to cover the school fees. Her father frequently threatened to stop her education, however, and marry her off, but Khushboo resisted and managed to finish the tenth grade at the top of her class.

They said I am growing up; I should be married. It was then that I started saying that I want to study and not marry right now. But, I never used to say this in front of Father. I used to tell Stepmother only. I told her that if I get married, I won't be able to study, won't ever be able to do anything. That, as she needs to ask for money from Father, I will end up doing the same thing. She seemed to understand this a little bit. So she agreed to let me study till class 10. And I also agreed to get married after tenth. . . . So, I managed to stay in school. . . . When I refused marriage after tenth grade, they said they won't let me study either. When I said I would not marry, Father said he had done enough for me. If I wanted to study further, that would be my husband's decision. I could study further only if he allowed me. And it was then that I started speaking in front of him [Father] as well. And then he thrashed me. He said this has never happened—that how can I, being his own daughter, defy him, talk to him like that—that how can I try to teach him how to treat me.

Asked if her father beat her often, she said:

A lot. I used to get thrashed very often. Like when I went home in the evening, if I did not feel like cooking, or if I ever was late coming home from school, I would ask Stepmother if she could cook that day, instead [of me]. She would ask me why. I would tell her that I am very tired. But she said that she never asked me to go to school, so it's not her problem. So if I didn't cook I would get beaten up. She would tell my father. Once he was drinking at midnight and asked me for food while I was sleeping. I said that I was tired. That day he thrashed me badly with a stick. And it was then that Grandmother came to school and asked for help.

The father was determined to pull her out of school after she passed tenth grade. Despite the Prerna staff's persuasion and counsel, he insisted that if she wanted to study further she would have to leave his house and he would wash his hands of her completely. During this meeting in my office, Khushboo stood at the back and kept repeating, "I am going to study, no matter what." Her father yelled at her in front of me, berating her for defying him. Though he did not yell at me in deference to my official status as director of his daughter's school, he was not persuaded by me to change his mind, either.

Later that night he beat her again for her defiant behavior. He kept repeating, "It is this education that has given you teeth of rebellion. It has to stop."

Unable to stop the beatings, Khushboo's grandmother sent word to Laxmi, who called the principal. Childline, an NGO for child protection, and the police were asked to intervene. After this, the father turned Khushboo out of his house, and her grandmother, who lives with her younger son, took her in and she continues to live with them now.

Talking about her life and how she feels about it, she says:

Wherever I am today, I want to go much ahead. I am happy. I was very scared when my father turned me out. I cried a lot that day. But now I can take care of myself. I am not afraid of being by myself now.

She does worry about her future though, feeling homeless and insecure and wondering where she will go after her ailing grandmother dies, since her father has washed his hands of her. She feels getting herself a home is her first priority.

I am worried for my life sometimes. What after my grandmother? Uncle [her grandmother's son] doesn't talk to me properly, even if I take up a place on rent; my father and uncle are strange people. I wonder what they will do. I am a little scared of them.

She attributes her resilience and persistence in the face of violent opposition to the support and love of her teachers and friends and to the education she received in school:

Environment in our school is very good. Just like a family. So, I got a lot of support from the teachers. . . . The critical dialogue classes used to give me courage to say what I feel, to talk about what I think. And for me, if I can say what I think, I feel like something's done. So I could say this to teachers. They used to tell me what is what, how to study, what to do.

Preeti

Preeti is a young Dalit woman, born in a very poor neighborhood in Lucknow. She is 21 years old, has been working at DiDi's as the manager of her unit.[3] Today she feels well in control of her life:

Preeti

I make my decisions myself. I do what I think I should do and want to do. Where I feel something is right, I do it. Even if somebody says otherwise. I feel I am intelligent enough to take my own decisions.

Preeti has two younger sisters. Her mother is illiterate and works as a domestic helper. Her father has had a little schooling—she is not sure how much—and can read some Hindi. He worked for a little while as a low-level office boy in a neighborhood school until he was fired for drinking. He has been drinking ever since Preeti can remember:

When I was small he used to beat my mumma. When I was in sixth class, he hurt my mother with a stone because he wanted money for alcohol. Soon I began to work with her. From age 11, I started working. My mother works in five to six homes, making 6000 rupees [\$90] a month. My father never supports us in any way.[4]

Preeti was enrolled in a local government school when she was six years old and studied there until second grade. Then she had to leave school when her sister was born, and dropped out for two years. A friend told her about Prerna, saying it would cost little and was in the afternoon. She enrolled in the second grade, and after a month she was tested and promoted to third, then to fourth at the end of the year. In one year, she had made up her two lost years.

Her mother was very keen that she go to school. Her younger sister stayed home to take care of the third sister who was just a baby, and then both joined her at school when the baby turned three. Preeti used to bring both sisters on her bike.

My father doesn't care about anything. My mother wants all of us to be educated and be in a good place. Even though she is not educated she wants us to be. She wants a better life for us.

Preeti completed high school in 2012 at the age of 17 and now is in her third and final year of her work toward a bachelor's degree. Until recently she worked part-time in a tailoring unit as a supervisor. She was promoted and earns 9000 rupees ($135) per month. She has bought herself a motorized bike with her own money, the first Prerna girl to do so. This has raised many eyebrows in her neighborhood:

They got jealous. They said—"how did she buy it? She must be doing wrong things." When I come for work, they think that I am doing the wrong kind of work. Like you know—and they say it openly that the girl has a bad character. That she is making money from wrong sources.

She said this with a good-humored shrug and went on:

My big goal is to build my own house, for my mother and myself. We don't have a house. I want to see myself in a good place, at a good height. The issues with which I am dealing right now, I want to come out of them. Like there are a lot of problems at home. There still are. Like when I go home after working here all day, my father comes drunk. He yells at us, sometimes abuses us, which we don't like. I work all day and still it's the same because of Father. . . . Because of him no one wants us in a good neighborhood. I want to live in a good neighborhood. So we have to think if we leave our father, then people will gossip. Because our society doesn't allow that we leave the head of our household. I have decided, if he keeps doing this, then when I will have my own house I will not allow him there. Right now I am still struggling, trying to figure out how to make all this happen.

Preeti attributes her present strength and firm resolve to rise above her circumstances to her school education:

> Because I have learned so many things from here. So this is my base. Teachers were like our mothers. They were caring; supporting, too. When I was small, I was so scared. I couldn't speak to anyone. But now I can speak fearlessly. Our teachers told us about all the right and wrong things which are happening in our society. And how to come out of that. We shared so many things, all our problems with our friends and our teachers and became strong.

On her third attempt, she finally won a competitive, one-year scholarship, sponsored by the U.S. government, to attend community college in the United States in May 2016.[5] Winning the scholarship raised her status tremendously in her community and even with her father, who was very proud when he learned about it. "He is very proud of me, since everyone at his work is congratulating him. They are all amazed—wondering."

Her mother says her father has reduced his drinking and his abusive behavior since Preeti got this scholarship because he says he has to live up to the respect Preeti has earned for the family. He worked hard at saving so he could give Preeti 5000 rupees ($75) for her trip to the United States. She is thriving at her college in Santa Rosa, California, excitedly sharing her pictures and news via Whatsapp and e-mail.

Kunti

Kunti is a 24-year-old Dalit woman who has successfully completed her MBA program. She works as a personnel manager in a food enterprise, managing over 40 employees. She says, "I feel confident, mature, and strong. Now I speak up for myself, even in front of my brother." Talking about her future she says, "Going forward, I want to establish my own business and I want to marry someone that I choose."

Kunti was born in 1992 in Lucknow and is the seventh in a family of eight children, with one brother and six sisters. Her mother is illiterate and her father was schooled up to tenth grade. He worked in the army as a *sepoy* (private), then left due to ill health. Her mother worked at different jobs, sometimes as a domestic helper or as a day laborer at construction sites, sometimes other work. She was the only earning member in the family with many mouths to feed.

Kunti

Kunti remembers days when there was very little food to go around. Smiling, she also remembers a time when she and her sister slept under a plastic sheet, trying to shield themselves from the rain, because the roof was missing over their part of the house. Shivi, Rama, Kunti, and Gyanti are the youngest of seven sisters and the only ones to have studied in Prerna, as the older sisters were too old when the school was established. While Shivi stayed only for six months and dropped out, Rama, Kunti, and Gyanti stayed and finished. They are also the only ones among the seven sisters to have completed twelfth grade. The older four sisters were married off before they turned 18, without going past eighth grade; one of them completed only the third grade.

Rama graduated from Prerna in 2009, has a bachelor's degree, and is now enrolled in a master's program in women's studies. She was married at 24 but found the courage to walk out of the marriage when she realized it would not work for her. Recently remarried, she seems happy and is continuing her master's studies. Gyanti has just graduated from twelfth grade and has enrolled in a bachelor's program. Their only brother was sent to a boarding school, has an undergraduate law degree, and is working in a local company as a low-level executive.

Kunti's father stopped working a long while ago, due to ill health, and has been bedridden. The burden of raising his large family fell to her mother until her brother got a job. When interviewed by Kunti, her father told her how guilty he felt that her mother had to bear the entire burden of their large family alone for so many years. Her sisters all worked as domestic help before they were married. Kunti and Gyanti, however, have been fortunate and have never had to work in other people's homes.

Kunti said her mother was warned by her in-laws not to bring home a daughter when she was about to deliver her, and this is why, for many years, no one ever celebrated her birthday. "But my mother always gives me money on my birthday," she said, speaking with great fondness and compassion about her mother. Of her childhood, she notes:

> I remember once my father yelling at my mother. He yelled at her so much that she was crying. I was sitting in the other room and listening. My room was very close to her, so I could hear. I was listening and feeling very angry. So I went to her. . . . I tried to calm her down. She didn't want me to see her like that, you know, so she asked me to go, but I really felt bad about it. It's not nice to see your mother [this way], for girls especially. It's very hard. It happened many times. I didn't see him hit her, but my sisters did. It was really painful.

She said, however, that in recent years her father had stopped yelling at her mother completely. "He doesn't say a word when she goes on at him about things." While she appreciates that her father has never stopped her from studying or wearing anything she likes, she also recounted many instances when she and her sisters were slapped around by her father and brother:

> If we did not cook what they liked, or if we didn't clean the home, or if we left too early in the morning.

Kunti had attended a government primary school, like her other sisters, before she joined Prerna in the sixth grade in 2003. When someone in the community told Kunti's mother about Prerna, she enrolled Rama and Kunti there, and later Gyanti, as well. Kunti says they left the government school because it was too far from home, and very few Hindus were there. As a minority, she said, without elaborating, "there were problems." Speaking of her old school, she said:

> It's like if you haven't done your homework or you have done something wrong, you got slapped. Like till I came here, I didn't know the basic

spelling of words like apple or cat. No one really taught you; we studied ourselves if we were interested. They never motivated us or helped us see we had skills.

"When I came here, I saw that I have many skills. I can write poems, even," she notes, laughing self-consciously. Her mother has been extremely supportive of the girls' education and was glad to find a school she could afford. Kunti's brother, however, has often said to Kunti and her two sisters that he thought sending them to school for so long was a mistake.

He still thinks like that. He thinks we have started talking back to him because of our education in Prerna. I think he is sorry that he has lost his superior status at home. Now I say what I think even when it is in opposition to what he thinks.

Her mother, on the other hand, is very proud of them and brags about their school and her daughters' educational achievements to anyone who will listen.

Kunti excelled in school, displaying many leadership qualities, was head girl in her final year, and graduated in 2009 with a high score. In 2012, facilitated by Prerna, she won a community college scholarship to the United States for a year (the same one Preeti won in 2016). She acquitted herself remarkably well there, too, and returned with laurels and a renewed confidence.

After she got her diploma in business management, Kunti applied for and was offered a job in a corporation in Delhi, but chose, instead, to return to Lucknow and work in DiDi's Foods, where she is personnel manager. She earns a monthly salary of 20,000 rupees and manages over 40 employees. Her manager is full of praise for her and finds her competent, mature, and confident, which is how she feels about herself, too. Asserting her sense of being equal she says:

I was so scared to even open my mouth in front of my brother but now I can give him [or anyone else] fitting replies, now I have the knowledge. I know so many things. I don't feel less than him in anything. I'm the same as him so why should I just agree with everything he says? [Why should I] put up with all his high handedness?

Speaking about Prerna, she says:

It has helped me become what I am today, made me strong and independent, so that I don't have to depend on anyone, now.

She showed me a picture of her boyfriend on her phone and told me in a firm voice and a twinkle in her eyes that she was determined to marry him even though he belonged to another caste.

Kunti seems to be well in control of her own life, saying that she is un-afraid now and feels she can face anything. She has also supported and helped her older sister get out of a very abusive marriage, handling all the court pro-ceedings and paperwork herself. Kunti and her sisters have been the main providers in their family for some years now, and she is the chief decision-maker at home, her mother seeking her advice on all matters.

The girls' stories, although each unique, sound familiar notes. Although Aarti and Sunita are Savarna girls, their lives have been impacted as much as their Dalit friends by poverty and gender. Though still precariously positioned, all the girls have managed to navigate an inhospitable social terrain, found some control over their lives, and are forging ahead, swimming determinedly along, albeit on uneasy, often troubled waters. Khushboo fights traditional notions of "home" for girls and dares, though nervously, to look for her own home. Aarti, Preeti, and Laxmi struggle to build lives for themselves and their siblings while dealing with abusive, alcoholic fathers. They are caught between societal notions of filial duty along with their own love for their fathers and their desire for a life of respect and dignity for themselves and their mothers. Angry and frustrated, they still try to understand the compulsions faced by their fathers, saying that they drink because of the frustrations of poverty and the stress caused by being the only breadwinner in the family. The girls say they have been enabled by their school to survive the unholy combination of poverty and gender, to stay and complete school and emerge empowered.

The chapters that follow take a closer look at their school, Prerna, to unveil what it did to enable these life outcomes, not just for Laxmi and her friends, but for hundreds of girls with life circumstances much like theirs.

3

Educating Myself
Valuable Lessons for Self and Others

It was at the ripe old age of 28, mother of two, that I found the understanding that had eluded me all these years: I was an equal person! I woke up in the middle of the night and whispered to myself, "You are an equal person. You have a legitimate right to everything anyone else has."

Here I offer a brief description of my own personal and intellectual journey to shed some light on my motivations for establishing Prerna. The valuable lessons I learned on this journey have informed and guided the educational purpose, goal, and pedagogy of the school.

Growing Up

I grew up in a middle-class Savarna family. My father had been forced to flee his home in Rawalpindi—then in undivided India, now Pakistan—leaving behind everything he owned. He settled in Pune, India, and married my mother soon after. He was 20 and my mother was 16. Circumstances did not allow either of them to complete high school. They lived in a small two-room apartment with my father's two younger brothers.

My father began his business from scratch. After many early failures, his company grew, eventually becoming a nationally known brand of packaged foods, Weikfield Foods Pvt. Ltd. We moved to a bigger house in an upscale neighborhood when I was two years old and my older brothers were four and three. My brothers and I were educated in an English medium coeducational army school until sixth grade. It was a small school in a modest building, run by army wives, and had a diverse student population, with children from low- and middle-income backgrounds. I remember it with great fondness as a caring, inclusive place. After sixth grade, we were moved to high-status, single-sex English medium missionary schools, my brothers to the boys' school and I to the girls' school.

These were established, 100-year-old schools in elegant buildings, with many amenities and high academic standards, catering to students from middle- to high-income families. The schools sought high learning outcomes and worked rigorously at achieving these. I studied diligently and soon began to achieve good scores. During this time my parents were struggling to build their lives and fortune and had very little time to think about us beyond providing for our creature comforts and ensuring our good education. As a result, they paid very little attention to our studies, and especially mine since I was a girl. If my father saw me reading at home, he would ask me, "Don't you have any work?" I took to hiding my books when I saw him approach.

Like many other girls in such families, I faced differential treatment at home early on, which became particularly marked as soon as I became a teenager. Restrictions were placed on my mobility, clothing, and extracurricular activities at school, most of which were forbidden since they involved staying after school. I was supposed to stay at home when I was not in school and help my mother in the kitchen and with other household chores. On many evenings, my brothers played cricket while I ironed clothes or took care of my younger siblings. I chafed at these constraints and at the clear discrimination. Seething with anger at the unfair constrictions on my life, I felt suffocated and caged. I complained often to my mother and siblings. My brothers were sympathetic and supportive and my mother, though she sympathized, advised graceful acceptance, saying, "Remember you are a girl."

Pitaji

My father's school education was unfortunately truncated at age 14 by his own father's untimely death.[1] In the ninth grade, he had to drop out of school and take over his father's business. An extremely intelligent man, he taught himself to read, write, and speak English, read voraciously, and was able to converse analytically about national and international political and economic affairs. Fiercely independent and fearless, he held strong opinions and was unafraid to go against the current. A dynamic entrepreneur, he was ahead of his times and progressive in many ways, but he held strongly conservative views regarding gender norms. Like many men of his era, socialized into a patriarchal ideology, he was fully convinced in the rightness of traditional roles for women in the home and society. They were meant to be good, obedient, docile, appropriately deferential wives, daughters, and daughters-in-law, to be seen and not heard, sexually chaste and pure. He believed these traditional norms were the only way to maintain the stability of society. I once asked him if he would still feel this way if he had been born a woman. He said that he would, but admitted that he was glad to be born a man!

Pitaji was the quintessential patriarch and his word was absolute law. I was too afraid to oppose his authority and never saw my mother do so. We were all fully cowed by my father's temper and his almost god-like powers and authority in our home. My mother was a hard-working, obedient wife, homemaker, and mother, doing her best to juggle all her roles to please everyone in our large family, making sure everything was according to my father's wishes. This power structure was a fairly typical one in many middle-class Indian families. I never saw my father physically abuse my mother, though none of us was spared his sharp tongue-lashings or spankings if we dared transgress his rules.

After I finished high school, I was enrolled in a Home Science college, chosen for me by my father because it was an all-girl institution. He simply could not bear the thought of his teenage daughter in college with boys her age. Though completely uninterested in the course, I agreed. Despite my high-quality school education, I had no aspirations beyond hoping to get a good husband, one who might be kind to me and, perhaps, more liberal than most, so I could have a freer life. My brothers, meanwhile, pursued college degrees in science, commerce, and engineering.

Getting Married

Within a year my father found a suitable husband for me. He seemed considerate, and I was engaged after a few hours' meeting at the age of 17, and married after a year. I entered my marriage in Lucknow, a new city over a thousand kilometers from Pune, where I knew no one. Welcomed by my husband, who was not an unkind man, and my mother-in-law, a kind matriarch, the conventional role of a "good" daughter-in-law was expected of me. I understood very quickly that, far from being freer, I was now further restrained by my role of wife and daughter-in-law. I now "belonged" to a man seven years my senior, whom I barely knew, and my security, my livelihood, and my happiness all depended on pleasing him and my mother-in-law. I lived by their pleasure and permission. As the glamor of being a new bride wore off, the reality of my situation dawned on me, and I quickly tried to adjust to it, attempting to learn all the rules of my new home and family and abide by them.

Educating Myself

Most girls of my caste and class, from my community and generation in India, were expected to have at least a bachelor's degree, acquired while a suitable match was found. A girl with a degree was even considered more desirable in the marriage market. Since I had always enjoyed my studies and was fairly good at them, and also because I felt deprived of the minimum education most of my friends would get, I enrolled in a bachelor's program in Pune University immediately. There was no provision for a distance-learning bachelor's program in the university, but I found my way to the registrar's office and explained my situation. I appealed to him to waive my attendance and allow me to study independently and take the examination as a regular student. To my surprise, he allowed it. I think he was a little taken aback by my request and touched by a young married girl's earnestness to continue her education, and he responded positively to my special situation and its constraints. I am ever grateful to him.

My mother-in-law and husband were amused by my eagerness to study, and since it did not involve my going to college, they indulged me. On my part, I made sure not to allow my studies to interfere with the functioning of the household and my duties. I had signed up for a political science major with economics and sociology as minor subjects. Since there were no lectures or notes to depend on and I had to try to make sense of texts myself, I read my textbooks very carefully, interacting with them thoughtfully and dialogically. I found libraries in Lucknow and continued my education, alone.

I was trying very hard to be happy in my new situation, finding spaces for myself wherever I could. My studies provided one such space. I had ceased to actively look for personal freedom, because I understood, if unconsciously, that when I married I had forsaken claims to that. I would not permit myself to think too much about myself, because it seemed to be dangerous territory and intuitively I knew that some doors were better kept shut for my own peace of mind. I kept up my studies, and three years later I was awarded my bachelor's degree. I still remember my joy and the great sense of achievement I felt. I had beaten my destiny and achieved a college education despite the fact that it had been denied me. It seemed like a huge victory. I felt I had acknowledged and vindicated myself.

Becoming a Mother of Daughters

One year later, after four years of trying, many fertility tests, and much stress, guilt, and tension, I delivered my first child and then my second the next year—both of them daughters. Much to the disappointment of the whole family, my parents, and my in-laws, I had failed to give my husband a male child. Though I swallowed my own disappointment the first time, I wept bitterly when I bore my second daughter, crushed by the weight of the entire family's disappointed hopes and expectations. The cold reception given to my second baby by almost everyone broke my heart, but, finally, it made me angry. Thankfully, I was able to stop feeling guilty long enough to be angry. Anger, my friend Rakesh once told me, is a revolutionary emotion, and so it was for me.

I named my second daughter Nidhi, which means "precious treasure," and held her close to my heart. I insisted that my mother-in-law celebrate her arrival with the traditional distribution of sweets to friends and family. I began to demand that she be welcomed with joy. This was, perhaps, the beginning of my journey as a feminist. For once I openly refused to go along and play the traditional role of the guilty and penitent daughter-in-law and wife. Both my daughters, Shibani and Nidhi, have grown into strong, independent, thinking women and continue to be my strongest supporters and advisers.

A Rude Awakening

In 1982 a cataclysmic event changed my life forever.

One day I got a call from my mother telling me that my cousin had been burned by a stove blast and was in critical condition in Delhi. She was three years my junior, then only 24, with a four-year marriage and a two-year-old daughter. I was shocked and distressed but could not imagine that it was anything other than an accident. I left immediately for Delhi, but she died before I reached her. When my mother informed me it was a suicide, I reeled in shocked disbelief. We never found out whether it was, in fact, suicide, but such suicides by burning were coming to light every day in the 1980s. She had not been happy in her marriage, always afraid and on edge.

When I asked her mother if she knew whether her daughter had been so unhappy, she replied heartbrokenly, "But which woman is happy in marriage? We all learn to adjust." My father was furious that she had brought so much dishonor to the family. His older sister, who had been in an extremely abusive marriage herself, commented, "This younger generation has no endurance. One is supposed to endure patiently." Her daughter-in-law, also suffering an abusive husband, sighed, "She is liberated! Good for her!"

My cousin's husband and in-laws maintained a defensive silence, making all the customary sounds of condolence, but refused to give many details about her death. She was cremated traditionally, in her bridal attire. My cousin was educated in the same elite, private school I had been to, and she had a college education. My imagination failed me as I tried to conjure up the image of her dousing herself with kerosene and setting herself aflame. Even if she were desperate enough to take her own life, she would have chosen a less gruesome way of doing it—pills perhaps. I still have difficulty accepting that her death was by her own doing.

The rest of the family refused to delve deeper into the matter. They were too afraid of the consequences, particularly for her infant daughter, who was in her father's custody and daunted by the difficulty, inconvenience, and continued pain of pursuing this matter in Delhi. My cousin's death went uninvestigated. Her younger sister and I went to a local nongovernmental organization and tried to file a complaint. But we were too young and inexperienced, too afraid to go against our own family, and the matter went no further.

Her death made a deep impression on me. I wondered why she had not confided her misery to anyone. Why was there no one to go to for support, for help? Savarna women were taught to be stoic and keep their marital problems to themselves; discussing them was like washing dirty linen in public and would bring shame and dishonor to both families. This expectation meant that many girls like my cousin blamed themselves and suffered in silence. The more educated they were, the more sensitive they were about keeping personal and family honor intact.

I returned home, still numb with shock and grief. Unable to put it aside, I decided to start a helpline for women in distress. Older and wiser heads counseled me to start a formal organization, and together with a few other women and men, including my husband, I founded the first family counseling center in Uttar Pradesh in 1983, called Suraksha, meaning "security" and "protection."

I was the secretary, and the office was housed in my home. This was my first step into the public sphere.

Through the center I made tentative moves into what I learned later was liberal feminism, propelled by a concern for domestic violence. I was stepping gingerly and warily into what was completely unfamiliar territory for me. I had read no feminist texts; I had no feminist role models; I had no conceptual tools to help me, and no gender training. What I had was the shock of my cousin's untimely and unnatural death and the experience of being a girl and woman in a society that was very gendered and discriminatory.

With no training in counseling or in gender issues, and with more enthusiasm than maturity, I dealt with many cases of domestic violence and tried my best to help. I had no idea what I was up against. Others in the organization had a paternalistic view and we made no attempt to effect structural change or change social norms. My work with Suraksha took me to middle-class and working-class homes, in both rural and urban areas, and broke some of the insularity of my social class. The poor rural women who had seemed so "other" faced the same problems and met the same level of violence that had ended the life of my rich, urban cousin.

Learning I Was an Equal Person

My interest in philosophy led me to Vinita Wanchoo, a much older woman, and one of my first mentors, who took me under her wing and introduced me to Indian philosophy. She insisted that I do a master's in philosophy. My husband resisted, saying that a bachelor's degree was enough.

Despite the silent disapproval at home, I enrolled in the master's program at Lucknow University. Often women and members of other subordinate groups learn to find ways of resisting quietly and surreptitiously, one small step at a time. I did the same. By the end of the year, my mother-in-law and my husband caved in and accepted my studies and in the years to come they supported and respected my ventures.

My master's coursework included political and social philosophy and ethics. I read all the Western political and ethical philosophers: John Stuart Mill, Hobbes, Locke, Rousseau, William James, Karl Marx. My readings taught me to think analytically about political and ethical systems, and I began to develop a growing understanding of inequality. It was around this time, at the ripe old age of 28, mother of two, that I found the understanding that had eluded me all these years: I was an equal person! I woke up in the middle of the night and whispered to myself, "You are an equal person. You have a legitimate right to everything anyone else has." I had enough sense to say this quietly, not out loud, because I knew it might not be taken kindly by everyone.

Recognizing yourself as an equal person is an important precursor to asserting and realizing your right to equality. This was one of the most important lessons I learned, and a key driver of my life. I later took this invaluable lesson to Prerna.

My public work with Suraksha was liberating me in ways I didn't understand at the time. Even though my marriage had impacted my life so strongly, it was in my gender workshops with young girls and their mothers that I understood how the full force of patriarchy exerted control through marriage. I began with the idea of discussing dowry and its pernicious effects for girls, wanting to raise awareness about this, but prodded by a (male) friend, I realized I needed to go deeper and discuss marriage, its purpose and structure, with girls directly. This was the beginning of my developing a feminist consciousness.

I started to visit girls' schools and colleges wherever I could gain entry, and spoke to them about gender equality and the need to examine institutions like marriage and family and the place of women in them.

Starting My Journey as an Educator

My gender workshops in high schools led me to thinking of education in schools. Reflecting on my own school education, I realized that though school had equipped me with reading and writing skills and academic information, it had not taught me that I was an equal person. It had not given me the conceptual tools to critically examine my life as a girl in a strongly patriarchal society. Most of the schools I visited were like mine. They did not address many of the existential questions that students have; they did not teach their students how to live.

I began to read about alternative schools, and in my search for more I visited the Krishnamurti Foundation school at Rajghat and met Ahalya Chari, the director, a very wise woman and educator. She was a proponent of a free-thinking and student-centric, student-driven, inquiry-based pedagogy embedded in a gentle ethic of care.

She suggested I start a school. I was taken aback. That had never been my goal. It seemed too large an undertaking, way beyond my ken. I told her I had no experience or degree in education. She told me, "You have all the right questions." I was surprised to learn you could start a school with questions.

Emboldened by a teacher I had met at my daughters' school, Geeta Kumar, who I invited to partner with me in the enterprise, and supported by my husband and mother-in-law, I soon took the plunge and started a pre-school, which we called Study Hall, in my garage.

For some years, I was fully involved in setting up my school and working at developing a child-centric pedagogy. The school catered to rich middle-class children, and it met their needs well. I read many educational philosophers, including Maria Montessori, John Dewey, Friedrich Froebel, Krishnamurti, Tagore, and Sri Aurobindo. They all spoke of education in apolitical terms. While I learned a great deal about developmental psychology, child-centered pedagogy, and activity-based learning, I continued to be oblivious to social class distinctions.

Raised Aspirations

Three years into the school's establishment, I began to feel I needed to learn more. Encouraged by Ahalya di[2] and supported by my husband, I applied to universities in the United States for a master's program in education. I chose the University of California at Berkeley, which had a reputation of being radical. Leaving my daughters with my mother-in-law and my husband, I left for Berkeley, excited but also with a great deal of trepidation and guilt at doing something for myself and leaving my children. My older daughter Shibani, who was only 12 at the time, encouraged me, saying: "You must go. It is such an opportunity."

And she was so right! Going to Berkeley probably was one of my best decisions. It was there I found some distance and was able to define myself anew, outside the bounds of my identity as an upper-class, Indian wife, mother, and daughter-in-law. At Berkeley I found myself divested of my class privilege and in a position of relatively less power and status because of my color and my developing country citizenship.

I was fortunate in my advisers, Anne Dyson and Herb Simons. Apart from the excellent academic guidance they provided, they treated me with respect and completely accepted who I was. They took the trouble to know me, learn more about where I came from, understand my context, and then encouraged me to make the course work for me and my native culture. I felt respected and accepted as an intellectual. I gained from this an important lesson—that the teacher-student relationship must be one of mutual respect, response, acceptance, empathetic understanding and care. This lesson has guided my work as an educator ever since.

Though I had gone there only for a master's program, Anne persuaded me to continue and work for a Ph.D. Like Vinita di and Ahalya di, she helped me raise my aspirations.

Learning That Oppression Is Systemic, Not Individual

My years in Berkeley were formative in more ways than one. Living alone for the first time in my life without a man's protection, working at my Ph.D., meeting the rigorous demands of the doctoral program—difficult and stressful as those years were, they were the making of me. It was there that I learned my struggle was not against my father or even my husband, but against a cruel, unfair, unequal social structure that left me powerless because I was a woman. That was the second liberating understanding that had eluded me thus far. I was beginning to perceive that though my struggle was personal, it was embedded in a social and political culture of domination, in which I and my husband, my father, and other men were equally embedded. It was not their fault. They were good men, living out the gender roles they had been socialized into, just as I had been socialized into mine.

This new understanding was very liberating because it freed me from the guilt of blaming and resenting my father and my husband. The men in our lives are important to us, and treating them as the enemy is alienating and painful. Two of my brothers, for example, have been strong supporters in my work and through my personal struggles. Dropping the burden of 35 years was such a relief! This new understanding was both freeing and overwhelming. Freeing because I could shift my attention from the men in my life to society and move some of the burden to society's shoulders. Overwhelming because social structures are large, omnipresent, and complex. How was I ever going to fight those?

During my stay at Berkeley, my parents visited me briefly. I was frantic with worry. How would my parents feel about staying in my tiny, World War II barracks-like apartment? All my fear of my father welled up again and I was back to being a young girl under his control. What I did not realize was that my father was seeing me in a completely different context for the first time. It was a learning experience for him, too. For the first time he acknowledged my intellect. One evening I showed him all my certificates, my bachelor's and master's degrees, and my certificates of proficiency from universities. He perused them slowly and in silence. Then to my utter astonishment I saw tears rolling down his cheeks. He was sobbing quietly, his face buried in his handkerchief. I was taken aback. I watched him helplessly, not knowing quite what to do. After a while he looked at me and said in a choked voice, "*Shabash beta* [well done]! I am so proud of you! Well done! I wish I had had the opportunity to go to university. I am so glad you have." I wept with him.

For the first time in my life he truly saw me as a person, not as a girl, his daughter. And I, too, caught a glimpse of him as a person, with dreams and struggles. Coming to a distant land, he was able to put aside his patriarchal lens, if only briefly. Also, I think the shift in my position, caused by my changed self-perception, forced him to shift his recognition of me. In the university setting, away from India, he was able to look at me afresh and see me not just as a daughter, wife, and mother but as a person, with a mind, an intellect, capabilities, competencies. A new respect for me was dawning and I rejoiced. I must add here that my father ended up becoming a strong supporter and the largest funder in my girls' education work. My childhood fear of him as the patriarch turned to ever-increasing love and respect. He was a social leader in his community and subconsciously in many ways, my role model.

I have spoken very little about my mother in all this. I saw us as being alike, both subordinate and unfree, as on the same side. My mother did her best for me, trying to protect me from a violent backlash from society and family, as she watched me protest, fight, and transgress, counseling patience, caution, and, often, just acceptance. She did not feel there was anything more she could do. I included her in my struggle, urging her to find her voice and the courage to protest. She was too afraid to rock the boat, to shatter the peace of her large family, to upset my father, whom she loved deeply, as did I. But she began to resist quietly, became increasingly more vocal and supportive of me, lending me her strength and drawing upon mine.

Expanding Social and Political Understandings

At Berkeley I made friends with a lovely young African American woman, Antoinette Mitchell, and we have remained lifelong friends. It was through Antoinette that I learned a great deal about race in the United States and racist oppression in general. I saw many parallels between racist oppression in the United States and caste oppression in India. In our classes we often discussed multiculturalism, and I could hear the pained voices of marginalized communities, such as those of Hispanic Americans and African Americans, crying out for inclusion and recognition.

My understanding of other oppressions and power relations grew every day. Though I began to understand the intersectionality between caste, class, and gender, for me gender oppression loomed large. It was the primary oppression. I understand now what bell hooks means when she writes: "It is the practice of domination that most people are socialized to accept before they even know that other forms of group oppression exist. . . . Challenging sexist oppression is a crucial step in the struggle to eliminate all forms of oppression."[3]

The courses at Berkeley enabled me to view education from a social and political perspective to see that education is not socially neutral, that differences must be acknowledged, attended to, and responded to. Berkeley is a public university with a highly diverse student population. All the discussions around education were about education in public schools, and my understanding of education expanded.[4]

Since 75 percent of the population in India lived in villages at the time, and 87 percent of Indian children went to public schools, I decided to choose a rural public school as the site for my research. It seemed like an opportunity to learn about both public schools and poor, rural populations. I began to view my own Study Hall School, still in my garage, differently. It now seemed a small private school for a very small section of the Indian population. So immersed had I been in my personal struggle against sexist oppression that I could not see the other oppressions in my culture, and there were many: class, caste, region, religion. I was blind to the culture of domination around me and to the fact that, as a member of a dominant class, I was a participant in it. My search for personal freedom had consumed me, even though my struggle was enhanced and supported largely by the public action I had taken as a result of my work with Suraksha. Becoming conscious of social class was the first step I took in recognizing other oppressions.

Being introduced to Paulo Freire through his book *Pedagogy of the Oppressed* was another major turning point in my intellectual journey. Though my own education had been the key instrument in my liberation, I was still oblivious to its emancipatory power. I had been engaged in critical thinking for many long years, since my teen years, through all the books I read, the diary I used to write about my daily travails, my private readings and dialogues while studying for my bachelor's degree, the fiction I read, my study in philosophy, and my discussions with the girls and communities during my work with Suraksha. I had been engaged in critical thinking, in critical dialogues, for many years without calling them this. I was finding a new vocabulary through Freire's work. And through this I realized I had been naming my reality all along. In naming it, my life had been transformed, slowly and painfully. As Freire taught, literacy can be life-changing, it can be revolutionary, but only when it enables us to critically examine our own social and political reality and then to understand it.

All these words resonated with me, illuminating past experiences with new understanding. I saw that education, to be real and authentic, must be relevant to our lives. It must respond to our condition, and it must illuminate it.

In our work with Study Hall School we were trying to make it child-responsive, relevant to children's lives. It was limited in its scope by the fact that these children were all rich and privileged middle-class children, with no struggles that I could see, except that their right to childhood be recognized and respected. What I didn't see was that there are children *and there are children.* They are not a homogeneous group. They have different lives depending on, among other factors: their class, their caste, gender, and where they live. Poverty, gender, and caste truncate their rights much more cruelly, and an education cannot be liberating unless educators take cognizance of and address the realities of children's lives.

While my personal struggle continued, gender in a social context took back stage for me. This is not surprising given that I was reading Freire and his associates, who all expounded on pedagogy for liberation in very sexist language and referred mostly to adult men. I began to think about children—both boys and girls—living in poverty and how education should be designed and organized to help them. I knew it was more than equipping them for livelihoods. It had to aim at personal empowerment and liberation, and that is what I used my research to explore.

I spent four weeks simply observing the classroom, watching as teaching and learning unfolded. The school was under-resourced, with no furniture and only two rooms. The second-grade class I was observing was conducted under a tree, with strips of cloth serving as floor mats on which the children sat and a blackboard and chalk as the only teaching material. There were 40 children in this class. I observed the hierarchical structure of the school, which mirrored dominant social structures of gender, caste, class, and geography. The principal was an upper-caste rural male, the teachers were all upper-caste, middle-class, urban women, and the children were almost all lower-caste and rural. The principal's authority reigned supreme; he made all the decisions. The teachers held complete sway over the children, with the boys clearly getting more attention than the girls. It was also a culture of neglect and uncare. The children were given minimal attention and, consequently, learned minimally.

I could not bear to simply watch and record what seemed to me a dismal situation. I designed my research as an action research and included a participant phase. This involved my engagement with the students to construct a language arts curriculum and practice together. The children and I worked together for eight months. I taught them three times a week, following their cues and constructing the curriculum as it emerged and recording their writing development. I learned that children develop both cognitively and as persons when they are treated with respect, attended to, and responded to respectfully as persons. Together we developed a language arts curriculum based on story, poetry, drama, and song. The students called me their "drama" teacher even though I was teaching them writing. Their writing proficiency developed in leaps and bounds because it was situated in their life worlds and because they learned they could use it for their own purposes.[5]

I returned home from Berkeley in July 1994 as a new person, intellectually and personally validated, and with my vision expanded. Though my struggle as a woman was still important to me, I began to perceive myself as more than just a woman. Because I had begun to accept myself more, I was less angry with myself for having been born a woman.

My education as well as my personal struggles provided an important avenue for self-work, self-reflection, and construction. The time at Berkeley was particularly important because it allowed me to divest myself of my cultural accouterments and look at myself anew, to rise above my personal struggle and align with other struggles. It gave me a new way to look at myself and at life, at social and political structures. I returned with enlarged theoretical frameworks, greater social and political understanding, and a deeper and wider understanding of myself, all of which has guided my work as an educator ever since.

Post Script: Prerna and Me

At risk of being too biographical, I have described the journey of my own personal, intellectual, and political development at some length because it is from this personal experience of being a girl and the development of my own feminist consciousness that my work has emerged. I also hope it makes clear my position in relation to the students of Prerna. As a Savarna upper-class woman, I was born to privileges and a security that my students and their families, most of them Dalits, were denied by their working-class lives. Their inequality was constituted by caste, class, and gender. However, we did have one important thing in common. Despite my class advantages, I also had felt unequal and unfree compared to the men of my class. My experience of sexist oppression, though, was specific to women of my class and different from theirs. Their caste membership condemned their families to lives of hard physical labor and many material deprivations that I was spared. While I complained of having to iron clothes when my brothers played cricket, Laxmi and Sunita had to clean other people's homes at the age of seven! Though I had to spend many evenings babysitting my younger siblings, I was never in danger of being pulled out of school. All the girls in this story, on the other hand, were compelled to drop out of school because there was no money to pay for childcare.

Despite the vast, stark material differences of our lives, it was the common experience of being discriminated against as girls that gave us some common ground on which to relate despite differences in our social power positions. It was through the lens of this common experience that we found some degree of mutual understanding. However, I am conscious that our class distance has imposed its own limits and a certain mutual opacity, which might have influenced my perceptions and my telling of their stories. That is why I asked the girls to read their stories and confirm or object to and revise the authenticity of their voices as they are rendered in this book.

4

The Story of Prerna

Girls loved coming to school. Before this there was no purpose
in their lives, nothing to look forward to. They used to cook
and clean and just stay at home. But now they looked forward
to getting ready and coming to school. They felt very important, like they had found a purpose.

—*Rachna, the founder teacher*

P rerna, which means "inspiration" in English, is an outgrowth of the Study
Hall School. It is a formal all-girls school covering pre-school to twelfth
grade. Prerna is run, as is the Study Hall School, by the private Study Hall
Educational Foundation (SHEF),[1] of which I am the founding president.
Prerna is also housed in Study Hall School's now fairly large, well-equipped
and well-furnished building, with security guards, and runs in the afternoon
at the end of the Study Hall School day. Prerna was established in 2003 with
these goals: to provide a quality education defined broadly and comprehen-
sively to include social, emotional, and political learning, a rights-based approach, and a strong focus on child-responsive and respectful pedagogy.

Prerna is an all-girls school by design; we wanted to reach girls who are deprived
of an education because of a paucity of resources at home. We also wanted to have
a clear and undiluted focus on girls and their needs. Furthermore, we knew that
parents are more comfortable sending their daughters to single-sex upper primary
and secondary schools. There is evidence of psychological and social benefits
for girls in single-sex classes, and when given the choice, girls generally prefer

Girls in school

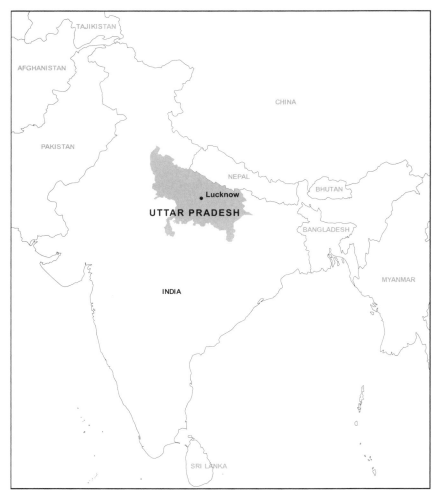

Lucknow

TABLE 4-1. *Literacy Rates (Percent)*

	All	Male	Female
India	72.99	80.89	64.64
Uttar Pradesh	67.68	77.28	57.18
Lucknow	77.29	82.56	71.54

Source: Census of India 2011, "Population Enumeration Data (Final Population)," 2011 (www .censusindia.gov.in/2011census/population_enumeration.html).

single-sex classes. Furthermore, research reports that single-sex classes assist in breaking down sex role stereotypes and gender segregation of subject areas, whereas coeducational settings tend to reinforce them.[2]

Prerna is located in Lucknow, the capital city of Uttar Pradesh, the most populous state of India, with more than 199 million people, of whom more than 59 million are below the poverty line, the most of any Indian state.[3] Uttar Pradesh has a gender ratio of 908 females per 1000 males, with the female death rate for the age group zero to four years exceeding the male death rate by 22 percent.[4] The state also has a 20 percent gender gap in literacy rates (see table 4-1); 9.2 percent of girls age 11 to 14 have never gone to school.[5] According to the National Family Health Survey, 58.6 percent of women age 20 to 24 were married by age 18.[6] The Annual Plan 2007–08 reported that 75.37 percent of girls in Lucknow were married before the age of 18.[7]

Prerna's neighborhood is Gomti Nagar, an area like many in Indian cities where posh residential homes sit side-by-side with low-income shacks known as slums. Most of the students come from the poorer parts of Gomti Nagar, some traveling from other, more-distant low-income neighborhoods.

A Typical Day

Most Prerna students walk to school, typically in groups of six or more, both for safety and social reasons. They often arrive before the school's 1:30 p.m. start time and crowd around the gate, waiting to be let in. They wear their school uniforms: a red-and-white checked shirt and white salwar (baggy pants) for the older girls and a red-and-white tunic for the younger ones. They all carry a small school bag, which they deposit around the quad area as they line up for assembly. The school day starts with a 15-minute assembly led by the principal, who recites a short verse or prayer, taking care to cover

The Study Hall–Prerna campus

prayers from all religions, which the students recite after her. Students may then read the headlines of the newspaper or present a brief skit, speech, or poem. After a group song, the students walk or run to classes with their teachers.[8]

A school day is broken into six periods of 35 minutes each and a 20-minute recess, during which students are served by the older girls a small high-protein meal sponsored by DiDi's Foods (see chapter 6). They sit around the yard chatting and eating during this break. A bell marks the end of each period. A visitor to the school is struck by the happy sounds in the classrooms, of children engaged in discussions, answering questions, and sometimes reciting poems or math tables in a chorus. Students can be found engaged in drama, music, or dance on the stage or in their classes, playing sports in the yard, or learning martial arts. The environment may be more sober in the principal's office as she listens to stories of violence and abuse from her students, talks to parents, and counsels them. The school ends at 5:30 p.m. Most of the girls leave in their groups, though many can be found playing in the yard or chatting with each other and their teachers. Some remain for after-school help.

Social Profile: Who Comes to Prerna

Prerna's enrollment in 2016 was 880 girls, with an average of 35 students in each class. There are 35 teachers, including the principal and vice principal. The students' family backgrounds are much like those of Laxmi and her friends, described in chapters 1 and 2.

The students come from very poor families, with an average family income of 8900 rupees ($133) per month and an average family size of 6.9 persons. Approximately 82 percent of the students come from historically disadvantaged groups—Scheduled Castes (SC) and Other Backward Classes (OBCs).[9] In addition, 19 percent of the children come from homes without electricity, 18 percent have no lavatories at home, and 48 percent live in huts or temporary homes. Many of the students are first generation learners, with 39 percent of the fathers and 70 percent of the mothers being completely unschooled. Of the fathers, 22.5 percent have a primary education, compared to 15 percent of the mothers. Only 10 percent of the fathers and 3.7 percent of the mothers have completed tenth grade. A large proportion of the students, approximately 43 percent, are engaged in work outside the home. High rates of domestic violence prevail, and 26 percent of the fathers are reported to be alcoholic. Aarti thinks the real alcoholism rate is much higher:

Homes of Prerna students

BOX 4-1. *The Study Hall Educational Foundation (SHEF)*

SHEF began its work in 1986 to empower children's lives and achieve equality through quality education for all. Through its schools and programs, SHEF has reached out to children from urban and rural backgrounds in and around Lucknow, including government schools in the states of Uttar Pradesh and Rajasthan.

SHEF's schools and programs include:

- ⁙ Study Hall School, a K-12 co-ed school for middle-class children, with an integrated program for children with special needs: 2000 enrolled

- ⁙ Prerna Girls School, a K-12 school for girls from low-income backgrounds: 880 enrolled

- ⁙ Prerna Boys School, a K-12 school for boys from low-income backgrounds: 150 enrolled

- ⁙ Vidyasthali Kanar School, a K-12 rural co-ed school in Kanar, a village near Lucknow: 435 enrolled

- ⁙ Digital Study Hall, SHEF's outreach arm where SHEF's best practices are shared using simple technology

- ⁙ *Gyan-Setu (Bridge of Learning)*, a cluster of Community Education Centres in low-income communities and migrant labor colonies for out-of-school children who are unable to attend Prerna Girls and Boys School: 600 children enrolled in 14 centres across Lucknow

Altogether SHEF, with its dedicated team of more than 300 men and women, reaches out to approximately 60,000 students, teachers, and student teachers through its schools and programs. SHEF works closely with the state governments of Uttar Pradesh and Rajasthan. SHEF is also part of several state, national, and international consultative bodies and networks working for educational reform and universalization of quality education, where we lend our expertise, experience, and unique perspective.

See Study Hall Educational Foundation (www.studyhallfoundation.org).

Most fathers are like this only; in my class [the one she currently teaches] there's not a single girl who can say, "My father doesn't drink or doesn't hit my mother."

Get Them into School and All Will Be Well

Like many others, I believe education is extremely important for girls and for gender equality. I also know that poor girls are left out of education because poor parents do not find it cost-effective to spend scarce resources educating their daughters. For these reasons, Prerna was established with the charitable motive of providing access to a quality school education to girls from low-income backgrounds who were either unschooled or had dropped out of school.

Initially, I issued a call for volunteers, and one of the primary teachers from Study Hall School, Rachna, stepped up; she wanted a second job. Rachna was given the task of recruiting girls from the neighborhood. She was given no special training but just told to go into the community and convince parents to send their out-of-school daughters to school. How did she do it? What were the responses from parents and how did she convince them?

In the scorching heat of a north Indian summer, where temperatures rage at 45°C (113°F) or higher, Rachna visited more than 100 homes over a period of two months. Every day from four to seven p.m., register in hand, she went to every house in Guari Gaon, a very poor neighborhood close to the school, and introduced herself as a teacher from Study Hall School, then fairly well known locally. She then described the overarching mission of the foundation and, more specifically, that of Prerna: "We want to educate girls who haven't had the opportunity to go to school." She conducted a survey, asking parents about their children—how many did they have, were there any daughters, and were they in school? Rachna found many girls taking care of siblings at home while their brothers were in school. She reported that often, while the parents gave poverty as a reason to keep their daughters out of school, on further questioning she learned that sons were going to school and sometimes to low-cost private schools.

Poorna was one of the girls recruited during this initial campaign. Now one of our alumnae, she completed twelfth grade in 2013, has a bachelor's degree, and is an assistant art teacher at Prerna. Her mother relates her own encounter with Rachna:

So when Rachna aunty came to our house, she asked me, "Why don't you send your daughters to school?" So I had three of my six daughters admitted. I didn't even mention I had three more. I didn't tell their father I had admitted them, because he would get angry. That's why I didn't get all admitted. But Rachna aunty found out and came back to ask about the others. I also started thinking that if they don't get educated their future will get ruined; thinking that when I will go to get them married, then people will ask how much education she has, then if they are illiterate—what will I answer? I would fight with their father, telling him this. I would cry—that my daughters are completely illiterate. . . . So then at last, I got the others also admitted. Then all my six daughters came here.[10]

Rachna reported that, unlike Poorna's mother, many parents did not see any value in educating their daughters, given that marriage, domestic work, and reproduction were the only aspirations they had for them. They said they didn't think education would make a difference to their daughters' lives or their own. Rachna then bent her efforts to persuade them that an education would benefit both their daughters and their family. She often cited herself, saying that she was able to contribute to her family income and educate her child because she was educated. She made special efforts to convince the mothers, telling them that their daughters might have a better life materially and earn more respect at home from their husbands and in-laws if they had an education.

She invited the girls and their mothers to just come see the school but was met with hostility by some parents, especially fathers, who were more vocal. Parents also expressed some skepticism about charitable efforts like Prerna, saying, for example, "There are many programs like these that open, people get funding, and then they shut them down." Rachna did her best to convince them that this one was here to stay and that SHEF was a well-established foundation and very credible.

Rachna worked hard at winning their trust, making repeated visits to homes. Often she was refused admittance or parents would refuse to discuss the subject. Mothers were more willing to listen, although some, often stepmothers, said they needed the girls to work at home. Some mothers did want their daughters to be educated but were afraid of their husbands. Most of the fathers either refused to speak to Rachna or seemed indifferent; a few were interested but said they had no money. Rachna focused on the mothers, leading several group sessions with them separately, trying very hard to point out other more specific advantages of sending their daughters to school. One point she made was, "They will not only learn, but also get clean water."

She finally managed to persuade some parents to send their daughters to school, offering a free trial. She shared her address with them, saying she would be available to answer any questions. In the beginning only 30 girls came, and then after two or three months the word spread and more parents started sending their daughters. As Rachna says, "When they saw that children were learning so much, other parents started sending their children too."

Rachna thinks a large attraction was that it was almost free and that it ran in the afternoon, so girls could work and still study. Prerna began with a token fee of 10 rupees ($0.15) per month. This is a "commitment fee," based on the belief that anything that comes completely free is not valued and that when someone pays, however small the amount, that person makes a commitment and is more likely to feel more responsible and respected. Also the size of the building and the fact that Study Hall School was well established were impressive and reassuring considerations. It seemed like a solid program, not some fly-by-night operation.

Reminiscing about the early days, Rachna says:

> The girls loved coming to school. They enjoyed themselves a lot. Before this there was no purpose in their lives. They had nothing to look forward to. They used to cook and clean and just stay at home. And now they looked forward to getting ready and coming to school. They felt very important, like they had found a purpose.

And so we began our journey with 30 girls and two teachers in July 2003. The first 30 girls had never been schooled or had dropped out to take care of their siblings or to supplement the family income by working. After that some students transferred from other schools, initially for additional tutoring in the afternoon and then, when they were convinced, the parents withdrew them from those schools and enrolled them in Prerna. Now we are in our fourteenth year and have an enrollment of 880 girls taught by 35 teachers.

From Learning Outcomes to Life Outcomes

In the first two years we saw our task as providing literacy and numeracy, bridging girls' lost years of learning and helping them transition into age-appropriate grade levels. We adopted the state board syllabus. Even though our enrollment grew steadily and reached 160 by the end of the second year, the girls' attendance was erratic and retention was precarious and volatile, despite Rachna and her coteachers' efforts.

Learning from Girls' Lives

It was then that I took a closer look at our girls. Clearly we needed to do something more. I sat down with a group of girls, about 14 to 16 years of age, the first batch to graduate from twelfth grade with us, and began to explore deeply with them their life experiences with the hope of learning more about them and of finding a possible answer to the retention problem. I began to talk to them about their lives, and wherever I found a resonance, I shared mine with them. We became real persons to each other. I engaged them in an arts project, described in chapter 8, where they shared their fears about being girls by way of images on paper and dramatized these in the class. Together we examined these images critically and reflected on our lives and the underlying cultural and social conditions and structures. My role was that of listening and providing gentle and often not-so-gentle "cultural prodding" by leading them to question the unquestionable culturally defined gender norms and traditions that framed their lives.[11] They then imagined possible lives in possible worlds for themselves and constructed these on paper and through drama.

At the end of six to seven weeks, I emerged with a much greater understanding of the girls' lives as, possibly, they did, too, of their own lives. By their own testimony, this was the first time they had engaged in a reflective self-examination. I also saw how the girls used the classroom and our sessions—the art, drama, and literacy work—as spaces for "self-work." As one of the girls said to me at the end of the session, "We feel we now have a self; we are somebody and can be somebody. Before this we just existed." This project had given the girls the time, space, and some tools to examine their lives critically, individually, and collaboratively with their peers and with me, their teacher. I also saw how the students felt respected and cared for, because a teacher, a valued adult, had taken the time and trouble to look at them as persons, to address them fully, to solicit their considered response and express interest in their lives. It made them believe their lives were valuable, *they* were valuable, and they could aspire to better lives for themselves.

I remembered then what Freire taught, that for education to be life changing and transformative, it must enable us to reflect on our own lived reality—personal, social, and political. It must respond to our condition and illuminate it.

This group remained with the project for a year, and these dialogues became an integral part of the school curriculum. The exercise taught us that children learn best when they are addressed fully as persons and their whole lives considered as valuable and relevant. A key ingredient is respect; when we are treated with respect, we all learn to respect ourselves. It also taught us that when teachers and students inhabit different worlds, caste-class worlds in the case of the Prerna teachers, understanding students' lives is imperative for teachers, whose perceptions of students and their lives are colored by class, caste, and gender. Dialogue and arts projects like ours are effective means of reaching out to each other over differences.

Rakhee, the principal of the school for the last 12 years, said in her interview:

> When I joined in 2003, I didn't fully understand all this. I used to teach very diligently, but I didn't talk to the children much. The first two years the school was not like it is now. We were only trying to teach the kids their Hindi, math, and science. In fact, there was a teacher, Vatsala [who has since left], who had no faith in the children—she would say to me, "Why are you wasting your brains and effort on these girls. Don't you see where they come from? They will just do what they do. Don't bother." I didn't feel like that, but I didn't understand empowerment till you did the first critical dialogues with Kunti's cohort, back in 2005. You used to tell us "talk to them, talk to them." I think Prerna as an empowering school really began from there.

Redefining the Task Ahead

We realized that as well intentioned as our efforts were, we were not doing enough at Prerna. We redefined our task in response to the girls' needs, recognizing that unless their education taught them they were equal persons, and enabled them to deal with the challenges they faced in their lives, they might not finish school, might not learn, and most important, their school might not make any difference to their life outcomes.

Guided by the question "Why do we want to educate girls?" we began to move our thinking from "learning outcomes" to "life outcomes." The girls should be educated so they may have better lives or, to put it in terms of the capabilities approach proposed by Amartya Sen and Martha Nussbaum, so they may be capable of living lives that are fully human.[12]

We shifted from an exclusive focus on the girls' learning to a broader focus on the girls' lives. The teachers were trained to learn about their students' lives and to keep those lives center stage in the classroom. We learned also that we needed to work alongside our students to fight all the problems created by the conditions of their lives. In doing this we realized it was important to build strong relationships with the parents, to work together with them as allies and partners in the endeavor to educate their daughters.

My life's work thus far as an educator and a women's rights activist came together as we developed and defined the educational goal of Prerna, understanding that such a goal continues to evolve and is never final. My own feminist struggle came alive as I engaged in critical dialogues with my students, and I came to see how their education was incomplete and far less effective unless it was linked closely with a feminist objective. Though their lives—at the intersections of caste, class, and gender—were impacted hugely by their poverty, most of their concerns were about gender. During our talks the girls did not focus on their caste, but they did discuss being girls and being poor. We chose to concentrate on gender first because it emerged again and again as an important theme for them. They felt much worse off than their brothers, with less to eat, less claim over the meager family resources, less freedom, less mobility, less control over their bodies and lives, and much more vulnerable at home and outside. Based on this treatment, they had learned their lives had little to no value.

Gerda Lerner lays the blame for the internalization of oppression squarely at the door of patriarchal structures. Patriarchy insidiously and invisibly captures the minds of men and women, exercising hegemonic control by becoming "naturalized." For our students to perceive themselves as valuable, they needed to learn about patriarchy and other structures of domination, learn to critique them, see how they shaped their lives and minds, how they severely limited the possibilities of their lives, and how they had been co-opted into perpetuating them by their silent acceptance of it. Understanding age-old all-pervasive structures of domination was important if they were to find a way of resisting and challenging them. Raising the girls' feminist consciousness, thus, became an important goal, perhaps even more important than mastery of the official curriculum mandated by the state. That is, literacy and numeracy would serve them only if it could lead to an understanding of themselves and their lives.

Learning Redefined: Looking at the Students

Teacher: Why do you come to school?
Laxmi: To study.
Teacher: Why are you studying?
Laxmi: So that our lives get better.
Teacher: What life do you want? It can be like that—just like you want it to be.
Laxmi: Aunty, which is full of happiness, where life is good!
Teacher: And what is a good life?
Laxmi: I don't know—where I don't have to work like this and my little sister doesn't have to work like this, where we can be something, anything that I am able to be, become something.

We looked at Laxmi and her life and asked: What did she need to learn to have a better life? What did Aarti, Sunita, Khushboo, Kunti, and Preeti need?

These are some questions that shaped our thinking. Tentative answers developed that guided our work. The girls needed to learn how to deal with the challenges their lives posed. And to do this they needed to learn first and foremost that whatever their caste, class, or gender, they were persons worthy of respect, intrinsically valuable in and of themselves, equal to everyone else in the world, with a right to autonomous control over their lives, and free to be who they wanted to be and do what they wanted to do. They needed to learn to act as equal persons in a world that treated them as socially inferior.

They also needed to question and understand why they were not treated as equals. What was it about society in which their sex, caste, and class made them inferior? Why did they have so little power? Why were they not allowed any control over their lives? Why could their fathers beat them and their mothers when they were displeased? Why could Khushboo's father cast her out if she did not do as he desired? Why did the girls have limited mobility outside their homes? Why did they not have the right to plan their lives, to decide who they could be? Why were they not important enough to educate? Why was their education not as important as their brothers? Why did they and not their brothers, even when older, have to drop out of school and take care of their younger siblings?

Most important, they needed to be empowered with the knowledge and the subsequent aspiration that they had a right to a better life, to a fully human experience. As Karen Oppenheim Mason writes:

> Women's empowerment involves not only their gaining new individual capabilities, but also the emergence of new beliefs about their right to exercise these capabilities and take advantage of opportunities in their community.[13]

Prerna's Educational Goals

We organized Prerna's structure, content, and pedagogy around the goal of achieving not just empowering learning outcomes but also, even more important, empowering life outcomes.

We came to define our overall goal this way:

> To empower its students. To raise their feminist consciousness and to help them emerge as emancipated women with a perception of themselves as equal persons having the right to equal participation in society, and to be equipped with the appropriate social, emotional, conceptual, and academic skills to live a life of their own choosing.

To reach the overall goal, a girl must:

↠ Learn to read, write, and successfully complete the government-mandated syllabus up to twelfth grade.

↠ Learn to recognize herself as an equal person.

→ Emerge with a sense of agency, of control over her life, of aspirations for her future, and have the confidence and the skills to realize them.

→ Gain a critical understanding of the social and political structures that frame her life and determine its limits and possibilities, which would, in turn, enable her to push the boundaries and reconstruct her life in more empowering ways.

5

Building a Universe of Care

And then I came here, then everyone, all the teachers were so
friendly, everyone was trying to understand my problem, so even
if I came late or had any problem, I would share everything—
there was no hesitation. So I felt like Prerna was my family, like
there is someone to take care of me.

—Laxmi, Prerna alumna

On the surface, the official organizational structure of Prerna is similar to
many other schools. Prerna is headed by a director, a principal, and a
vice principal. The principal and vice principal are responsible for recruiting
teachers; mentoring, monitoring, and supporting them; admitting students;
managing the daily operations; assigning classes to teachers; conducting planning meetings with the staff; organizing assessments; and planning and
organizing all school activities and events, including monthly meetings with
parents. Together the director, principal, and vice principal also provide intellectual leadership, taking care of the academic health of the school. They se-
lect the textbooks in consultation with the teachers and track teacher and
student performance. In addition, the director guides innovations, does professional development of the team, raises and manages funds, budgets alloca-
tions, determines salaries, and networks with the larger education community
in SHEF and outside.

When one digs deeper into Prerna's structure, it is clear that the underlying ethic that pervades the organization is what makes Prerna unique. The

management style is consultative and democratic. The entire staff work as a team with few hierarchical layers. Though the principal and the vice principal are technically the heads, they view themselves more as mentor-leaders and work alongside the teachers, ready to offer guidance and support when needed. The school has made a special effort to foster a culture of care. It is organized as a web of mutually supportive relationships, with the needs of the students kept at the center. The students call their teachers "aunty" to reduce the traditional hierarchical distance between teachers and students. In India, *aunty* refers to maternal and paternal aunts, as well as any older woman, friend of a parent, or neighbor. It connotes greater familiarity than the official "Miss" or "Ma'am" traditionally used in schools, though some schools, government and private, do use *behenji, didi,* or *akka* (meaning older sister).

Chetna, one of our most senior teachers, believes this culture of care is the main reason Prerna is successful in terms of retention, completion, and achieving high learning and life outcomes. Explaining, she says: "It's all because of a feeling of connectedness with the teachers and the school."

Respect Is the Guiding Principle

Most of the 35 teachers (two of whom are part-time) come from a middle-class background. All are women except for a part-time music teacher. This has been done by design to provide a safe and secure environment for girls and to make the gender focus easier and less contentious. Eleven of the teachers have been with the school for over five years. The others were recruited as the school expanded.

The first teacher, Rachna, was a full-time teacher at Study Hall School and volunteered to work in Prerna as a second job. She served as the head teacher for two years and ran the school with two other teachers she recruited from the neighborhood. All subsequent teachers have been recruited similarly, through personal connections or by word of mouth.

Along with the required academic qualifications, teachers must be willing to work with an egalitarian mind-set in light of the low-income background of the students. A bachelor's degree is the basic requirement, and we try to get teachers with a teaching credential or a B.Ed. degree, but we are open to recruiting those without one. The school believes in training teachers on the job and engages them in continuous training with a strong focus on gender training and critical pedagogy, organizing several workshops each year. Teachers

Prerna staff

are mentored continuously by the director, principal, vice principal, and senior teachers.

Fifteen of the teachers have a master's degree, one has a physical education teaching credential, and the remaining twenty have bachelor's degrees. Nineteen have a teacher training degree or diploma and the others are pursuing one. Three of the teachers—Sadhana, Poorna, and Aarti—are alumnae of Prerna. Aarti joined as a teacher's assistant after she graduated from high school and later became a full-time teacher after she got her bachelor's degree. Preeti, Neetu, and Poonam also are Prerna alumnae and work in the administrative office.

The majority of teachers are Savarna middle-class, only four are OBCs, and all need the income.[1] Their average family income is approximately 35,000 rupees ($523) per month. Several are single women, divorced or widowed, and many face marital problems. During our teacher-training sessions, which take the form of critical dialogues, it emerged that all of them have experienced sexist oppression, either in their natal or marital homes, some of which is described in greater detail later in this chapter.

When dealing with poor people, the tendency of the middle classes is to adopt one of two approaches. The first is a "deficiency" approach, assuming that poor people have deficits that need to be filled, or that they are not intelligent enough, not teachable enough, and in some way are responsible for their poverty. This approach often leads to poor treatment of marginalized groups.[2]

The second approach is a "charitable" or paternalistic attitude of *noblesse oblige*—the do-gooder attitude, which, though it means well, is condescending and based on an acceptance of the unequal social positions. This approach seeks to help people from subordinate groups without treating them as equals or ever expecting them to become equals.

Our teachers have come with elements of both these views. However, after they join, the teachers are given extensive orientation and training, particularly focused on getting them to view and treat the girls with respect, to understand with sympathy and empathy the unfortunate and grim ways in which poverty limits their lives—without blaming them for it or viewing their poverty as causing inherent deficits. Respect is the key guiding principle. Teachers are also led to reflect critically on their own unearned class privilege, to understand class as a social construct, and to guard against an inadvertent class-based perspective. We require our teachers to be conscious of the students' poverty and of the distance caused by class difference and to work at surmounting the barriers it creates to mutual understanding or communication. Prerna's activity-based curriculum, with an abundance of drama and other cultural activities, helps increase mutual involvement and participation by both teachers and students to help reduce the distance between them. An ethic of care—based on respectful, receptive, and responsive attention—is emphasized and inculcated formally and informally to the teachers through continuous mentoring and by example.

As Rakhee, the principal, a kind, mild-mannered person, said:

> We invite new teachers with smiling faces and whenever we feel she is not doing things like we do, together we tell her that "No, this is not how it's done in Prerna, but you will learn. Don't worry about it." See, when they come new, they obviously make mistakes. They are used to the ways of other schools, which are very different from ours. I call them to my office and speak to them privately, and then my senior teachers' group, the ones who have been here for a long time, from ten years, they keep a watchful eye to see that no one is violating our culture, or behaving in a misguided manner; that no one is hitting the kids, for example. We explain to them that they have to be understanding of the children's lives, talk to them, understand them.

The focus group discussions with the teachers revealed they had come to understand clearly the need to take a respectful, responsive stance when interacting with the students. Some admitted they had joined the school motivated by a charitable instinct, because they knew it was for "poor girls," and also agreed they had come with a deficit view of "poor children." Their perception of a teacher's role had been a narrow, minimal one of "teaching the syllabus and nothing more." One teacher went on to make a concession:

> I expected to teach the syllabus, but with more examples, so that the concepts were clear to the children, because I knew they were poor children, and slow to understand.

The teachers say they were led to an expanded view of their roles as a result of their induction into the culture of care. They learned several things, but most important, they understood it was key that they got to know their students, learn about their lives, win their trust, and build a bond of respect and care with them.

Building a Relationship of Trust with Students

At the foundation of Prerna's pedagogical activity is the establishment of trust. Trust is the ground on which other learning stands. To build trust, before any teaching can happen, teachers focus on knowing the students and responding to their students' lives. One teacher said:

> After coming here, I realized that it is of prime importance that the girls feel connected to me . . . till they feel free to talk to me about things that are happening to them, I can't really teach them anything successfully.

Another one added, "If a child is a low achiever, then I need to ask myself—what's going on with her—in her life, at home?"

Knowing Your Students

According to Nel Noddings, who studied caring in school contexts, "The one-caring [or carer] is first of all attentive."[3] In line with this, Prerna teachers pay close attention to the circumstances of their students' lives, and are very watchful, especially for signs of silent or sullen withdrawal. As Chetna said:

When you are teaching, you see every child. You know what they are doing—their eye movements, their body language; how much they are listening to what you are teaching. If they are involved, and if they look withdrawn suddenly, you can judge from all this.

Noddings further draws our attention to caring as a relational concept, writing:

It is not enough to hear the teacher's claim to care. Does the student recognize that he or she is cared for? Is the teacher thought by the student to be a caring teacher? When we adopt the relational sense of caring we cannot look only at the teacher.[4]

The students felt their teachers took the trouble to know them, their life circumstances, and their problems—and that they were there to mentor them, counsel them, help them, and enable them. The students often refer to the school as "family." As Sunita said:

I felt very good after coming here because mother didn't have that kind of time for me. She would go in the morning and come back in the evening. So I used to feel like all the aunties are mothers. She worked hard and paid all the bills, but it was here that I felt that I am with family. We never even felt that we are away from home; like they are our people.

Sunita distinguished between the care she received at home and in school. Her mother's caring expressed itself in "working hard" and ensuring that her children were fed and clothed. Those tasks took up all her time and energy so she was unable, though not unwilling, to give Sunita the attentive and responsive care she got in school.

In all the discussions, the students repeatedly mentioned their strong relationships with their teachers and the immense support they drew from this. When asked why the students thought they were cared for in school, Laxmi, who had no mother and lived with her alcoholic father, responded:

Because people were listening to me here. In my house, my neighborhood, I couldn't say anything to anyone, no one listens. . . . Here everyone would listen. So I felt like the pain that was there was reduced. If there was even a slightest problem, people would try to know what happened and they would listen and tell me what to do. Like there is nothing to be afraid of, from anyone. We would tell them everything.

Aarti, who had been a student at Prerna for eight years before becoming a teacher, commented on the value of being able to discuss personal problems with teachers:

I hadn't seen this in any other school that you can go to a teacher and talk about personal problems. It will be just about studies, but here discussing our issues was part of it. As a student all this was very new to me, to others as well. Because I don't know if there is any other school where problems of students are discussed [in the class]. Now as a teacher I understand it well. It's very important to talk to the students. To know them.

When a student is admitted, the school requires her parents to fill out a social profile form, sometimes with help. The teachers also interview their students, parents, and other caregivers, for example, older siblings in the case of younger children. This is the official way of getting to know the children. Shabana, one of our teachers, noted:

In Prerna our girls get an identity. We all know our children. In other schools I have taught in, they don't even call them by their names. They don't know their names. In our school, each teacher knows every child's name, along with her family history and circumstances. What her dad does, how many siblings there are, whether the child works or not, how they live. So the children know that we know them. They feel so connected with the teachers and the school. That's why they are so excited to learn; they come running, "Aunty, what are you going to teach us?"

Care theorists also mention "reciprocity" as being an integral part of caring. Aarti, who teaches 32 children in her class, said she got to know her students by sharing her own life with them once they got "attached" and trust was established. Sunita talks about how she appreciated this:

After coming here and seeing our teachers, that they are also women. So, we are [the] same; we can [also] study and go ahead. We came to know them. Teachers would tell us about themselves, that they were also married early, still they managed to do all this. That made me very strong. If they can, so can I.

Responding to Children's Lives

Teachers are also guided by the belief that building trust and respect involves perceiving students as ends in themselves, honoring their intrinsic worth and dignity, and, most important, being prepared to see the world from their point of view. This means also being flexible to adapt classroom rules and pedagogy accordingly, as illustrated by Rakhee, the principal, who described an incident with Laxmi:

> I used to teach science, and there was a test one day. She [Laxmi] had come late because of her job. I asked her, "Child, you have a science test today, and it has started," so she said, "Can I give it after half an hour?" I asked her, "Why? Everyone else has started!" She said, "Please give me half an hour's time. I will study, because I haven't studied and I will fail. I was working till very late last night and my father was drunk. Just let me study and then I will give the test." I allowed her to do that. I told her to sit in the corner, learn the lesson and that I would give the test afterwards.

This incident made Rakhee realize how stressful a student's life could be at home. Following this incident, she:

> Put a system in place so that we teach them here only, make them learn here, because they don't have time or support at home. They have to cook at home, they all work outside and many don't have electricity at home. I explained to all the teachers that they should give the first period to study. . . . If school is opening at 1:30 p.m., then the exam will start at 2:30 p.m. This gives girls a chance to revise if they haven't studied at home. Kids appreciate our understanding.

An important lesson for all educators and teachers is that teaching and learning do not happen in a vacuum; they happen in the social contexts of students' lives and their worlds. Unless educators and teachers are responsive to these contexts, they cannot teach successfully and children will not learn. Had Rakhee not responded sympathetically to Laxmi's condition and her life circumstances, Laxmi would not only have failed her test, she would have also learned to see herself as a failure.

Another teacher, Roli, mentioned the case of a girl called Shanti. She was not in Roli's class anymore, but she knew her well.

> She was a very active girl. During recess, I noticed that she looked very silent and quiet, and I wondered why her face was not the same as before; I tried to find out what was wrong. We found out later that her father was abusing her at home.

Roli took the matter to the principal and together, with the help of Suraksha, a women's rights organization, which also runs a family counseling center and child protection services, they worked at stopping the abuse, which was by no means an easy task.

Shanti's mother's first response was to deny the abuse and accuse her daughter of misunderstanding, even lying. After several sessions with a trained counselor from the organization Suraksha, she admitted the problem, along with her own helplessness. She and her four children were completely dependent on her husband. She had done her best to protect her daughter at home but had chosen to be silent publicly about the abuse because she did not know how they would survive without his support were he to go to jail, along with the fear of her daughter being shamed and losing "honor" in the community. Suraksha worked hard to show her alternatives—that she could be helped to find a job and that she could seek assistance to stop the abuse. Representatives from Suraksha also spoke to Shanti's father, making him aware of the legal consequences of his actions. They worked at deconstructing the location of shame and honor, pointing out these consequences actually lay more in the act of the abuse and less in its disclosure. Shanti's father was not prosecuted, but the public disclosure and intervention resulted in his stopping the abuse. Though we did not think this was the ideal outcome, either ethically or legally, in this case, as in others Prerna had to leave such matters in the hands of agencies more experienced and better equipped to deal with them.

The girls also appreciate their teachers' understanding and support and do not hesitate to share their life worlds with them. Chetna affirms this with confidence:

> The children believe that if they face any problem, the school is there with them. That the school will give them every kind of support—be it physical, mental, even financial—as far as that is possible, given any problem they have—social problem or in the family. That they can

share their problem and that they will definitely get help from here. So this gives them a lot of confidence. If they have any problem, they come and tell us.

Speaking very firmly, she said:

I must repeat—that it is because they know that somebody is listening to them and supporting them that they start talking about their lives and problems and finding solutions.

During a focus group discussion, one of the teachers, Roli, told me about a nine-year-old girl who had developed a habit of stealing and had stolen 500 rupees from the principal's purse. I was struck by the manner in which all the teachers recounted together how they dealt with the issue. They spoke of the student with compassion, sympathy, and a lot of good humor. What was particularly striking was a complete absence of blaming and shaming. Roli, assuming the air of a clairvoyant having magical powers, made a game in questioning the child:

I am not going to ask you about the money. I don't even want to know what you did with it and I don't want it back; we can talk about it later. I will just look into your eyes for a while, and as I will see I will immediately get to know everything—when you took the money! How you took it! What you did with it! I will know everything. So if I just look into your eyes for a bit, I will know. So why not just tell me?

The child confessed to the "all-knowing" teacher, giving great detail about how the money was stolen with the help of a friend and that she had spent it. Roli went on to say that the most important thing was trust; the child needs to know that the teacher will understand and support her despite the transgression. Roli and the other teachers understood that poverty compels people to do bad things; that rather than punish, a teacher should work with the child to bring about better behavior.

The teachers spoke to the girl's sisters and finally called in her mother. They discovered:

Actually her mother used to beat her [and her sisters] a lot. . . . So we talked to the mother and explained to her that if she treats them like this, then her daughters will definitely repeat such behavior. The mother needs counseling, too. She has to work all day, poor thing, and can't find much time for her kids.

Roli's and Rakhee's examples, as well as Neetu's story (see box 5-1) illustrate well the importance of looking at students' behavior in the classroom holistically, assessing it thoroughly, looking for explanations, and responding sympathetically.

Expanding the Notion of "Quality Education"

According to Noddings:

> Caring teachers listen to their [students] and help them acquire the knowledge and attitudes needed to achieve their goals, not those of a pre-established curriculum.[5]

She goes on to point out that there is a problem with having a preconceived notion of what an educated person must know:

> The world is now so enormously complex that we cannot reasonably describe one model of an educated person. What we treasure as educated persons may be very different from the knowledge needed by other educated persons. Therefore, we cannot be sure (beyond a small but vitally important set of basic skills and concepts) what everyone needs to know.[6]

Repeatedly the girls expressed the value of being able to share the difficulties of their lives and how this sharing helped them acquire the necessary knowledge and skills to face their problems and resolve them. It is clear they need to know much more beyond the state-mandated curriculum. Prerna demonstrates that the notion of what constitutes "quality education" needs to be expanded.

Research shows that many teachers would like to be caring but their schools' conditions do not permit it. The culture of the school, large class sizes, the pressure of standardized testing, a top-down, syllabus-driven pedagogic model—all these crowd out any attention to students' needs or interests arising from their own lives. Most of all, there is no expectation that teachers should spend the time to listen with care to their students and attend responsively to them.[7]

BOX 5-1. *Neetu Returns to School*

Neetu and her daughter Ishika

One of our returning students, Neetu, was pulled out of school in grade nine, at the age of 17. Despite our best efforts to prevent it, she was married off by her parents, who believed it was the best they could do to secure her future. Five years after being in an abusive marriage she returned to Prerna, along with her two-year-old daughter, seeking enrollment for them both. She graduated from high school in 2016 at the age of 25, is currently enrolled in a bachelor's program, works many jobs, and is determined to buy herself a small house. Her daughter is thriving in grade 2.

She tells her own story of how she was able to return to school and how her life was influenced by her teacher and the school. Her story is also a particularly interesting example of the teachers' sensitivity and ability to be flexible and responsive to a girl's special needs.

No. I never wanted to get married, but like it happens in the family, my grandparents and father decided that I should be married—and I am the eldest one in the family—so that [the] rest of my sisters can also get married, my father and grandfather forced me and I said yes. At that time I also thought that since I am the eldest one, and we are three sisters, I felt that if

Father doesn't get me married, how will [the] rest of my sisters get married, you know that feeling! But now I feel that my parents should not have married me off this early. Now, I have a younger sister; I won't let them marry her off.

After being married, Neetu left school without notice. Her husband soon took to drinking and beating her. He gave her no money, so she ended up working in homes as domestic help to support herself and her little baby daughter.

One day, I was washing other people's clothes, and I was thinking that my mother also, because she was uneducated, used to wash clothes, so I was wondering if my life also would remain the same. My mother was uneducated, and she was washing people's clothes, getting beaten at home. Would I also be doing the same thing in my life? Then I felt that I should go to school and talk to aunty once because teachers always said that "there is no age for education. It can be done at any age; you should just be motivated to finish." I was wondering, "How will I go back to school after five years?" And then I thought of my Principal— Rakhee Ma'am—so I went to her house. And it was like seven or eight in the morning during the summer holidays. I was wondering how I would talk to her and tell her that I want to return to school and finish. I was embarrassed, because I had left school without even informing her about anything, but I thought she will understand, so, though I was a little scared, I went to her house, and told her, "I want to finish school. Please can you help me." She was very welcoming and supportive. She asked me to come back to school.

When I went to school then, she supported me in every way, and other teachers, when they learned about my story, they were very supportive and glad that I was completing grade 10. Everyone supported me a lot! So, because of that I was able to complete school. *(continued)*

She added with a great deal of pride:

I had never thought that I would be able to reach grade 12. Because I had got married in 2008. Now I am enrolled in a bachelor's program too. If not for my school, I would not have been able to even think about this! If I had gone to any other school, they would have rejected me right away, that after this age, you can't study.

Understanding the barriers to girls' education, girls are taken at whatever age we get them, and encouraged to finish school irrespective of their age. Neetu's story, like that of others in this chapter, is an example of ways in which schools need to actively and sympathetically respond to the needs of children's lives, endeavoring to bridge the gap between their difficult circumstances and their desire to come to school.

In contrast, Prerna has made an ethic of care an important part of the school's organization and pedagogical practice. Dialogue with the students and building a caring relationship with them have become an all-permeating premise, in effect the hidden curriculum that is just as important an enabler for learning as the official curriculum. The other supports provided by the school, also a manifestation of the culture of care, are described in detail in coming chapters.

Teaching to Be Equal

At Prerna we work with the view that a girl's self is a relational being constructed in and by her relationship to others. She becomes aware of her personhood as it is reflected in and by her relationships; it is in being treated with respect that she learns to respect herself.[8] However, as later chapters elaborate, this sense of self-respect eludes girls, even middle-class girls, who have been positioned as having less value than sons, as burdens to be unloaded and handed off to another family by marrying them as early as possible.

The students testify that the teachers help them counter this negative self-perception and develop a positive, strong self-image because of the respectful care with which they are treated. Srishti, the vice principal, distinguished Prerna's goals from those of other schools where she had taught:

> But here, first it's about empowering the child, teaching them how to speak up [have a voice] and not stay silent, having an understanding of what's right and wrong, and being alert about their rights.

The teachers view enabling girls' empowerment as their most important teaching goal. They recognize the need to help girls become self-advocates and work at this so that their students can be respected by society and lead happy lives.

They also want the girls to find worthwhile jobs and to become economically independent. They all want them to raise their aspirations and push the boundaries of their lives. One teacher summed it up nicely:

> Now when I ask my children what they want to be—one of them wants to become a bank manager and she has also worked out the steps. The children are thinking of how to get there. I want them all to aspire high. I keep trying to stretch their aspirations. They must have big dreams and once they have big goals, then they will definitely try to reach them. So that's what I work at.

That teacher represents a voice I heard too little during my own research,[9] where I saw classrooms filled with young children who would have been eager to learn if their teachers had only been more encouraging and caring and shown an interest in their students' futures. Teachers must be ambitious for their students and be able to develop in them a capacity to aspire and the strength to transgress the narrow boundaries laid down by the gendered norms and roles prescribed for them by their families and communities, whose expectations are constrained by poverty, a lack of education, and a conviction of the invincibility of caste, class, and gender boundaries.

Teachers and Students Empowering Each Other

One reason most of our teachers have taken so easily and quickly to the ethic of care and respectful response, in my opinion, is that they are all women living in a strongly patriarchal culture like India. Almost all of us have faced sexist

Rakhee

oppression. The girls' lives resonate with us despite the class and caste differences; this is the common experience that helps us understand and communicate with each other. Described here are the life experiences that Rakhee and Chetna brought to bear on their work in Prerna.

Rakhee, who came to Prerna as a principal, wished to enroll for a master's degree in science after she graduated with a bachelor's, but her wish was crushed by her family, especially her older brother, who, as breadwinner, had the decisive voice. He noted that she would need a more qualified husband, who would be hard to find because boys in their community weren't very highly educated. Though she was angry, Rakhee did not resist:

> I couldn't say or do anything. Very soon, my brother found me a husband and I got engaged. I didn't get any support from my family to study any further. I wasn't aware of my rights, because our society was like that, so I felt that whatever my mother is doing is right for me.

Rakhee said she became more aware of her own rights after she joined Prerna. Conditioned to obediently accept her parents' decisions for her before her marriage, and then those of her husband and mother-in-law, she says:

I would never speak up. But now I think of my rights. I have learned that I have the right to speak up, to do what I want. I have changed a lot. Even my husband notices it.

Many of the teachers echoed her, saying they had become aware of their rights and had learned to fight for them.

Rakhee and several teachers have been empowered to take up their education once again, in some cases after 10 years and more. Rakhee is now contemplating enrolling in the master's degree program that her brother denied her.

Chetna joined the school in 2004 as a teacher. Her first husband, whom she had chosen herself and whom she loved, died suddenly a few years after her wedding, leaving her alone with a daughter. She was coerced into marrying again by her father, who maintained that an unmarried woman was an aberration. She felt emotionally blackmailed by her family:

They used to tell me—"you have taken one man's life, will you take your father's life also [by disobeying him]?" I didn't want to live with this guilt also, so I had to marry.

She married her second husband half-heartedly but separated soon after when she realized he had lied to her about the number of children he had from his first marriage. He had mentioned two in his newspaper advertisement, while there were actually four. Returning to her parents' home, she was allowed to stay, grudgingly, though they made every effort to send her back.

Now needing to work, Chetna started looking for a job. She had a bachelor's degree but no training. One of her friends who was teaching at Prerna told her about the school and what a caring place it was. She applied and was accepted, and was happy to be in such an accepting environment.

Chetna tells us what Prerna had meant for her:

The condition in which I came here, it was very important for me to feel accepted at work. You don't get that easily. . . . I was very depressed at that time. I felt I had nothing, I was nothing. So, the fact that someone accepted me in that condition was a very big thing for me. And that too without diminishing me.

Chetna

She says she gained confidence and respect and learned to be creative in Prerna:

> I never knew I had so much inside me, but then when someone trusts you, you feel there must be something in you. I have gained so much.

She went on to describe the supportive, caring culture of the school as she experienced it as a novice:

> Because here nobody will make fun of you or put you down. Here, they let you grow slowly. Everywhere else, whatever they give—they need returns quickly. They feel they have to get their money's worth right away. It's so stressful! Here, there's no such transactional approach. Here, a space will be given to you and in that you can grow. So, what happens with this is that people feel that they have to do much better. And when one person feels that they received this support from senior teachers—like they never degraded us, they kept guiding us, so that we can do much better. They have faith in us, so we begin to have faith in ourselves.

Teachers also talk about how they were inspired by the students' lives and the resilience and courage they showed in the face of odds. Chetna recounts her own transformation:

> When I came here, I used to think that I have nothing. And then when I would see these girls, I mean they have nothing at all, no support, sometimes not even enough to eat two rotis [Indian bread], and they often come to school with an empty stomach. Yet they are happy. They can be so energetic and creative and respectful! That was a great thing! These were the things they taught me; these kids had a very big role in making me who I am today. I found confidence by just seeing them, understanding their lives and who they were.

Care Is Empowering

Our teachers are introduced to our ethic of care even before they are trained in critical feminist pedagogy. As noted, teachers go through several orientations and workshops during their induction and are regularly mentored by senior teachers. Most important, they are infected by the all-pervasive "aura" of the school, as Rakhee calls it. The main points are the ethic of care and the importance of paying close attention to the girls and their worlds. Formal structures are in place, like profiling children's socioeconomic backgrounds, which teachers are required to do themselves. In classes beyond grade 4, the critical dialogue sessions provide this space. Beyond that is the general culture, the expectation that the teachers will be watchful, will try to know and understand their students, will be available to discuss their problems, will invite their lives into the classroom—all in terms of the examples they use, the informal conversations they have with them, and the deliberate reduction of conventional distance in teacher-student relations. In our teacher workshops we continuously emphasize respect for the girls.

The teachers indicate that they have learned to expand their job descriptions or roles at Prerna. While they had arrived with a different, rather limited idea of what they were to do as a teacher, interactions and encounters with their students changed their conceptions. Their role now encompassed being mother, mentor, counselor, teacher, and advocate for students' rights, as is evident from Roli's story. They saw the need to take care of them in multiple ways, particularly emotionally.

And from the students' viewpoint, it is evident they saw their teachers as playing these multiple roles. As Khushboo explained:

> The environment in our school is very good. Just like family. The relationship is not just that of a teacher and student. They treat us like their own. The love I got here I should have got from my mother.

The students said repeatedly that they felt listened to, understood, and supported, and they emphasized how important that was to them, how it helped them study better and feel better about themselves. For example, Kunti noted:

> Teachers were supportive and understood us. Like every single time, when we felt we are not able to study, we are not able to focus, they tried to talk to us about life in general and about us, about our family. So it was really helpful to concentrate on studies because when we got people to share our things, we feel better, we feel comfortable. For me, like in my case, it was very important that I was able to share my personal problems.

The key is being attended to and responded to as whole persons, not as objects. By confirming each other and rendering each other valuable, our lives are made visible and valuable, thereby acquiring value. Prerna is organized as a universe of care, every part of it being supported by the other: teachers supporting each other, the students supporting each other and being supported by teachers. As bell hooks says in her book *Teaching to Transgress*, "To hear each other, to listen to one another, is an exercise in recognition. It also ensures that no student remains invisible."[10]

The "daily reciprocity of caring" is an intrinsically good, ethical way of interacting with anyone, leading to the nurturing development and growth of everyone.[11] In my opinion, the world would be transformed if caring could form the foundation of all organizations and institutions—families, corporations, healthcare institutions, government institutions. In a caring relationship, human beings meet each other as equal persons, with a full recognition of their humanity, which is a fundamental way of challenging patriarchy.

6

Enabling Learning
Building a Web of Support

Here they support you for everything. My fee was waived off whenever I had no money and they show you how to make your way in life, how to make progress. That is very important. Whenever I felt lost, my teachers would counsel me and I would find solutions. I learned how to fight for my rights, how to manage my life, and I would not have completed even though I wanted to, if not for the continuous support I got here. If I was absent some days, even that they would understand; they understood my compulsions and helped.

—*Poornima, a Prerna alumna*

Though caring, respectful, responsive teachers are the main source of support for our students, the school's culture of care expresses itself in other forms of support as well. Prerna has recognized that the girls face several challenges that can keep them out of school and prevent them from staying when they do enroll. The school has tried to support them to meet these challenges, only some of which are visible on the surface.

Making Education Affordable: Financial Support

From the stories the girls tell us, it is clear that poverty is a major barrier to girls' education. Poor families are unwilling to spend scarce resources on their daughters' educations. Rachna, the founder teacher, found this when she went on her recruitment drive, and Laxmi and her friends all tell us the same story. If not for the very low fee at Prerna, she and others could never have attended school. Many of the parents interviewed said they were able to send all their daughters to school because the fee was so affordable.

Government schools are free for all children until grade 8, as per the Right of Children to Free and Compulsory Education Act of 2009, and books and uniforms are provided free to girls and children from the Scheduled Castes (SC) and Scheduled Tribes (ST), with special cash scholarships for children belonging to these two groups.[1] However, parents are reluctant to send their daughters to government schools. They see little value in doing so, both because of the high opportunity cost, since the subsistence of poor families is heavily dependent on the productive labor of girls, and because of their perception that the quality of education in government schools is poor.[2] A 1999 report on the Indian educational system noted it is a myth that elementary education is free. Although admission fees in government schools are minimal, several hidden costs deter parents from sending their children to school. "Recent surveys indicate that the cash costs of education play a major role in discouraging poor families from sending children to school, especially when the quality of schooling is low," the report said.[3]

Prerna began with a nominal fee of 10 rupees per month in 2003, and the fee is still highly subsidized at 100 rupees per month ($1.50) up to grade 8 and then 250 rupees per month ($3.75) in the secondary classes. This is a commitment fee so that parents value what they get and feel respected that it is not a handout. Need-based scholarships are given to those who cannot afford even this much. Around 20 percent of our students are getting full scholarships because their family incomes cannot support even the nominal fee or because there are too many daughters to educate. Several families have six or seven daughters studying in Prerna. A very inexpensive uniform has been prescribed, largely because parents feel a uniform dignifies students. The school has also made an effort to prescribe very affordable books. Uniforms and books are provided at a subsidized cost, often free in cases of extreme poverty. The entire uniform package for the summer and winter, including a sweater and sports gear, costs 1065 rupees ($16) for those in grade 6 and above and 830 rupees ($13) for those in pre-nursery to grade 5. The book package, including stationery, is 400 rupees ($6) per year.

Parents' testimony indicates that even when they are prepared to send their daughters to school and to pay for it, money can be a deterrent. Students have shifted to Prerna from approximately 40 schools in the neighborhood, both private and government-aided, and parents revealed that they come because of the affordable cost, distance, convenient schedule, the good-quality education, and the reputation the school has of being caring and safe.

Prerna is committed to supporting its students and alumnae in every possible way to ensure that they have good life outcomes. A scholarship of 5000 rupees ($75) is awarded to all students who finish grade 12 successfully and who intend to continue their studies by enrolling in a college degree program. According to one of our alumnae, Moni, all the girls in her cohort wanted to go for a bachelor's degree and some had already saved some money from their incomes; for those who had no money, the scholarship came as a blessing because it would have been impossible to fund their college education without it. She also mentioned that even though the scholarship covered only one year's tuition, once enrolled, the girls found the money to cover the remaining two years' expenses. In the last seven years, 93 of the 96 girls who have graduated have benefited from this scholarship.

A scholarship of 20,000 rupees ($300) is also awarded to Prerna alumnae who gain admission to a master's program. Moni's sister Soni, who was among the first to get this scholarship, said her parents would never have supported her postgraduate education if not for the scholarship. From the parents' perspective, a high school education would have been sufficient and a bachelor's degree was definitely more than enough. But once the scholarship was offered, their reaction was "If your school is giving you money for studying further, then go ahead and study." She is in the second year of her master's degree in education.

Two of the graduates gained admission to an unaffordable MBA program. In response, Prerna began a student loan program for girls such as these. Jyoti, a 2011 Prerna graduate, also graduated from this program. Though the 20,000 rupees scholarship was a great help, she needed further support, so she was given an interest-free loan of 50,000 rupees ($748), which she is paying off slowly (see box 6-1 to learn more about how programs are funded).

Adapting the School to the Girls' Lives—Convenient Timings

Though Prerna is an afternoon school by default, it has turned out to be a boon because many of the girls are compelled to work in the morning to support their families. As noted, 43 percent of our students work as domestic help to supplement family incomes, starting as young as age eight. The average income from this is approximately 1900 rupees ($28) per month and is essential to the

BOX 6-1. *How We Fund Our Programs*

The Study Hall Educational Foundation (SHEF) bore the entire cost of funding the Prerna School for the first four years. In addition, Prerna students in the afternoon could take advantage of the fully equipped building and playgrounds of the Study Hall School, whose students attended in the morning, saving Prerna significant infrastructure costs. At that time, SHEF's main source of funding was the fee received by Study Hall School. We used any surplus to fund Prerna and kept costs very low. The Study Hall parents are aware of the Prerna School and how it is funded and have not objected. In fact, many have come forward to support us additionally in recent years.

When the number of students reached 300, we began to need outside funding. My father came to my rescue. He helped tide us over and has continued to be our largest funder, even posthumously. Subsequently, we sought and received annual sponsorships for individual girls, by individual donors and organizations such as the Indian Institute of Management alumni fund and the Mona Foundation. The number of these donors increases every year and currently accounts for nearly 26 percent of our funding. Study Hall students raise another 5 percent for Prerna every year through fundraising programs, such as dance nights, raffles, and fetes. The swimming pool owned by Study Hall School is open for use after school by the parents and neighbors for a fee, all of which goes to Prerna, accounting for 8 percent of the funding. The surplus from Study Hall School funds the balance.

I began the undergraduate college scholarship, the scholarship for postgraduate studies, and the student loan program with personal

families. Laxmi, Preeti, Sunita, and Khushboo all could not have come to school if the school was not in the afternoon. If the girls and their families had to make a choice between work and school, many girls would not come to school.

The flexibility of the schedule has enabled many girls to get an education and emerge from the cycle of poverty by equipping them for better jobs. Laxmi, for example, has finished her bachelor's degree and is now working as

Laxmi being awarded scholarship for college

funds, which are now supplemented by donations from friends and family.

I have learned from my experience that, if you are fortunate enough, the best way to fund ideas you believe in is to start small and invest frugally with your own money. Once you prove your concept, donors do step up to help. This helps you work at your idea without the stress of meeting contractual demands made by donors. We do, however, keep looking for donors who believe in our work, and we hope to find a long-term donor partner. SHEF is committed to supporting Prerna in perpetuity, and we are in the process of setting up a corpus fund for Prerna.

head sales manager in a company with a salary of 25,000 rupees ($374) per month—a very fair middle-class salary. Many of our girls have similar success stories.

Teachers at Prerna do not support child labor and campaign against it continuously with the parents. However, since we see no alternative for these families, and since there is no government social security or safety net for the girls, we would rather our girls come to school while working than not enroll at all. Available data on labor-force participation clearly indicate that only a small minority of Indian children are full-time hired laborers. The vast majority work as family laborers at home or in the fields, not as wage earners. This distinction has a bearing on the relation between child labor and schooling because family work hours tend to be more flexible and can be adjusted to schooling.[4]

Girls have punishing schedules, as recounted by Laxmi and others, but they come cheerfully to school and maintain a high average attendance, as high as 83.6 percent—which is far above the national average for government primary and upper primary schools at 72.1 percent.[5] This is despite long hours of work at home; many work for eight hours in addition to coming to school for four hours. As Sunita says:

> It was good that the school was in the afternoon and it cost very little.
> I would work in the morning and come to school in the afternoon.

Similarly, Khushboo's grandmother was able to argue with her son, Khushboo's father, who objected to her schooling. Khushboo could be spared for a few hours in the afternoon, she said, after she had finished the housework in the morning, and could do more in the evening after school.

This demonstrates that if we want girls to come to school, stay, and complete, then we must accommodate school to their lives and the challenges therein, rather than expecting them to fit their fragile and precarious lives into rigid school schedules and rules. Given the reluctance of parents and the low value they place on the education of their daughters, given the pressures of poverty and a gendered perception of their roles, schools must adapt themselves as much as possible to the conditions of these girls' lives and work around the constraints and limitations that prevent them from getting an education.

Taking Care of Physical Needs

Many of the girls looked malnourished and were coming hungry to school. Beginning in 2011, we started a meal plan. A small, protein-rich midday meal is provided at no charge to all students up to grade 8. This is provided by government schools, as well, both to fulfill the nutritional needs of children and to serve as an incentive for children to enroll and attend.

Apart from this, the principal and teachers are responsive to their students' healthcare needs. Even though the government has free healthcare for those who need it, the care is highly deficient in quality and very hard to access. Recognizing this and the fact that our students' lives are vulnerable to disease given their poor and precarious living conditions, the school has responded in several ways. Medical, dental, and eye checkups are organized at the school regularly, often by local doctors on a volunteer basis or supported by organizations such as the Rotary Club. In addition, SHEF has started a medical aid fund and provides help when the girls are found suffering from serious illnesses like typhoid, jaundice, and tuberculosis.

The teachers have often gone the extra mile personally and helped to find subsidized healthcare for students and their parents when they have applied for help. For example, Mona required an expensive eye surgery without which her vision would have been severely impaired. Rakhee, the principal, appealed to a highly regarded ophthalmologist in the neighborhood who agreed to perform the operation free of cost. In another case, a student's father fractured a leg and was unable to work, causing the family, with no savings, serious financial deprivation. Prerna teachers raised money and used their connections to ensure that he was treated. They helped support him medically and financially for the next three months until he was able to go back to work. Thus, Prerna not only enhances social capital by providing financial support, it also opens up access to middle-class networks, which are often off limits to poor, lower-caste families.

Early Enrollment and Multilevel Accelerated Learning

Since the initial door-to-door recruitment of students for the first class, girls and their families or friends have initiated enrollment on their own. Students are brought by parents—mostly mothers—neighbors, other Prerna students, and community organizations. Though every effort is made to encourage the community to send children to preschool starting at age three, many girls who have fallen through the cracks are brought in by current students, others in the community, or self-enroll at much higher ages. Sunita asked me to accompany her on a home visit to a 10-year-old girl who had never been to school.

Aunty, she has no mother and so has to stay at home and take care of the house. I've tried to talk to her—that she can come in the afternoon, it's only a few hours, and she [can] manage her housework, also. Like all of us. But she is too scared to ask her father. She might listen to you.

I did visit the child and tried to persuade her father, who refused outright. However, Sunita persisted and after repeated visits was able to persuade her to join the school.

The school turns no girl away; the oldest girl to have come to Prerna without having any prior formal education was 15 years old. Prerna applies a multilevel learning model and accelerated program so these girls can learn at a different pace; they are transitioned to higher grades as rapidly as possible.

The Bridge Course

Our goal is to ensure that students achieve a primary grade education as early as possible and are transitioned to the upper primary level and finally to the secondary school. Because parents often wish to marry off their daughters as early as possible, it is important to ensure that girls finish a basic education as quickly as possible. In the earlier years, when class size was small, the accelerated learning was done informally by individual teachers. But as the number of girls requiring this accelerated program grew, along with class size, we started a special bridge program for girls who were older, had dropped out for several years, or had never been to school.

The bridge course began in 2012–13 with 12 girls. Two of Prerna's alumnae, Sadhana and Sushma, took on this class under the guidance of Rakhee and other senior teachers. The program has now grown to 40 girls in 2016. The age range is 10 to 18 years, with the average age being 14. On average, the girls have been out of school for approximately four years, with some girls returning after a six-year absence. Of the current cohort, 22 percent said they had been pulled out because parents thought they were learning nothing at school, and 30 percent said they had to be pulled out because the family migrated to another location where they found work. The rest said they were pulled out to work or to take care of siblings at home because of the ill health or the death of mothers.

SHEF developed its own materials for this course called Chhota Raasta (Shorter Path) based on the state-mandated curriculum. The class is divided into two levels, and a multi-grade teaching method is used, with each student developing at her own pace and being helped to move up the levels. Level one covers the course of grades 1, 2, and 3, while level two covers the course of grades 4 and 5. The students participate in all the cocurricular activities and

The Bridge Course students

have critical dialogue sessions once a week. Older peers provide support in school and at home. The teachers' goals are to restore girls' lost confidence and self-esteem and to instill in them the belief that they can learn. They are then put through an accelerated learning program with the goal of transitioning them to the mainstream school in the closest age-appropriate grade.

In her study of several accelerated or bridge programs around India, Vimala Ramachandran, a well-known scholar specializing in primary and girls' education, pointed out the value of such programs in helping girls who had "missed the school bus or simply got off the bus too early" to realize their right to education. She emphasized, however, that since most of these were informal programs, it was important to forge "effective linkages with the formal system to ensure continuous learning."[6] The success of Prerna's bridge program lies in the fact that it is embedded firmly in the formal school and in students' lives.

Our bridge program has enabled many girls who would have not enrolled or not stayed in school to get an education. It has recorded a 46 percent transition to age-appropriate grades each year. However, despite our best efforts, some girls do drop out, either because they feel they are too old or because they just don't want to be in a classroom. We are trying to see if they can be guided into vocational courses instead.

Becoming Girls' Advocates: Engaging Closely with the Community

The school engages closely with the community, understanding that the community and families need to be supported in raising their aspirations for their daughters' lives and recognizing education as a pathway to improvement. Prerna works at getting them to recognize the school as a partner in the project of educating their daughters and has put certain practices and systems in place to achieve this goal.

All new parents are required to attend an orientation meeting where they are introduced to the school's goals, the philosophy of empowerment, and our rights-based approach to education. Parents are required to sign a bond confirming they are aware of the law concerning child marriage, affirming they will abide by it, and agreeing to support their daughters to finish school. Though the bond is not a legal document, it creates an awareness and instills a minimum commitment. So far only one parent has refused to sign the bond and none of the parents has criticized this practice.

Parents are invited for monthly meetings and gender workshops where their children's academic learning is discussed, along with other important social issues, like child marriage and girls' right to education and to lives of their own choosing. In most meetings, students put on small performances where they visually express their feelings when they are subjected to abuse, neglect, and early marriage. In one meeting, after the performance and discussion, the first batch of our alumnae were presented scholarships to attend master's degree studies. Neetu, the returning student mentioned in chapter 5, raised her hand and asked to speak. She came right up to the front and said:

> I want to say something to the parents here. These girls getting the scholarship and going for their master's studies were my classmates. This is where I could also have been, had my parents not married me off in class 9.

Bravely, she narrated her story and ended with an appeal:

> Please don't do this to your daughters. Give them every opportunity you can to study. Marriage is simply not the only answer for their future security.

Similarly, we encourage parents to speak up in support of girls' education and their rights. We have found this practice effective in influencing reluctant parents. At a parent meeting during a discussion on early marriage, one of the mothers who had been persuaded not to marry off her daughter, Priya, who had completed her bachelor's degree, asked:

> But tell me, now that my daughter has studied so much, she will need a more qualified boy; he will demand a higher dowry. So where am I going to bring this much money to get her married?

One father responded:

> Listen to me, if she is educated, she will manage herself. She will start earning money and you just see, then the boy's family will not ask for dowry. You just let her study as much as she wants . . . you don't have to feel so burdened.

Parents are also introduced to community and government organizations providing protective services to children and women, like Childline, Suraksha, and the recently established Women's Power helpline in Lucknow, 1090.[7] Prerna works at informing communities about the law, particularly laws that protect women and children, in our monthly meetings and whenever the opportunity presents itself. Our effort is to help community members recognize themselves, particularly women and girls, as citizens and to construct constitutional identities to give them a more equal status than the traditional identities they wear.

When a proposed child marriage comes to light, we intervene actively and immediately. When necessary, we have found it very useful to invoke the law, even though we know it is very hard to mobilize the police. One of our students, Rinky, a ninth grader and age 16, faced an early marriage. Her family had pressured her into believing it was her duty to protect the family honor by marrying the groom chosen for her, since they had already given consent. We called in the parents and informed them that the marriage was illegal, as she was underage, and her consent did not make it legal. The parents insisted on going ahead, saying all the arrangements had been made and now the honor of both families was at stake. Rinky was silent and scared to oppose her parents, but glad for our support. We tried hard to counsel her parents against this action. Her mother cited poverty as one of the reasons for marrying her daughter off early: "You don't understand. We are poor people and we have to marry our daughters as soon as we can." I argued, though unsuccessfully, that

Rinky's early marriage would not diminish the family's poverty, that it was not the only option to secure her future, that education offered other pathways; if Rinky was educated she would be able to earn a better living and help the family. After many unsuccessful sessions where we collectively tried to persuade the parents to postpone the wedding until Rinky was 18 and had finished her school education, I finally called her fiancée, who was 22. He implored me to back off, saying all the arrangements had been made, the invitation cards printed, and it would be a major loss of face for his family too. "I promise to let her study after we get married," he said.

I heard him patiently and then invoked the law. "You do know that this is illegal, and you could be arrested for statutory rape, right? She is 16 and you are 22; even in cases of mutual consent it is illegal to have sex with a minor." He said he was unaware of this law but seemed to be more willing to listen to me.

"Here is what I suggest," I continued. "You only have to wait for two years till she finishes her school education and is of legal age and then you can marry her with an easy conscience." He sounded very noncommittal as he hung up, saying he would talk to his parents. I was delighted and a little surprised to hear a few days later that he was able to convince his parents to postpone the wedding. He ended up marrying Rinky three years later, soon after she finished twelfth grade. Her parents, who had been less than happy at the intervention, have since thanked us, grateful that Rinky was able to finish her education.

Even though it is difficult to get the police to act in cases of child marriage and we are reluctant to take the matter to those lengths for fear of alienating our parent community, simply invoking the law has proved to be very effective, as in Rinky's case. Though we have met with some failed attempts—for example, in the case of Nandini, whose early marriage we could not prevent— we have succeeded in preventing many child marriages. The teachers and the principal fight to keep the girls in school and to ensure that their rights to realize their full human capabilities are respected. We do not have exact figures, but Rakhee and her teachers report that they are facing fewer cases of child marriage every year.

Despite the law against child marriage in India, passed in 2006, "convictions have been few and far between."[8] In 2014 convictions were secured in only 14.6 percent of cases.[9] Organizations like UNICEF and other local NGOs, however, have actively campaigned against early marriage, and SHEF has been part of these efforts, as well. We regularly participate in seminars and conferences to share how we organize ourselves as a school to prevent early marriages. And we advocate strongly that other schools and teachers expand their roles to include advocacy against early marriage and other violations of girls' rights.

Over the last 14 years, we can say with some conviction that we have been able to change parents' mind-sets toward their daughters—their right to education and their lives—to some extent. While we have had confrontations, like the one just described, we do not view ourselves in an adversarial relationship with our parent community. We believe that when we work in the best interests of their daughters we are supporting both the parents and their daughters. Our goal is to build an awareness in all our parents, especially the reluctant ones, to perceive their daughters' education as a common goal, as a way of enabling them to lead better lives, which would in the long run mean better lives for the families, too.

Technically, we have no jurisdiction over the parents' personal decisions regarding their daughters so the parents could easily tell us to mind our own business. Yet, it is interesting that, in most cases—sometimes after repeated requests—parents do come and sit through these counseling sessions, even when they don't agree with us. The unequal social power position of the school and the parent community, and fear of legal repercussions, might help explain why parents are willing to listen. I believe the main reason, however, is that they know Prerna is a school with its students' best interests at heart, even when the school's views run counter to their own.

In early 2016 we conducted a community survey to understand Prerna's impact in the community in terms of changing attitudes and mind-sets. One of the questions was, "We encourage girls to speak up against child marriage and domestic violence in school. Do you think school should be educating girls thus?" All the respondents, mostly mothers, agreed and 27 agreed very strongly. Some of their responses included:

It is very good that the school teaches them this; it will have a good impact on future generations and make them stronger.

Yes! This knowledge is very important for girls to keep themselves safe from violence and exploitation.

It is interesting that our enrollment has grown steadily every year, even though we often are swimming against the cultural current—against the accepted practices of the community. In the same community survey, we asked a follow-up question: "Girls are taught their rights in school. Do you agree with this practice?" All but one of the 80 respondents agreed it was a good thing, and 29 of these agreed very strongly, one parent saying, "All schools should teach girls their rights." Others commented that awareness of their rights was important for the girls because it led to greater self-confidence and independence, gave them strength, and was good for their daughters' futures. One said, "It will teach her to fight for her rights in the future also." Another said that "the school teaches her everything that we can't teach her," and another commented, "My daughter teaches me everything she learns in school." One father recommended that "all schools should have such programs."

Being Responsive to the Community's Needs—DiDi's

Our girls and their families come from extremely poor backgrounds. Mothers and their daughters bear the brunt of the unholy nexus of poverty and patriarchy, suffering long hours of work and, in too many cases, abuse by violent, drunken husbands and fathers. While 75 percent of our mothers are employed, not all of them have full-time work. Many of them work as domestic help, washerwomen, or construction workers with intermittent work, at a daily wage. One-fourth of our mothers are unemployed, rendered even more vulnerable by their economic dependence on their husbands. In response to the economic needs of some of our mothers, a sister organization—and a multigenerational workplace—was established with the dual goal of empowering the mothers and their daughters economically and emotionally. Called DiDi's, it is a social enterprise providing services and employment, while also making a profit to support the educational mission of Prerna. In addition, DiDi's provides the midday meal free to Prerna students and also uniforms at a small cost. So the business provides livelihoods to the mothers while helping educate their daughters. Everybody wins.

Veena, a Study Hall teacher, took charge initially, and DiDi's began with the management of the Study Hall School cafeteria by two mothers.[10] It has grown since, employing 65 women, and has become a leading caterer for corporate offices and individuals. It also tailors the uniforms for all the SHEF schools and two other schools. It employs mothers of our most destitute girls and other women from the community who need employment. In addition, it provides employment and training to girls who graduate from Prerna. Veena is part of the Goldman Sachs' "10,000 Women" program and has successfully participated in three of its training and mentoring programs.[11]

The mothers have found economic and emotional support, since DiDi's works on the same principles of care as Prerna. They have also found social status as a result of their economic independence and because they are working in a company.

Sheela, whose daughter Sandhya is a Prerna alumna, became DiDi's delivery van driver. She was the first professional woman driver in Lucknow and felt a great sense of dignity working for an organization rather than as a domestic helper. She said:

> At first my neighbors criticized me for driving, saying it's not a woman's work. But I didn't listen. Now they have stopped talking. I have started seeing the world outside. Earlier I knew nothing; now I drive and go to so many places. I feel very good.

She is a great role model for other women to venture into areas not traditionally meant for women. Completely illiterate, Sheela demonstrates great confidence, has been greatly empowered by her work for DiDi's, and now has even higher aspirations, inspired by Kunti, who went on a plane to the United States for her community college scholarship. She said, "One day I will also fly on an airplane."

Monika was a single mom in need of work. She had a small daughter whom she enrolled in Prerna and she worked in DiDi's.

> Since I joined DiDi's my life has changed a lot. I have done so much, I have grown here only. That's why I like it here. I feel very safe here.

Many parents find both Prerna and DiDi's very safe places for their daughters and do not apply mobility restrictions when the girls go to either Prerna or DiDi's late in the evening or even on holidays.

Khushboo, Preeti, Jyoti, Kunti, and Kunti's sister Rama all worked at DiDi's while pursuing their higher education. Very few organizations allow their employees the flexibility to work and study at the same time. The money the DiDi's girls earn is an invaluable support to their families and for their own higher education. They gain valuable marketable skills, giving them an advantage for future employment. Kunti and Jyoti, graduating from Prerna in 2009 and 2011, respectively, were both able to gain admission to an MBA program because of their work experience at DiDi's.

Jyoti and Kunti have returned to DiDi's in managerial positions after completing their postgraduate management diplomas. They are now deputy managers earning 20,000 rupees ($300) each. Jyoti is in charge of business development and sales and Kunti handles personnel and client accounts. We hope they will take complete charge of the enterprise in time. Jyoti says:

> When I first came here, I joined because the salary here was more than anyone else would pay [me] and also because no one would allow me to study at the same time. But now after my postgraduate degree, I feel my whole ambition has changed. Now I feel that this is the place that helped me grow, Veena Aunty is the one who helped me gain admission to the MBA program, so I should work toward finding more opportunities [for this place] . . . so that other girls like me and their mothers can also join and benefit, like I have. . . . If I use what I have learned here and in my college, then probably we can improve and more people can join us.

DiDi's presents its own challenges and tensions, especially in a country like India where age differences are governed by rules of deference to the elders. The younger girls are educated, while most of the older women are either illiterate or minimally schooled. The girls had to negotiate the terrain carefully. In the beginning they often ran into trouble but learned to navigate more successfully with time. As Kunti said to me when discussing her relationship with the older women she must manage:

> I see what I can learn from them and what they can learn from me. So the whole process is about learning and understanding each other. . . . Also all these elder *didis* are like my mother, very similar. They face many of the problems my mother has had to face, so helping them is like helping my own mother. That feels very good. . . . We can build their skills, so that they can stand on their own feet. I love this effort for my community.

What about Our Boys?

Some years after we started Prerna, the parents asked that we educate their sons too. We heard often:

While our daughters are being educated so nicely here, our sons are becoming *goondas* [gangsters] and street urchins. What about them? They also need education.

Our first instinct was to ignore the request because we wanted to use our resources for those who were most disadvantaged, the girls. But the parents persisted, and we found ourselves opening a primary section for boys in July 2009 with 50 students. In 2015 we opened a senior school for boys, guided by the understanding that boys need to develop a feminist consciousness as much as girls do, so that they find a way of critically examining the ways in which patriarchy constructs masculinity and how men and women both are deprived of mutually enriching and nurturing relationships. We now have 150 boys enrolled, 100 in the primary section and 50 in the senior section. Though this effort is in a relatively nascent stage, I describe this separate program briefly in the epilogue.

Pedagogy

We believe that schools must provide a safe and caring environment first, because this creates the fertile ground in which sound pedagogical practices can bear fruit. Without these supportive conditions, the best pedagogy will have only limited success. The reverse is also true, of course. Caring without competence has little value for students and parents.

Delivery of a poor education continues to be a strong deterrent to retaining girls from disadvantaged groups in school, even when education, uniforms, and textbooks are free and monthly scholarships provided.[12] The 1999 study mentioned earlier found that even when parents are highly motivated to educate their children, they are reluctant to send them to school when they were not convinced of the quality of education provided by the school.

Parental hopes of quality education are often massively frustrated. This, in turn, discourages them from sending their children to school regularly even when they have a genuine interest in education.[13]

As already explained, Prerna works hard to support girls' learning in the classroom and beyond. The pedagogy is engaging, interactive, participatory, and activity based. Though we use a standardized government-mandated curriculum (see box 6-2), students' individual abilities are kept central and are addressed by the teacher. Using a developmental approach recommended by developmental psychologists and child theorists, the teacher focuses on children's inherent strengths and abilities and helps them move forward on the learning curve.[14] This is a view of:

> Children as social, cultural and historical beings growing, learning and developing in a social context, as part of a social and cultural process, using cultural tools, their competencies linked with the competencies of others—developing into a wider and wider realm of meanings.[15]

As Chetna, a teacher, has noted:

> When I or any other teacher knows that the child is not able to do something, she puts extra effort into that child. We try to harness her talent in some other area, so that from there, she can gain confidence. That's the most important thing—confidence that she can learn! We work very hard at that. And when a child makes a mistake, we don't scold, we try to help her. . . . We don't classify them according to their marks. They are all equal and we tell them that.

The teachers apply their pedagogy based on the daily circumstances of the girls' lives, keeping the lesson relevant by using examples from their lives and contexts. They use interactive, participatory methods of delivery to engage the girls in their own learning. Even though the teacher clearly has the authoritative role in the classroom, the attentive, listening, and responsive pedagogic stance of the teacher makes the classroom more participatory and democratic. Teachers work hard to make the materials accessible to the students by using activities, role-playing, and small group work. Most important, they show they care about their students' learning. They demonstrate their faith in their students' ability to learn and provide every support in school, conscious that there is very little support at home; often none. They are also alert to signs of abuse or other problems at home that interfere with learning, and are quick to investigate and take appropriate action.

The teachers are trained via regular workshops, critical dialogues, and training videos that model the same pedagogy. They are also trained to adopt a clear, critical feminist perspective when conducting the empowerment classes that form a key part of the curriculum and are described more fully in the next chapter.

Enriched Curriculum

Prerna follows the state-mandated syllabus, with a focus on reading, writing, and numeracy skills in the early grades. The primary language of instruction is Hindi (also the mother tongue for almost all our children), with English as a second language. English is added as a second language in grade 1 and taught aggressively to ensure students have mastery over a language that continues to be necessary for getting better-paid jobs in the state and in India. In response to popular demand, the state has introduced English in all its public schools at grade 1.

In addition, students receive instruction in social studies and simple science in the primary grades. The syllabus grows in complexity in the upper primary and secondary grades (see box 6-2).

The academic curriculum is enriched with sports, martial arts, music, art, and a strong focus on drama. The students are encouraged to develop a strong voice and to use it in a variety of forums. They have several opportunities to express themselves and participate in public-speaking events and to give presentations and performances, to which parents are regularly invited. Girls are given every opportunity to develop leadership skills. Grade 6 and above are divided into groups called "houses," each with a distinct name and identity. In Prerna they have been named after legendary Indian heroines: Laxmi, Gargi, Sarojini, and Ahalya. These houses are led by senior girls, who organize and lead their members for the various events organized by the school, such as debates, dance, music, and art competitions. All the events have gender justice as their theme. For example, one topic for a declamation contest was "Is marriage the only goal of a girl's life?" Other themes include "Democracy and equal education for girls"; "Democracy and patriarchy: Are they consistent?"; "Honor killing: Whose honor are we defending?; and "Child marriage or girl slavery?"

The school organizes an elaborate concert and an equally elaborate sports day, on alternate years, ensuring that every girl participates. Parents are invited to these events and turn out in large numbers. Rakhee reports that the number of fathers at all our events and meetings is growing substantially. These are opportunities for the parents to see their girls shine on the stage or the sports field and to be proud of them. The teachers believe the girls not only enjoy sports very much, but also gain a great deal from them. As one teacher explained:

> Sports keep the girls active and very happy. It refreshes their mind. . . . [Outside Prerna] they never get the opportunity to play. They never

BOX 6-2. *Curriculum*

Primary (Nursery to Grade 5): Hindi, English, math, science, social science, computer science, sports, drama, critical dialogue (from grade 4), dance, and music

Upper Primary (Grades 6 to 8): Hindi, English, math, history, geography, science, computer science, critical dialogue, sports, drama, dance, and music

Secondary and Higher Secondary (Grades 9 to 12): Hindi and English as compulsory subjects, plus any four electives of the following: math, history, geography, science, home science, psychology, sociology, Indian culture and history, and computer science. Sports, drama, critical dialogue, dance, and music classes, along with career counseling and vocational training provided as an additional option

have a chance to play. [Here] they play basketball, badminton, and the sports day! That's huge! When they march with the flag, they feel very proud and so confident. Parents also feel so proud. They come and tell us that they never imagined their girls could be so good.

In India one rarely finds girls playing in the public playing fields or the empty plots where children play informally. International Labor Organization data show that girls are engaged in household chores for more than 24 hours a week, which is twice as much as boys.[16] Boys, on the other hand, are found playing cricket or football, depending on the season. Girls should have an equal right to play. Other than the developmental benefits of play and sports, girls have a right to be happy and to engage in activities that are fun. Prerna makes sure they have opportunities to exercise this right in school. Understanding the empowering potential of sports, Prerna's students are encouraged to participate in local, district, and even state-level matches. One student, Sandhya, won a gold medal in a district-level basketball tournament and was selected for the state basketball team along with Shalu, recently selected and sponsored by the Uttar Pradesh government for a coaching camp, from which the national young women's basketball team will be selected.

Sunita, Khushboo, and Laxmi on their Sports Day

Playing basketball

Making Sure Girls Attend Regularly

The teachers monitor their students' learning and attendance very closely. If a child is absent for more than two or three days, the teacher pursues the absence aggressively—calling the parent, asking girls who live nearby to find out why the child is absent, and if all fails, the teacher makes a home visit. This practice sends a strong message to the parents that the school is serious about girls coming to school regularly and will track students' attendance closely. Many planned child marriages have come to light, and some foiled, because of this tracking. The teachers share their monthly average attendance with the principal and director. As a result, the annual average attendance of the school is 83.6 percent, well above the national average for government primary and upper primary schools at 72.1 percent.

However, Prerna continues to be responsive to the exigencies of the girls' lives. Since several of our students' parents are migrant laborers, they leave for their villages when there is no work, taking their children with them, returning after a few months when they again find work in Lucknow. Girls often return after months of absence due to this practice, and Prerna has taken them back and tried to help them make up for the lost time in school.

Supporting and Tracking Learning: Flexible Low-Stakes Assessments

Teachers track their students' learning zealously but are careful not to make their assessments threatening, stressful, or judgmental. They make sure students are well prepared and give them time in school to practice and prepare. Teachers are sympathetic to the constraints faced by the girls at home and are willing to make necessary adjustments. It is common for a student to ask the teacher for more time to study for a test, as Laxmi did, "because there was no time to study last night. I was cooking till late." And it is equally common for a teacher to allow the student this time.

With support and supervision by the principal and academic head, teachers create their own tests until grade 9, pitching them to the ability levels of the majority in the class. Teachers aim to design assessments that enable learning and also give children the satisfaction of knowing they are learning. Our students seem to take their tests seriously, as teachers report a spike in attendance on the days of tests and exams. Students are tested every month, with summative assessments at the end of the first term, called half-yearly exams, and at the end of the academic year, when children are tested on the whole year's coursework. Test scores are shared and discussed with the principal and director at the end of every month, along with attendance averages. Student reports are shared with parents on a quarterly basis; in problematic cases more frequently. Parents feel respected by this practice because it shows the school feels accountable to them for their daughters' learning. This shows them that, because they know their abilities and struggles so well, teachers care about their children. Parents also like to know that their girls are learning; they enjoy seeing their progress and are encouraged and further motivated by it.

Grades 10 and 12 have national board examinations, made and conducted externally by the National Institute of Open Schooling (NIOS) in Delhi. The NIOS is the board of distance education, under the Union Government of India, established in 1989. It is a special education program meant for children in remote areas who have special circumstances or needs that prevent them from taking the regular, very high-stakes, state or national board examinations. The syllabus and materials are designed by the board in Delhi and provided to individuals, centers, or schools that use their board exams. The NIOS board certificates are recognized nationally and internationally by universities and given equal consideration with the other state and national board exams during admission.

We have chosen the NIOS board because of its wide range and flexibility in choice of non-compulsory subjects. The learning materials, such as textbooks, are carefully sorted in terms of complexity according to grade level, and the lessons are clearly and simply presented, making them accessible for the students. Additionally, we supplement these with our own materials. Most important, NIOS offers a very easy, flexible examination schedule, allowing students to choose the number of subjects they want to be tested on at one time. Students are allowed to repeat a test if they fail, or if they want to improve their grades, without the first grade appearing on their final transcript. Since only the highest grade is recorded on the final transcript, it is a low-stakes examination, allowing girls many chances to succeed.

Research reports that high-stakes testing, with only one chance to pass or fail, is unfair to students such as those from Prerna, who, with all the challenges they face at home, have difficulty keeping up regularly with their studies and, consequently, with passing the gatekeeping exams at each level, which leads to their repeated failure and eventual dropout.[17] It is also the case that the high-stakes state and national board exams serve as gatekeepers for university admissions supported by a large academic coaching industry, which even middle-class families are barely able to afford, thus giving them a distinct advantage over poorer families. As PROBE reports, this is particularly frustrating and "hard to bear for those who cannot afford private tuitions and are unable to create a learning environment at home."[18]

In the shadows of this high-stakes testing industry, the NIOS course has become stigmatized over time, perceived as a course for children who are deficient intellectually, as lacking in rigor and not of equal status. In my view, rigor should not be confused with a stressful high-stakes testing system. Our students work very hard, as do our teachers, and emerge with the competencies required for admission to law, commerce, and humanities courses in colleges and the local state university. In fact, our students have faced no trouble in getting admission into state universities and colleges.

What the NIOS board provides us with is flexibility. It gives us a fair amount of freedom to design our curriculum as we wish, which we value greatly because we believe that our enriched curriculum is the main driver of our success, even academically. Its assessment format is flexible, allowing students many chances to pass their exams—something that, according to the principal Rakhee, "is a very comforting, stress relieving feeling for the student and teacher both."

Given our students' circumstances, like that of Neetu described in box 5-1, this model allows us to take them at any age, and helps to motivate and keep them in school. Another of our alumnae, Poornima, also a returning student, was able to finish grade 12 because the NIOS allowed her flexibility in attendance. She was compelled by her circumstances to work full-time after tenth grade. Rakhee allowed her to attend part-time and gave her extra help when she needed it. She took three years instead of the usual two, but she completed twelfth grade. Poornima expresses her gratitude to Prerna, saying she could never have become whole again if she had not returned to school:

If Rakhee aunty had not brought me back, I would never have come back to school. I felt so scared, ashamed, and I would have been married off by now.

About the future she says triumphantly:

Now I want to do my B.A. and then I will see what I want to do. Right now, I'm so proud of myself. No one in my family has studied so much. I could never imagine I would even finish tenth grade! Look at me!

Computer Education

Computer education is provided to students from grade 4 onward. Though they learn to use computers in traditional ways, learning to do school-level coding and other tasks, students in secondary school are encouraged to use the Internet, make digital movies, and use the electronic medium to express themselves and expand their connections with others in the world, thus giving them a more cosmopolitan view of themselves, their lives, and the world outside. Laxmi, Khushboo, Preeti, and Sunita were part of a multination student network and engaged with students in other countries in various ways for three years as part of a research project led by my friend and colleague, Professor Glynda Hull at the University of California at Berkeley. In this project, youth from a variety of cultures and countries—South Africa, Norway, the United States, and India—communicated and exchanged digital artifacts such as stories, pictures, and videos via a protected online social network called Space2Cre8. The program provided a platform for all the participating youth to "reimagine themselves in relation to their local communities and the world around them and to develop an awareness of their positionality relative to and in conjunction with others." Our unique use of computer education is described more fully in an article in *English Education*.[19] Since then, our students have learned to become active on social network sites, and as a school we have tried to engage them in using the electronic medium as a site of self-expression, self-construction, and self-expansion.

Vocational Training and Career Counseling

Prerna students receive vocational training while working as apprentices in the schools and constituent units of SHEF from grade 9 onward, when they are at a legal age to work (see box 4-1 for more about SHEF). Each year 25 girls get this opportunity, assisting at the reception desk, in the science and computer labs, and in the library for three hours each day in the morning before school. They receive a small stipend of around 1500 rupees ($22) to 3000 rupees ($45) per month. Unfortunately, not all girls get this opportunity, first, because several of them are working in the morning and the opportunity cost of leaving their jobs is too high. Laxmi, for example, had to keep working in several homes through her school years to support her family. Second, there are limited outlets in SHEF. Several girls save the stipend and use the accumulated amount for their higher studies. Khushboo, however, who interned in

Students celebrating their achievements at Convocation ceremony

the computer lab for a year and in the DiDi's-run cafeteria for another year, used her stipend to pay for her grandmother's hospital bills.

Career counseling is provided regularly through a mentoring process with the aim of building each girl's aspirations for a better life and helping her plan ways to achieve them. Parents also are regularly counseled to encourage their daughters to pursue higher studies and careers, holding up examples from our alumnae. The goal is to build aspirations in our girls and their parents that education can help them break caste and class barriers that have constrained their lives thus far.

Celebrating Girls' Learning

At the end of each year the school holds a formal convocation ceremony to honor girls who graduate from grade 10 and grade 12; in recent years girls who complete their bachelor's and master's degree also have been included. It is a moving ceremony, where girls march fully attired in cap and gown and receive their certificates and prizes from their principal and some distinguished academic or local celebrity. Their parents and families are invited. We have found that parents also bring their neighbors to witness their daughter's achievement. In most cases their daughters are the first in their family to graduate from high school.

Aarti describes her graduation ceremony as:

> An out-of-this-world feeling. I felt so proud. In other schools nothing like this happens, so our families and our neighbors all wonder. They are fascinated! And they ask us what degree we have got! We feel very special, even our parents.

Her teacher added, "Even we feel so proud of our girls. They look so beautiful, all dressed up!"

Prerna's goal is to respect girls and their education. Rakhee reports that parents feel very respected. Our purpose is to encourage parents to value their daughters' education, particularly its completion, and to motivate others in the community to send their daughters to school and keep them there. We have started to celebrate our alumnae who have completed their bachelor's and master's degrees with the aim of raising the aspirations of parents for their daughters. Parents who have spoken at the convocation have expressed their pride, saying they are grateful that their daughters have achieved what they could not. As expressed by one father:

> I didn't finish school and I am so glad that Poonam has finished. I don't know how to speak English. But when she speaks English, I am so proud!

7

Developing a Feminist Consciousness
Dialogical Circles of Empowerment

Critical dialogues opened our minds, and we were forced to
think—[about] what happens to us, what should happen, and
why it doesn't happen. So that helped a lot.

—*Aarti, a Prerna alumna*

The girls in my story are all developing what Gerda Lerner, in her book *Creation of Patriarchy*, defines as a *feminist consciousness.*[1] They have reflected on their own condition; they know that what has happened to them is wrong and that the structural conditions in society have been responsible for their subordination and opposed to their freedom and equality. In listening to their friends' stories and problems, they have helped each other develop ways of changing their condition and have expressed alternate visions of their future.

So how did this happen? They refer to "critical dialogue classes," to drama, to writing of diaries and poems, to the fact that they were "listened to." In this chapter and the next, I describe how Prerna deliberately engaged in a pedagogy that was empowering. We channeled feminist pedagogy and critical pedagogy into our official curriculum through activities like critical dialogues, drama, and critical literacy not just to make students aware that they had a right to equality, but also to enable them to determine the direction of their lives and to free them from the fetters of oppressive social definitions and expectations.

111

Feminist author bell hooks describes a familiar experience for most of us who have struggled to make sense of our lives in patriarchal societies and families. She explains that, by continuously and painfully reflecting on our experiences, writing privately about them, and talking to whoever will listen to us, if we find the space, the opportunity, and the community to do so:

> One may practice theorizing without ever knowing/possessing the term, just as we can live and act in feminist resistance without ever using the word "feminism." . . . To me, this theory emerges from the concrete, from my efforts to make sense of everyday life experiences, from my efforts to intervene critically in my life and the lives of others. This to me is what makes feminist transformation possible. Personal testimony, personal experience, is such fertile ground. . . . While we work to resolve those issues most pressing in daily life we engage in a critical process of theorizing that enables and empowers.[2]

Inspired by this thinking, I set out to create a space in Prerna's official curriculum to practice feminism in the classroom, without ever calling it that, to help students theorize about and trust their lived experiences, to "read" their lives together in a way that empowered them. Dialogue, for Freire, is an existential necessity. According to him, it is by naming the world through dialogue that people transform it.[3] When you are denied the right to name your world, or when it is named for you by others, you are denied your historical and ontological vocation to become human, which dehumanizes you. To become human is to become more critically aware of our world and gain more control over it. I wove Freire's critical pedagogy into my feminist thinking to develop over time a practice of critical feminist pedagogy, suited to our particular context. This pedagogy aimed to raise girls' critical consciousness of oppressive social norms, power structures, and the gender relations that impact them. This approach enabled students to "name" their condition in a patriarchal world and to imagine an alternative self and life in a newly possible egalitarian social order and, most important, to work toward realizing it. Kunti describes our approach well:

> When we used to talk and listen to each other's stories, I got to know things about myself, about society, about other people. Like what's going on in society, with women, [and] about everything that is caus-

ing us problems. I came to understand more about my problems and how to resolve them, how to overcome them, and how to survive even.

Creating Dialogical Spaces of Possibility in the Classroom

Dialogue is at the heart of teaching and learning at Prerna. As the students, teachers, and I have pointed out in this book, education is relevant only when it helps us understand the personal, social, and political realities of our lives and equips us to navigate our paths through the complex terrain of those realities. This is especially the case given the girls' complex and challenging realities. Laxmi, Aarti, Preeti, Khushboo, and Kunti all relate stories in which the worlds they see and experience have been named and controlled by dominant others—usually fathers, husbands, and brothers. Their identities as girls and women, and their consciousness, have been constructed by dominant discourses of social tradition, religion, and patriarchy.

In developing an empowering education for our girls, the first thing we did was validate their experiences and realities. The goal was to help them deconstruct and then reconstruct their patriarchal subjectivities and enable them to relocate themselves in a mentally reordered world. We wanted them to emerge with the understanding that patriarchy has a history; it was begun in history and can end.[4] To that end, empowerment classes as a primary site for critical dialogues were held once a week. These classes began as an arts project, which provided the girls a safe space to express their experiences, feelings, and fears of being a girl. This led to critical dialogues about the girls' lives, which included the exploration of drama and dance as another medium for naming and learning about their worlds. This finally resulted in a rehearsed performance. This project is described in detail in the next chapter.

At first we conducted these dialogues only with the oldest students, above the sixth grade, but, at Rakhee's insistence, we began to conduct them with those as young as fourth grade—using an age-appropriate approach. She says that many of our fourth graders are teenagers and need to discuss these issues, too. Girls are vulnerable to child marriage as early as 11 and 12 years of age. They also need to understand all about "good and bad" touch as early as they can, as they are prey to sexual abuse at home and should be able to protect themselves. As a result many cases of sexual abuse have come to light and mothers have been alerted. Girls also learn how to demand equal treatment at home early, so that it becomes a habit.

Teacher conducting a critical dialogue

The development and refinement of Prerna's empowerment class has helped us understand the importance of creating official curricular space for girls to "read" their lives, not only so they can deconstruct and reconstruct them, but also so they are enabled to see themselves as active knowledge producers, not just knowledge consumers. In these classes, while the teacher has more power than the students as the "expert facilitator," the dialogues and reduced power-distance from the teacher make the classroom a more egalitarian space than a typical teacher-centered classroom in India. The teacher learns about her students' lives through the dialogues and shares her own personal experiences where they fit. At Prerna, the teacher is no longer the only source of knowledge, and students are no longer mere consumers. The girls are co-constructors of important knowledge that they need to live their lives.

In the following sections, I provide analytical descriptions of how Prerna has adapted the theory and practice of critical dialogues to the unique cultural context in which our students' lives are embedded. Excerpts of transcripts are provided here, but links to the videos with English subtitles, which were recorded in 2007 for instructional purposes, can be found in the notes.

Critical Dialogue: Early Marriage and Girls' Lives

Several of our dialogues are focused closely on marriage in patriarchal families. Rakhee, the principal, several teachers, and I all have experienced ways in which marriage, even between adults, severely limits our lives. Being women in a patriarchal society, marriage impacts our lives by circumscribing possibilities for us—physical, emotional, and intellectual. This is especially the case when marriage is not by choice. Rakhee attributes her truncated education to her brother, who thought a master's degree would render her marriage prospects more difficult. My own parents cut short my education when they found an eligible groom for me. In our focus group discussion, parents also expressed concern about meeting increased dowry demands from a more qualified groom for their educated daughters, never questioning the inevitability of marriage. In a short study in which Prerna students interviewed their own mothers, 95 percent, who had suffered untold miseries in their own (child) marriages, said that even though they believed marriage was an uncertain pathway to their daughters' happiness, it was unavoidable.

Nivedita Menon explains this well, describing the patriarchal form of family (and marriage) as:

An inherently violent institution that is gendered to the core, involving a complete reshaping of the self of the woman getting married. Women have to learn to remake themselves completely, but even more significant is the fact that the entire period of their lives before this singular event of marriage is spent in anticipating and preparing for this specific future, from the choice of career, education, to learning to be adaptable from early childhood.[5]

Menon identifies three main features of the Indian family: patriarchy (power distributed along gender and age hierarchies, but with adult men trumping older women); patriliny (property and name passing from father to son); and virilocality or patrilocality (the practice of the wife moving to her husband's home).[6] All three conspire to leave women vulnerable and completely under the control of and at the mercy of their husbands and their families.

In this excerpt, a group of eighth grade students are engaging in a critical dialogue with their teacher and peer leaders on the issue of marriage.[7] Kunti and Aarti, then in tenth grade, are the peer leaders. Kunti's cohort had engaged in a similar dialogue with their own teacher and were now facilitating the critical dialogues with the lower grades. The goal of this dialogue was to help girls gain a deeper understanding of the impact of child marriage on their lives. Notably, two of the students in this dialogue, sisters, Nandini (14 at the time) and Gangotri (17 at the time), are married and awaiting *gauna*.[8]

Peer leader: So everyone here is above 12, right? If you are married off now, what will happen? And also, if you are sent immediately to your in-laws' house, what will happen to you? How will you feel?

Nandini: Life will be ruined.

Peer leader: How?

Nandini: The girl will get pregnant and there will be all the household chores.

Peer leader: Tell me, what will happen to the girl?

Sudha: Her education, her freedom, whatever she has at her parents' house, it won't be there in the in-laws' house. So, she becomes pregnant, has to do all the work, even if she wants to study, she can't study. And if she wants to go out, that also she can't do.

Peer leader: So, like you said, that her freedom ends, what freedom? . . . What kind of freedom do you want? Even in your parents' home?

Gangotri: A girl should be allowed to play, have good food. She should be educated and learn many things. She wants to be happy, have much happiness. She has a lot of dreams to fulfill. But girls are married soon; they are physically and mentally not prepared. Her life is totally ruined. She is sent to her in-laws' house. She has to serve her in-laws and she gets thrashed by them and her life is totally ruined.

Teacher (intervening): Tell me, in your group, these two girls are married. Is this correct? Is it good?

All girls in unison: No, aunty.

Teacher: Why not?

Gangotri: [Because they] are small; [they] are under 18 years. It is [their] time to study, and do something in [their] life.

Teacher: So why didn't these girls protest and refuse to get married?

Kiran: Because their parents ordered them to.

Teacher (to all): So if your parents order you [to get married] then will you also say yes?

All in unison: No, aunty.

Teacher: Why? Why not? If they couldn't protest then how and why will you?

Teacher to Nandini: Child, why didn't you refuse or protest?

Nandini is silent. Her sister Gangotri steps in.

Gangotri: Parents yell at us and also say they will be dishonored if we don't keep their word. They say they will be insulted in front of guests. They talk us into it and we are forced to get married. We have to do whatever our parents tell us to do. Often, girls are not informed about their marriages. No one asks us. They tell us just a few days before the wedding when everything is ready and done. Generally they inform us when guests are already in the house. And suddenly they say you are getting married. And then parents tell us that they will be insulted in front of the guests. So the girl is also scared to refuse.

This scenario is exactly what happened to Nandini, who found out she was getting engaged only on the day of the engagement ceremony.

The teacher continues her questioning, trying to get the girls to explore solutions and imagine possible ways of resisting parental pressure: "So tell me, in this situation, what should you do?"

Nandini suggests mediation:

We should take somebody's help who can make our parents understand that this is not the right time to get their daughter married. Then too they might marry her off. But if the parents understand a little then maybe the girl will not be married.

The teacher turns the discussion to the value of finishing school:

Teacher: Say, if today you are married off and you are not able to complete tenth grade, then? How will that make a difference? . . . Tell me, Nandini, why do you want to complete class 10?

Again Nandini is silent and Gangotri answers instead.

Gangotri: So that if not much, at least I can get some small job, if I finish tenth grade. If I am educated, only then will I get some nice job . . . so that in future I don't have any problems.

Teacher: What kind of problems?

Gangotri: If my husband kicks me out, and if I have to go back to my parents' house, then I can get a job and take care of myself.

Teacher: Oh, okay. You tell me, Nandini? Like you two are now married, what do you think your life will be like? Think. So what will life be like after you get married? How will it change?

Nandini is silent, so another student speaks up:

Pooja: Aunty, after her marriage her life will be like this—her mother-in-law and her sister-in-law will taunt her, say all kinds of things to her. She will be told to do all the housework. Even though she might be the youngest in the house, still she will be landed with all the responsibility and work.

Teacher: Why so?

Peer leader: Aunty, that's what the in-laws want—I mean, they don't consider this girl who has come into their house, the daughter-in-law, as one of their own. [For them] this girl has come from another family, so she doesn't belong; she is like a servant, her job is to do all the housework.

Sudha: And she is scared and alone, so she can't refuse.

Teacher to all: So is this true?

All the girls nod.

Sudha: Aunty, they will keep her like a servant . . . and they will also hit her. If the husband is good then he might not, but mostly even he will hit her . . . so she will be entirely helpless.

Peer leader: If she has a job of her own, then will she tolerate this treatment?

Pooja: No, she won't. Because she would already know things.

Teacher: Then, what will she do if all this happens?

Pooja: A lot of girls silently keep on tolerating, and only very few don't, but girls should be like—they should definitely raise their voice. If in-laws don't listen, then she should file a report in the police station.

Pooja makes the point that it is important to protest against ill treatment. She invokes her identity as a citizen with rights, having recourse to laws and an authority beyond the family.

Teacher: Okay, Nandini, what will you do if this happens to you?

Nandini finally speaks up:

If this happens to me, I will tell my husband that "all this is happening to me, and that I don't want to live here, I can't work all day and still listen to your mother and father yelling at me, and that I don't want to live here." If I am educated, and I am working, I won't obey them.

Naming Their Reality

The dialogue vividly brings home the cruelty of both patriarchy and patrilocality—which is probably why Nandini was rendered silent. Nandini speaks up only at the end, as the comments by the teacher, peer leaders, and her classmates make her conscious of the implications of her marriage, even though she already has a vague impression that her "life will be ruined." I remember that, like Nandini and many other young girls who are married off early, I had almost no understanding of the life-changing commitment implied by marriage. In fact, like many young girls in my situation, I was completely distracted by the sudden attention, raised status, and the thought of many new clothes and jewelry.

Getting the girls to name the implications of patrilocality and child marriage is a first step to helping them see how unjust these practices are, even though so deeply ingrained in society. Sharing their feelings and experiences allows girls to look critically at such "normalized" practices and to use this space and dialogue for consciousness-raising and constructing an alternate reality.

Changing our consciousness about things is an act of change; one brick in the wall, yet a very important one. Gerda Lerner writes that "since women's thought has been imprisoned in a confining and erroneous patriarchal framework" for centuries, the precondition for change and for emancipation of women is to transform their consciousness about themselves.[9]

The teacher and peer facilitators' role in these dialogue circles is to use their persistent questioning to help the girls find ways of resisting. They push the girls to generate solutions and to imagine possible ways of countering parental pressure. Through this process, the girls can begin to see that the forced marriage need not be inevitable and irretrievable, as it is positioned to be. The girls are learning that education is a pathway to more control over their lives and that raising their voices in protest against injustice is important.

Though Nandini and Gangotri both remained in school for another two years, we failed to keep them to tenth grade, as the in-laws insisted on taking their daughters-in-law to their homes, and since they were older than 18, we could not take legal recourse. Much against their wishes, both Nandini and Gangotri saw their educations truncated. Their mother, however, upon being interviewed by our students, confessed that she had made a mistake and was determined not to do the same with her third daughter, Gayatri, who was thankfully married only after age 18.

I don't know why I did it. I wasn't well and it seemed like the best thing to do at the time but I know now that it was a mistake. I won't do the same with Gayatri.

Nandini has approached us recently with the desire to complete tenth grade. Gayatri has recently finished twelfth grade.

Critical Dialogue: An Identity after Marriage

In this dialogue with Kunti and Aarti's cohort, conducted before they became peer leaders for girls in lower grades, the teacher is wrapping up a module on marriage.[10] The girls had interviewed their own mothers to find out how they had experienced their marriages. All but one of the mothers had been married before the age of 15. In this excerpt, the teacher begins the dialogue by asking about the role of empowerment in a married woman's life:

Teacher: So, what does empowerment mean? We have been talking about that.
Kunti: To be aware.
Teacher: What does it mean to be aware?
Kunti: That a girl doesn't think that just because she is getting married, she just has to have kids and raise them, just [do the house] work, she should also think that if she has married, then how will that marriage be successful. That means she should not just tolerate any violence from husband or mother-in-law. And that just because she has married, it doesn't mean that she has to stay tied to the house only; she should do something for her own good, too.
Christina: That after marriage also, she should be able to give importance to her own life, that "I too have a life and I also can do something, not just doing whatever husband says or whatever mother-in-law says, I also have a right to think about my own life." Like it happens in a lot of homes, that [in-laws say]—"don't get the [tubectomy] surgery done till you have a boy," so this should depend on the woman also, that she can make decisions for herself. She also has desires; why does she have to do what society dictates? Like these days, even government says you should have only two kids. So she also should be able to say what she wants, that she wants only one [child], if that's what she wants—but then if her mother-in-law says—two—then what? If she has a [respectful] status in the home, then only can she refuse. "No, just one, I want to think of my life also."

Teacher: So, what does this mean?

Kunti: That we also should have a choice.

Teacher: Meaning you should have control over your own life; you should have a right, and an empowered person, male or female, is one who has control over his or her life, has choice. It's also called-self-determination. Like you say, "We want to stand on our feet." What does that mean? That I can live my life, according to me, according to my beliefs, according to my desires. My body is mine. My life is mine. My mother, my family also— those are also mine, so my relationships are also mine and we should care about those, too, and not like—only what I want should happen. We should listen to them also and to ourselves, too.

Here, the teacher emphasizes the relational nature of the "self" as against an overly individualistic view of it.

Kunti: Yes, so if mothers and family say something, then we shouldn't always say, "It's my life, I will live according to myself alone, it's none of your business what I do." This shouldn't happen! Meaning we should accept their good advice and argue about what we don't agree with.

Though it is apparent from the dialogue that the girls greatly value autonomy, they and their teacher point toward a relational autonomy.[11] The girls are learning to distinguish between being independent and being alone. The girls have always worked in groups, lending and borrowing skills from each other and building on each other's awareness to make sense of their lives collectively. Their dialogues illustrate that learning to be independent is a collective, social process. In this view, each person is not an atomistic individual, free from others and free to be alone, but instead a sovereign, autonomous person in a dialogic community of sovereign persons.[12]

Rama: I suppose one has to marry, but first we must study—so that before going to someone else's house, I can know myself, and can know society as well—that I, too, have a place in society. I also have a name; this doesn't mean that I should only be called someone's wife.

Kunti: My own name should be there, like it happens that the whole family adopts the husband's last name. Like if I am "Rawat," and I marry some "Sharma," I will be called "Mrs. Sharma." This should not happen. I should still be called "Rawat."

Kunti's comment here is particularly significant, revealing her comfort in her caste identity. Sharmas are Brahmins, while Rawats are Dalits. Kunti prefers to keep her Dalit identity. She does not feel "upgraded" by her marriage to the socially higher Brahmin identity.

Teacher: That means having an identity of your own. Why is that so important?

Sunita: Our education should give us an identity.

Teacher: Why? Who will be benefited by that?

Girls in unison: We ourselves.

Teacher: You will be respected more, right? Okay, why should we have an identity?

Jyoti: If we have an identity, then only can we think about moving forward; we can fight for our rights, if we have an identity.

Sadhana: Aunty, when you have an identity, then it's a different life.[13]

Teacher: How?

Sadhana: It's your own life; no one can say anything! And you are independent.

Teacher: And like we say—our rights. Now, how do you know that you have rights?

Kunti: You told us. We learned it here.

The teacher goes on to explain that they derive their rights from the constitution and their citizenship.

This dialogue illustrates the subtle but disruptive process of conscientization. It comes after several weeks of discussion, of sharing their feelings and experiences and trying to look at them analytically together. The teacher helps them move to an alternate way of looking at marriage. Kunti arrives at a very different definition of a "successful" marriage than how her parents, and mine, and our community might define it. They would consider a marriage successful if it remained intact, where their daughters successfully played their roles as obedient, cooperative wives and daughters-in-law; perhaps they would include "with less incidence of abuse." Kunti, by contrast, defines a successful marriage as one in which the woman refuses to tolerate any violence, physical or emotional, and is not restricted by the traditional role of the house-bound mother and wife; in fact, one where she can work for "her own good," too. In her interpretation and that of her classmate Christina, a successful marriage should be one where women have autonomy to "give importance to her own life" and have a voice that counts.

BOX 7-1. *Marital Status of the Girls Participating in Dialogues about Marriage*

Kunti is 24 and currently unmarried, although she had a boyfriend of another caste, who she bravely declared to her parents. After initial opposition, they accepted him

Jyoti is 23 and unmarried.

Aarti is 26 and unmarried. She says marriage is not her priority. She has to finish her degrees and build or buy a house for her mother before considering it.

Christina is 26. She is unmarried and has finished her bachelor's degree and a one-year diploma in nursery teaching. She is working as an assistant teacher in a pre-school.

Sadhana is 27. She has a bachelor's degree. She eloped and married a man from another caste.

Rachna is 26. She got married at 21, has one child, and is still pursuing her bachelor's degree.

Archana is 26 and finishing her bachelor's degree. She married a man of another caste of her own choice, after much resistance from her family.

Rama is 26 and was married at age 24 to a man of her parents' choice. She left him shortly after, saying the marriage was "a fraud." She has recently remarried, and is pursuing a master's degree.

Rinky is 26, married, with one child. She is still pursuing her bachelor's degree.

This illustrates how developing a feminist consciousness can lead to a reconstruction of their lived realities. The dialogue above is concluded by an interesting discussion of identity. The girls are very clear that they deserve to have an identity, because it will be good for them as individuals. Together with their teacher they are constructing an idea of what it means to be an equal, autonomous person and are coming to understand that being a person is integral to the conferral of rights; you must be a person to have rights.

The dialogue proceeded to a discussion (not presented here) of the centrality of having an identity as an equal person. The teacher pointed out the difficulty of this, turning the dialogue to a discussion of patriarchy and girls' place in it. Kunti could see that, for girls, being an equal, autonomous person is a fight and not an easy one "because the structure of society is that it doesn't want to see that the girls do something independently, have their own identity." The girls were determined that their lives would be different, as one said, "because we have a knowledge of our rights, of ourselves."

Our girls see very clearly that "a knowledge of our rights, of ourselves" is a crucial kind of knowledge. Prerna believes that education, particularly in the context of girls and other marginalized groups, is incomplete unless it includes this critical kind of knowing and knowledge.

Box 7-1 demonstrates how the girls in the dialogues translated their learning into their lives.

Critical Dialogue: Redefining Femininity and Masculinity

In another dialogue, the same group of girls were asked to describe what they saw as the defining characteristics of an ideal man and woman.[14] The goal was to help them develop alternate visions of masculinity and femininity by imagining what their own ideal conceptions of each might be. The students begin by responding that a man should be strong and able to earn money. Christina mentions that "he should give due respect to a woman." The teacher continues to probe the students for their thoughts:

Kunti: He must respect everyone. A man needs to think about a woman's aspirations and dreams, not just that he must also respect a woman.
Sadhana: He should give freedom to a woman.
Rinky: He should think about equality; he must consider that. He should also help with housework.
Kunti: He should respect everyone.
Christina: He should be employed somewhere.
Kunti: He must be wise.
Rachna: He should allow his wife to have a good job, work outside the home also.
Teacher: Okay. Now tell me about an ideal woman.
Kunti: She should be independent.
Christina: She must know about her rights.

Aarti: She must be educated.

Christina: Freedom is a must-have.

Sadhana: She should be aware about her own rights.

Kunti: She must make her own decisions.

Rachna: Women should be economically independent.

Jyoti: If she is educated then she also has some power.

Kunti: She should respect others and should be able to fight for herself.

Rachna: A woman must be educated and confident about herself.

This dialogue came after a series of dialogues, over a period of 10 weeks, in which the students describe marriage as their mothers, older sisters, and aunts had experienced it. The purpose of these dialogues was to help the students challenge the conventional notions of masculinity and femininity, which when internalized framed their ways of knowing, behaving, and constructing themselves in the world. The dialogical circles provide a safe place for the girls to risk definitions they are too afraid to articulate to their families and communities. They would be severely chastised if they were to ever express thoughts such as these. As is evident from the transcript, the students have arrived at definitions of masculinity and femininity that position them as equal persons, even though nothing in their lives at home or in society gives them an equal position. Even so, they are able to imagine the possibility of equality between men and women in what they know to be a very unequal society.

The Power of Possibility

Imagining possibilities is the first step in moving toward realizing them. bell hooks refers to Freire's work:

> In its global understanding of liberation struggles, always emphasizes that this is the important initial stage of transformation—that historical moment when one begins to think critically about the self and identity in relation to one's political circumstances.[15]

There were similar dialogues on topics like patriarchy, domestic violence, sexual violence, and gender-based discrimination at home and in society, dowry, menstrual health, reproductive rights and health. Recently—bravely, nervously, and with extreme caution—we embarked on a dialogue about the notion of honor (*izzat* in Hindi) and its location in girls' bodies. The subject of sexual freedom for girls, or their rights over their own sexuality, is fraught with danger and risk, given the often-fatal consequences for girls should they dare to transgress the strict norms around female chastity and sexual morality. Norms around sexuality are severe because control over women's bodies and their sexuality is central to maintaining patriarchal dominance.[16] Precisely for this reason, it is crucial that girls learn to critically examine and understand sexual norms and sexual morality.

The content of critical dialogues is continuously evolving, based on the emergent themes generated by the students' lives. We have not yet addressed caste and class directly in our critical dialogues because these issues were not raised by the girls. Gender-based oppression, especially in the domestic domain, seemed to be their most immediate experience of inequality, requiring the most urgent attention. We address poverty indirectly by helping them construct pathways to transcend their poverty through their education. We recently had a discussion with alumnae regarding the inclusion of caste in our critical dialogue curriculum, and they agreed it would be good to include it so girls learn to fight casteist attitudes in society and their families, especially as these govern their marriages. "Caste should not be a barrier to us marrying who we want," one girl said.

The critical dialogues are embedded in and informed by the culture of care that pervades the school. At Prerna we believe that care is empowering. The classes are very participatory, supportive, and enriched by improvised and performance drama and critical literacy, which I describe in greater detail in the next chapter. Each girl is made visible because everyone is included and heard. Even those who are rendered silent, overwhelmed by a conscientization of their reality, learn and eventually articulate the injustice of their lived experience. The process and the participant structure of the classroom, as much as the content of the dialogues, is empowering. As bell hooks writes, "To hear each other, to listen to one another, is an exercise in recognition."[17] Becoming visible to one another is a way of constructing oneself. I come to myself, mediated by another.[18]

Training Teachers

One of the school's major challenges continues to be teacher training as we work at getting teachers to adopt a more participatory, egalitarian approach in the classroom. This approach runs completely contrary to their prior training, their own schooling and teaching experience, and a culture in which deference based on age and gender difference is the norm. A continuous process of training is needed to move teachers from a didactic instructional mode to a more dialogical one where they listen to students, allow them to argue back, narrate their own experiences, and then build the lesson around this dialogue.

Teachers and students both come with the belief that teachers have the advantage of age, experience, and knowledge, and therefore justifiably occupy a superior power position in the classroom. In the case of Prerna, many of the teachers also have class and caste privilege. Stepping down and sharing their power with their students is difficult and seems to be counter-intuitive and countercultural. It takes a lot of support to move them in this direction. Students adopt the dialogic mode more easily, though girls who first enroll in the higher grades have more difficulty. One student who joined in grade 11 was very resistant to the approach, saying in some bewilderment, "Why are we talking about all these issues in school?" Her classmates explained to her the pedagogic rationale for the critical dialogues, along with their practical benefits: "We learn about practical living in [this school]."

Students discuss issues freely, with a lot of good humor, often disagreeing with each other and with the teacher, though less with the teacher because she is looked up to as the more authoritative voice. All the sessions involve drama and small group discussions, to enable full participation and more intense, uninhibited engagement and discussion. The teacher is trained to listen and follow students' cues. For example, in the dialogue on domestic violence, the teacher began the lesson by getting them to define the term.[19] She asked them to break up into groups to discuss what they understood by it and to develop an improvised play on how they might experience it in their lives. Once the girls had performed their plays, the teacher used them as the context for the dialogues. Listening to the students' rendition and narration of their experiences in this way guards against teachers framing the dialogues from their own middle-class perspectives. I personally learned a great deal about our students' lives through our critical dialogue sessions. It was an important way of bridging the differences of our lives.

The teachers continuously engage in critical dialogues among themselves as well, facilitated by more experienced teachers on issues of pedagogy, gender, and class. They reflect on their own experiences as women, as students, and as teachers, on their own class advantages, the differences and similarities between their own lives and those of their students, and how to negotiate these differences respectfully. They watch live and video-recorded critical dialogue sessions and are supervised by more experienced teachers until they feel comfortable about conducting these classes alone. This training is never a finished process, and some teachers take to the pedagogy more easily than others. Prerna alumnae such as Aarti have emerged as the most successful facilitators.

The teachers have a particularly difficult time working with issues of sexual rights and freedom as they struggle with their own fears around sexual freedom for girls. For example, Rakhee expressed the concern that an increasing number of girls were having relationships with boys and eloping. We engaged in extensive discussions with the teachers around the issue of girls' sexual rights, sexual behavior, and morality, and the difference between prudent and moral perspectives on sexual behavior.

Taking the Feminist Movement to Schools

Freire's critical pedagogy mostly addressed adult men, while the feminist pedagogy led by feminist educators in India and Western contexts has addressed adult women. Understanding the importance of the role of knowledge in achieving a gender-just world, Prerna seeks to bring the feminist movement to schoolgirls through its critical feminist pedagogy. The status of girls and women in countries like India shows that the work of the feminist movement is far from over. Educators can play a major role in building a more equal world provided we tap the enormous potential provided by the classrooms in our schools. They can and should be "radical spaces of possibility."[20]

8

Finding Self, Finding Home
Using Drama for Self-Work

We are learning to live strong.

—Kunti, a Prerna alumna

The goal of all teaching and learning, all education actually, is to answer the fundamental question: "Who am I and what is my relationship with the universe and others in it?" My view is closely aligned with educational theorists such as Anne Dyson, James Britton, Barbara Rogoff, Vivian Paley, J. Krishnamurti, and Jerome Bruner, who perceive the learning child as a social interpreter, using the cultural tool kit of metaphors, concepts, categories, and theories implicit in the language and multiple discourses, some inherited and some encountered. All these provide the cultural frames through which she makes sense of reality, reinterpreting and reinventing it along with her place in it.

One of the special features of Prerna is how it weaves together in its curriculum drama, reading, and writing, along with critical dialogues, to help the girls create a more empowering idea of themselves in the universe—so they feel more "at home" in an otherwise fairly hostile world. Here they can construct their own responses to the question "Who am I?" and attempt to place themselves in their social and political universe.

This chapter describes some examples of how we use drama to provide an interpersonal, social, and aesthetic context or platform for the girls to focus on themselves and each other. I will start by describing and defining briefly the underlying philosophical ideas and concepts.[1]

Edward Bond's Notion of the "Self"

Edward Bond is one of the world's leading playwrights and drama theorists. He writes extensively about the sense of self, a key theme of which is that:

> The mind works to find meaning and value and to understand the world, not only on the basis of a steady processing or assimilation of experience, but that the mind itself undergoes qualitative change in the process of encountering the world.[2]

This implies that the self is reconstructed every time it acquires new experiences, knowledge, skills, and memories. By integrating new meanings and stories into its existing self, it makes sense of itself afresh and this new self-knowledge leads to further self-creation.

In addition to this changing self, Bond further offers the idea of the "palimpsest self"—that is, this changing self is actually the accumulation of many selves existing on the same plane—a "series of horizontal selves." There is the core self, or inner self, which holds all the other selves together and gives coherence and composure to the self. It is this core self that Bond considers drama to have special access to. This resonates with a Freirian sense of our "essential humanity" from which oppression alienates us and which we must regain by overcoming the forces of oppression. Audre Lorde seems to be pointing in the same direction when she says that while there is much of ourselves that is historically and socially constructed, there remains a "deeper reality of feeling" within us, which is more intimately in touch with what it means to be human.

The palimpsest self leads to Bond's idea of the "gap," a sort of mini-nothingness between the self and the world. Animals have no gap; their contact with reality is direct, not mediated through culture. For humans, the gap is the site of a two-way interaction between the self and society/the world. It is the way we establish our volatile relationship with material reality. In effect, you might say we create ourselves, or define ourselves, in the gap. We are the total meaning we produce in the gap; the gap, therefore, is like the site of a self-theater. We do not live our biology in a mere animalistic way; we live the meaning we create in the gap.[3]

Self at "Home" in the World

I resonate strongly with Bond's conception of the child's right to be "at home in the world." As he puts it:

> There is a basic orientation of the newborn human toward the world, and of the world toward it. Intrinsic to this new center of awareness is its right to be; this is gradually articulated into its right to be at home, to make the world its home and for the world to be its home, which in time is articulated into the right of itself and others to be at home in the world.[4]

This "right to be at home in the world" is at the root of all conceptions of justice and struggles for equality. The common cry of all disenfranchised people—women, the colonized, the enslaved, the oppressed—is and has been that we have been denied our rightful place in the world. Innately we know the world is meant to be home to all of us, but someone has taken away that right from many of us. The Marxist idea of alienation; Paulo Freire's idea of being dehumanized and alienated from our essential humanity; bell hooks's yearning for "home"; all resonate with my own experience, pointing toward a kind of "homelessness" and a desperate attempt to find a place of belonging, one's home.

In this context, the self, in a perennial state of becoming, tries to locate itself in relation to the bewildering phenomena of the world and other selves, struggles to make sense or "meaning" of all its experience, and yearns to find its home or a way to belong to the world. It is always a developing self—an interpersonal construction, informed by all the conversations we engage in or are excluded from, the ways in which we participate or do not, the ways in which we are recognized and treated by others. The self is also politically constituted, depending on how we are positioned in social structures, how we participate in institutions, how much power we have or do not, and what roles we play within these structures and institutions. The self is an imagined self, constructed and created through the meaning we assign to the gap that connects us to the world we inhabit.

Feelings as a Source of Knowledge

The theoretical alienation of the self from home symbolizes the struggles experienced by Prerna students. Rendered "homeless" by society and family, many students arrive at Prerna with little to no sense of self after years of physical, emotional, and psychological abuse just for being girls. They never had the time or space for self-work, because, in India and many parts of the world, young women, especially those who are also poor, do not have selves; they do not have the right to "be." Like all oppressed, subordinate, and disenfranchised groups, the world is not their home and they are not at home in the world. Because of this, the core of Prerna's approach to self-work is the goal of bringing the self to consciousness and finding a place of belonging.

For feminist pedagogy, both experience and feeling are vital parts of this consciousness raising, a kind of "inner knowing," and "a guide to a deeper truth than that of abstract rationality."[5] Feelings or emotions are a way of knowing the world and ourselves in it; they are a way of connecting the self with the universe. According to poet Audre Lorde, recognizing our "deepest feelings" gives us the power to challenge the dominant definitions of truth that construct our sense of self and the way we relate to others in the world.[6] I have found that connecting to feelings can be highly impactful for both women and men. During my gender trainings, for example, I have found that it is only when male trainees *feel* the pain of women's lives that they change their perspective about sexist oppression.

But society rarely affords the opportunity for such inner knowing. For too long have schools operated under a dichotomous and, in my view, a flawed separation of reason and emotions, facts and values. This legacy has resulted in marginalizing and undervaluing those subjects most often associated with emotions, values, and imagination—for example, the arts—to the periphery of the curriculum or to the extracurricular realm and focusing disproportionately on reason and facts in the official curriculum. David Best tells us that feelings are a kind of cognition, a source of knowledge, and have immense educational value because we not only learn from our feelings, we also learn to feel deeply.[7] An emphasis on emotion and feelings does not mean we must reject reason and analytical thought. Rather, according to Lorde, it must be made clear that reason alone is not enough to gain a deeper understanding of the social, cultural, and political forces that shape our lives. Bond's concept of the "twinning" of reason and imagination helps show us that we need both of the mind's most basic processes to understand the material and human world. This framework—where knowing is a think/feel (and imagine) process, two sides of the same coin—fuels the epistemological premise on which we work in Prerna.

Our First Arts Project: Fear of Being a Girl

Inspired by Wendy Luttrell's book *Pregnant Bodies, Fertile Minds*, I embarked on an eight-week project with Aarti, Kunti, and their cohort in 2005, when they were in the ninth grade. This was my first attempt to do drama with them and to use art as a way of exploring our lives together. It led to the formulation of our empowerment classes, critical feminist pedagogy as we have been practicing it since then.

The students began by introducing themselves verbally, in writing, and in drawing. They did small role-plays to give a snapshot of their everyday lives. The girls then discussed the fear of being a girl/woman more specifically. We used improvised drama and still images to provide context and to fuel the discussion. This was followed by individual descriptions of what that meant to each of them through writing. Participating in this written exercise with them, we all wrote short reflective think/feel pieces, using our own experiences and lives as girls, which we read out to the group. The girls then made a collage of pictures illustrating graphically how they saw themselves and what their fears were. We discussed different ways of overcoming these fears, helped along with interspersed, small role-plays. The girls danced, using movement to depict bondage and release. They made another collage, this time about their dreams for the future, and talked to the group about their drawings. Finally, I decided to stage a performance with the students, based on my belief that students grow in strength as they work toward this type of activity and also because they loved performing. This group of girls had never been on stage or done any form of drama before this.

Following are excerpts from the girls' essays in which they wrote about their fears as girls.

We cannot go out of the house. If we go out then people look askance at us and say nasty things about us to our parents. So our parents do not let us go out of the house and scold us. . . . And when you are at home, everyone is forever nagging you, "Don't do this, don't do that." How should a woman go out? She is always afraid of society and of home.—Rachna

Society frightens you, of course, but mostly we are afraid of men, because we are made to fear them from childhood. Finally fear sets in our hearts completely.—Christina

I am afraid of being a woman, because there is no respect or value for women in society. People always look at women with a bad eye, mostly

people at home. So we have to live in hiding, almost, to protect ourselves. Even if we want to live fearlessly, our parents fill us with fear, so
that we learn to live in fear and can't rid ourselves of it.—Aarti

It is clear from the excerpts that the girls do not feel "at home" in the
world. In fact, they do not feel at home in their homes either. In our discussions, the girls and I shared our experience of always being reminded that our
parents' home was not our real home; we were often told, "when you go to your
own home . . ." referring to our marital homes, which are, again, likely to be
places of alienation and isolation. The girls reflected for the first time on this
special homelessness of girls and women. Of course, they had known it, but
they were articulating it for the first time and so were, in effect, seeing this
reality for the first time. Together we examined this reality critically, questioning its fairness. Many discussions around the idea of home ensued, and
their role-plays and still images depicted feelings of being servile, caged, and
under threat.

The girls' collages expressed similar sentiments, with images of their yearning to be free, to be treated as equal, to be allowed to study, to be loved by
their fathers, and—though sympathetic—not to be like their mothers, silently suffering. Christina's collage, for example, has an interesting mix of
pictures to which she has assigned brief descriptive comments in bubble boxes.
In one corner she has pasted a picture of a man standing and talking to a
woman. It looks like they are having an argument and the bubble box says,
"I am very sad when papa scolds mummy." Below that are two pictures of
young women, one happy and smiling, and the other sad and forlorn, with the
text box: "I am very happy when my father lets me go out." The collage also
shows a boy and a girl seated at a table where the girl is writing, while her
brother watches, smiling supportively, with the comment: "I wish I could study
with my brother like this." She has then pasted a picture of many children, all
happy, and writes, "And I could play with other children." Above it is a picture
of a girl with a trophy in her hand, and the text box says, "I am happy." Another picture shows a father and a daughter—both happy and smiling—next
to a picture of a girl's face, looking sad and wistful, with the comment, "I wish
my father also loved me like this." At the center of the collage is an image of a
young girl, smiling, strong, and free.

Christina's first collage

Self-Knowing Is Self-Creation

We did much reflective discussion around the role-plays and the collages. Our drama provided the girls with a "site" to do the self-work that is needed to "know" the self and "construct" it. This is not a place they had experienced before. They never had the time, the space, or the legitimacy to have a site for self-work. Christina asked me after the first dialogue, "Aunty, why are you talking to us about our lives?" She, along with the others, said this was the first time anyone had cared to talk to them about their lives or their feelings. As Rama writes:

> Girls cannot speak to anyone in society. They can't express their wishes to anyone, because no one cares what girls think or say and no one listens to them.

Kunti, Aarti, Rama, and their classmates used both their imagination and their reason to make fresh sense of their lives. Their initial creative efforts provided them the space and the physical tools to work on themselves and make meaning out of their experiences. Their discussion with their peers and me helped them engage in this self-actualization exercise. They came to understand their homelessness in the world and, more important, to question its injustice. Thus they created a new self in a "series of horizontal selves,"[8] questioning and trying to make sense of the position of the previous self, with reference to justice. Freire calls this process a "denunciation," that is, the naming and analysis of existing structures of oppression, followed by an "annunciation," or the construction of new structures, forms of relationship, and ways of being in the world.[9] Together and individually, the girls felt/imagined/thought while making their collages, using their felt experiences as the subject matter for the knowledge they were creating. In their culture circles, they also found a respectful, willing, and responsive audience who participated in the self-construction effort. They were learning the valuable and empowering lesson that critical feminist pedagogy aims to teach: they could be knowledge creators, not simply knowledge consumers.

Our Play

We worked on a play, *Rani Laxmi Bai*, for six weeks and finally staged it in a public auditorium. The play is the story of the great Indian hero, Rani (Queen) of Jhansi. She was born in 1835 to a Brahmin family, and at the age of 14 became Rani Laxmi Bai of Jhansi when she married the Raja of Jhansi. She was widowed in 1855. She was an extremely unusual woman, as she grew up trained in sword fighting, horseback riding, and wrestling. She trained all her maids-in-waiting similarly. When she was married, she built and commanded a women's army, which defended Jhansi against the British. Her most trusted generals were women, and her women's army fought in the infantry, cavalry, and artillery divisions. The British were stunned to see this women's army and were awed by the young queen's prowess. She was one of the main heroes of the first battle for independence in 1857, when she took on the British army almost by herself and died fighting on June 18, 1858. Legend has it that she fought with two swords, the reins of her horse held between her teeth, and her infant son tied to her back.

It is quite a remarkable story and an extremely inspiring tale for women. I chose this story for the girls to live through the possibility of a "self" like the Rani—a real historic figure and to give themselves the opportunity of self-creation in that site. In the course of their rehearsals, the girls learned to speak loudly and strongly, to walk tall, and to raise their eyes and hold a steady gaze—all things their real-life contexts taught them not to do. Parents, mine included,

Christina as Rani Laxmi Bai

specifically instruct their daughters to keep their gaze down, to not speak unnecessarily, to keep their voices low, to keep themselves out of sight if possible—in effect to be voiceless, self-less, barely visible, silent servers of everyone else in their families. For one scene in the play, the girls had to learn mock sword fighting. I asked them who were their present-day real-life enemies and how they would fight them. The girls said it was society, and sometimes their own families, too. "We have to be strong inside of ourselves to fight them," they said, affirming the need to unify within.

Classrooms as Sites of Self-Work

It is unfortunate that the official state-mandated curriculum does not afford opportunities or "sites" to allow students to work in this self-constructive way. Little help is offered in the search for "home," and very little legitimacy given to self-work or imagination by a majority of schools in most countries. The official curriculum is crowded with and often reduced to decontextualized and remote lessons in literacy, numeracy, and science.

Prerna has focused on making curricular spaces for such sites of self-work. We have learned that teaching and learning should be aimed at helping our students exercise their right to "be" in the world, "to be at home in the world," and to give them the tools "to make the world their home"; in other words, to locate themselves in a self-affirming, non-alienating relationship to the universe and others in it. Our drama project was a way of helping girls tap into their imaginations to learn, to recover their "radical innocence," and to find their essential humanity.[10]

My students say they gained more from this drama project than from all their studies put together, and I am inclined to agree. I believe that in the course of this project they found a site where they could use their imaginations, their feelings, and their reason to confront their world, to make sense of it, and to leap beyond the traditions and ideologies that governed their lives and had denied them a home. In the process, they began to work out, as Bond notes, "the logic of their own humanness." They were learning that they had a right to "be"; to be a person with wishes, with aspirations, and a "self." As Christina put it:

> Our parents are going to marry us off when they think it is right for us and there isn't much we can do. They won't change. But we can change and do things differently when it's our turn. Right now we have to do what they say.

Kunti contested this:

> No, we can certainly talk to them and have our say. If we are strong within ourselves, we can change them maybe.

Enabling each other, together, they began to imagine themselves at home in the world and started to see their world as their home, which was reflected in their own verbal reports and their second collages. In her second image, for example, Christina has pictures of girls happy and in control, writing and using a computer. She imagines herself getting educated, learning to use a computer, buying a house of her own, traveling and visiting a church that she wants to see, and she imagines herself as "happy."

Their second collages, made toward the end of the project, were in sharp contrast to the first ones and a delight to behold. Very upbeat in nature, they show an exuberant sense of life reaching out and upward to its possibilities, imagining and constructing possible worlds and possible lives. Rachna wants to be a sailor, Kunti wants to be a pilot, Aarti wants to be a dancer, Christina wants to be computer professional, and Rama wants to be a designer. All these

Christina's second collage

professions are very far removed from the circumstances in which they are living, making it twice as creditable that they have the courage to dream so boldly.

I believe that as the girls dramatized themselves, dialogized themselves, storied themselves, and imagined themselves working hard at self-knowing and self-construction, the self was stirred; it was "released," asserting its right to be, invoking justice. I asked the girls what they thought they were learning as we were rehearsing for the play and received many varied responses:

We are learning to walk tall.
We are learning to speak loudly and strongly.
We are learning to look up.

But the clincher was this one:

We are learning to live strong.[11]

I rejoiced! I believe that strong imaginations make strong individuals, as it shows them a way to push the boundaries of their lives.

The performance itself had a strong, empowering influence on the girls. Kunti recalls her experience:

> So it was the first time for me, to go on stage. Like we got the script and I thought, like what is this and how will it happen? I had never done anything like it. Then I told myself, if others can do it so can I; that if I managed to do this, it will change other things in me, develop things in me. Facing these many people is not easy. This was sooo good! When I completed it and people praised me, they applauded, it came in the newspaper, then everyone at home, my parents, my sisters—they were all like—that was you!

Christina, who played Rani in the play, recalls:

> In my family a lot changed. First my father didn't ever trust me. He came to drop me to the gate but never came inside, even for the parent-teacher meetings. And he didn't want me to study after class 10. Then he came to see my play. He was literally crying. "You did such a good job!" And after this his perception of me changed. I think he actually began to see me as Rani Laxmi Bai, my role [laughing]. Now I can study as much as I want. "I realize that girls should also go ahead," he said to me.

We took the important lessons learned from this early experiment and made sure we provided legitimate space in the official curriculum for vital self-work, for using feelings, experience, reason, and imagination to enable our students to make sense of their lives and worlds. Different art forms, particularly drama, dance, and drawing, became an integral part of our curriculum.

Disrupting Taken for Granted Social Realities

In this section I describe how we use "disruptive texts" to engage students in critical social literacies, which, as Elizabeth Yeoman points out, not only help us understand how dominant discourses shape us, but also give us a way to critically dissect these narratives, to re-read them and replace them with an alternative view of our social reality.[12] To this end, critical feminist pedagogy, among other strategies, uses "alternative literary texts," which can help to "re-articulate and re-traditionalize" notions of femininity.[13]

We engaged in critical literacy by working with an alternative text, *A Wife's Letter*, written in 1914 by the Nobel Prize winner Rabindranath Tagore.[14] I ask for the reader's patience as I describe the literary piece in some detail to make evident the "disruptiveness" or potential for disruption for our girls.

The story's central character is Mrinal, a middle-class Savarna Bengali woman who writes a letter to her husband 15 years after their marriage. Born in a village to poor parents, she was married off when she was 12 years old to the younger son of a middle-class Bengali family in Kolkata. An intelligent woman, Mrinal quietly resists the traditional role required of a daughter-in-law in such a household. Yet, she must conform overtly and would probably have lived her life as it had been given to her if not for a certain unforeseen circumstance.

Mrinal's husband's elder brother's wife, whom she calls Didi, also lives in the same house. Didi is forced to give refuge to her orphaned younger sister, 14-year-old Bindu, rendered homeless and penniless after their parents' death. With no money, and considered unattractive, Bindu is essentially rejected by the household, and only the rudest, most basic arrangements are made for her—a cowshed. She does all the housework and eats very little. Completely vulnerable and defenseless, Mrinal writes:

> *Bindu lived in great fear . . . as if there was no reason for her having been born into this great universe. And so she would always shrink away as she passed, lower her glance as she walked by.*[15]

Shunned by the family, Mrinal takes the young girl under her wing and gives her affection and care, much to the annoyance of the entire family. Bindu develops a firm attachment to her. To save the family's honor, the gods of matrimony are invoked and a marriage is arranged for her by the family. But Bindu is terrified of leaving the only person in the world who has shown her some love and care. She begs Mrinal not to abandon her.

> *Bindu came to me, and sat at my feet and cried. "Why do I have to be married?"*
>
> *I tried to explain things to her. "Bindu, don't be afraid: I've heard your groom is a good man."*
>
> *Bindu said, "If he's good, what do I have that he would like me?" . . .*
>
> *Bindu cried night and day; her tears didn't want to stop. I knew how painful it was for her. In that world I had fought many battles on her behalf, but I didn't have the courage to say that her wedding should be called off. And what right did I have to say that anyway? . . .*

Bindu said, "Just five more days before the wedding, can't I die before then?"

The day before the wedding, Bindu went to her sister and said, "Didi, I'll just stay in your cowshed, I'll do whatever you tell me to, I beg you, don't get rid of me like this."

For some time now, I had seen Didi wipe her eyes in quiet moments; now, too, her tears ran. But the heart could not be everything; there were rules to live by. She said, "You must realize, Bindu dear, a husband is a woman's shelter, her protector, her salvation, her everything. If suffering is written on your forehead, no one can avert it."

The message was clear: there was no way out. Bindu would have to marry, and she had to accept this as her fate. The marriage was solemnized at the future husband's home, but just three days later, Bindu escaped and Mrinal found her cowering in a corner of the cowshed. Bindu revealed the terrible truth—that her husband was insane.

Mrinal fought her family fiercely and refused to send Bindu back to her deranged husband's house, but to no avail. She had to return. Later, Mrinal tried to arrange a second escape for the young girl, planning to take her away on a pilgrimage. But before she could execute the plan, Bindu, in desperation and seeing no other way out, puts an end to her misery by setting herself on fire.

Mrinal writes:

People heard about it and were enraged. They said, It's become a kind of fashion for women to set fire to their clothes and kill themselves. You all said, Such dramatics! Maybe. But shouldn't we ask why the dramatics take place only with Bengali women's sarees and not with the so-brave Bengali men's dhotis [loin cloth]?

Devastated, Mrinal decides to leave her marriage and her home. In her letter she addresses her husband, trying to explain her action:

In your world I didn't suffer what people would normally call grief. In your house there was no lack of food or clothing; no matter what your brother's character, in your own character there was nothing that I could complain of to the Lord, nothing I could call terrible. So I don't want to raise my head in complaint about you—this letter is not for that.

> *But I will not go back to your Number Twenty-Seven Makhon Boral*
> *Lane. I've seen Bindu. I've seen the worth of a woman in this world. I don't*
> *need any more. . . . I too will be saved. I am saved.*
>   *Freed from the Shelter of Your Feet,*
>   *Mrinal*

It is a beautiful story and an eloquent, artistic, and poetic expression of the remarkable courage shown by a woman in 1914, where there was no place for a woman if she left the shelter of her home, however oppressive and cruel it was. She could either find her freedom in the brothel or in death. Mrinal chooses neither and saves herself by removing herself from the shelter her husband offers. As a powerful disruptive text it illustrates poignantly how the patriarchal family in a patriarchal society positions women, a cruel injustice that constructed women's lives in 1914, as they continue to do today.

We turned this letter into a script for a play and dramatized it as four monologues, interspersed with enacted vignettes. We first read the play and discussed it. The girls listened raptly, in awe of the story and the artistry of the language. They related to the fact that Mrinal had been married at 12 and to Bindu's plight, telling us stories of their orphaned aunts, cousins, and friends who were treated similarly by relatives. One mentioned how her cousin had killed herself to get out of a cruel marriage, and I shared the story of my cousin. Most important, they discussed marriage as a practice of "settling" women, as a way to earn their keep and find a home. They saw, maybe for the first time for some of them, the cruelty and the unfairness of this and how, in many cases, married women are rendered homeless by marriage.

As we rehearsed, the students not only discussed these themes and understood them intellectually in the context of their own experiences; they also *felt* with Bindu and Mrinal as they imagined Bindu's desperation and pain, Mrinal's helplessness, courage, and resolve. The students embraced the roles of both women, "exploring their own realities with and through the stories of others, against the backdrop of a larger world," in the words of Kathleen Gallagher.[16] As American Verbatim Theatre artist Anna Deavere Smith writes, "The theory of play is that an actor has the ability to walk in another person's 'words' and therefore in their hearts."[17]

The language of the text evoked deep emotions, the girls often crying as they rehearsed, moving each other and us to tears with their powerful renditions. Good literature has the power to stir our deepest feelings and touch our deepest selves. Lorde describes the transformational power of these emotions:

Kunti and Sunita performing Bahu Ki Chitthi

As we begin to recognize our deepest feelings, we begin to give up, of necessity, being satisfied with suffering and self-negation, and with the numbness which so often seems like their only alternative in society. Our acts against oppression become integral with self, motivated and empowered from within.[18]

The girls seemed inspired by the words, which had a disruptive effect on their understanding of their own lives as girls in a society that was not very different from the one in which Mrinal and Bindu had lived. We engaged in critical dialogues during which we discussed patriarchy, the social system that it constructed, and the place of women in it. We questioned its legitimacy and its inevitability. We deconstructed traditional notions of femininity, examined the social structures that fostered them, and saw how Mrinal had challenged them in a very difficult social context and time. The girls discussed how the tragedy of Bindu had finally helped Mrinal pierce the patriarchal veil under which she had lived, and they marveled at how she had found the courage to finally discard her chains and step out into the world, to claim it as her home and her life as her own.

Even though Tagore left Mrinal's story unfinished, the girls speculated among themselves about Mrinal's life:

And what will happen to Mrinal now?" Laxmi asked. "Where will she go? How will she live her life, support herself?"

"She should go into an ashram [a nunnery]," Aarti suggested.

"No, she should find a job," Khushboo countered.

"But she has no education," Kunti objected

"She can always clean homes," Laxmi said, cementing how closely the girls identified with this middle-class Savarna woman who would be unlikely to choose cleaning of homes as a way to support herself. "She is an intelligent woman; she can educate herself while she works and then find a better job."

Aarti asked, "Should she go back to her husband, if he takes her back?'

Laxmi exclaimed, "NO! That will be horrible for her! They will treat her very badly! Now she has taken a bold step; she should follow through!"

Aarti said, "But it will be very hard! Men will prey on her and people will not respect her when they find out she has walked out on her husband!"

"She's a very brave woman and if she has found the courage to walk out, she will find the courage to brave all the obstacles and find her way," Laxmi said quietly, but firmly.

The girls were feeling, thinking, imagining, and moving to a critical understanding of power structures and the power of transformation through resistance. They were also learning to define a new meaning of "home." It didn't necessarily have to be a parents' home or a husband's home, and it was possible to step out into the world, look up at the sky and see it as a roof over one's head and the world as one's home.

As Freire says:

It is not limit-situations in and of themselves which create a climate of hopelessness, but rather how they are perceived by us at a given historical moment: whether they appear as fetters or as insurmountable barriers.[19]

Using Improvised Drama with Critical Dialogues

Often we began our critical dialogues around a topic with an improvised drama, devised by the girls using their own experiences. The teacher does this so she can see how her students situate their understanding of complex concepts like patriarchy in their daily lives. This exercise, which helps provide a meaningful, locally relevant context for the dialogue, is illustrated in the following description of our discussion of patriarchy.

The grade 11 students were asked to break into groups of six. Each group was given the task of devising a play illustrating a moment in the life of one of their homes. Here is a brief description of one of these dramas:

The father wakes up at five in the morning and calls for his wife and daughters, who are still in bed, to make tea for him. Wife and the daughters begin to prepare the morning tea for the father. Mother gets the daughters started with the household chores. The older daughter asks the mother if she could prepare khichdi [an easy-to-cook rice dish] for lunch, as she is not feeling too well. The mother then asks the father if that is what they should cook. The father asks the son, "What would you like to eat, my boy?" The son replies, "Matarpaneer" [a dish of peas and cottage cheese]. The mother and daughters are then ordered to cook matarpaneer. One of the daughters asks the father for money to buy paneer. This request annoys the father, who starts asking the daughter to account for money that he had given her earlier. After a short argument the father asks the son to fetch money from his wallet lying in his room. The son is shown stealing some money from the wallet and sliding it in his pocket while getting money for his father.[20]

Later in the day, the lunch is cooked and served. The younger daughter is hungry and wants to eat. The mother tells her to wait till the father and the brother are done eating. Father does not like the taste of the food and yells at his wife and the girls. The son refuses to eat the food and complains that it tastes terrible. The father reaches for his wallet and gives the son some money to go out and eat lunch.

Mother timidly asks the father, "The girls were asking for permission to go to a friend's birthday party." Father tells the wife, "A girl going out of the house to meet friends is out of question." The drama ends with both the girls left to stand sad, disappointed, and alone.

Their improvised dramas showed the fathers in complete control over everyone's lives, dictating how the girls dressed, what they ate, where they went or not, how and where they worked. They also showed how sons get preferential treatment in terms of more and better food, more money and more freedom, and how they had power over their sisters. The mothers were shown as silently serving and quietly suffering, too afraid to speak out against their husbands.

In dramatizing this play and through critical dialogues afterward, the girls made a close, incisive analysis of the discourse of patriarchy defining their lives in their families and homes. Kathleen Gallagher, who used Prerna as one of her research sites, describes how the performance of drama "clearly gave these young women a forum for the public naming and shaming of previously private experiences of subjugation."[21] In the discussion that followed the drama, the girls illustrate how they begin to render the invisible visible.[22]

Khushboo: In our play, we showed how one day looks like, that how the father takes every decision—about everything, like who is coming and going from the house, what will be cooked—from the smallest thing to the biggest, everything is determined by him. No decision is in the mother's hand. We call this patriarchy.

Sunita: He alone takes all the decisions, and he's also preparing his son for the future.

Laxmi: And he is oppressing his daughter, not giving her a chance to get ahead, and the boy can do anything. Like the girls cooked, and then he didn't like the food, so he just went out to eat. He also got the money from his father for that; the girls didn't get any such chance.

Sunita: The boy can continue sleeping till 10 a.m., but the girl was woken up at five!

Priya: Aunty, it was shown that when the father got up, first thing he did was drink tea, and the son also. But the girls didn't do so, and neither did their mother. When food was cooked, it was first given to the father. When the girl asked, "Can I eat?" Mother said no, saying, "First let your father and your brother eat. We will eat after them!" Why does this happen?

Nishu: The son even stole the money his father gave him for some payment and even then father didn't say anything to him. And when the girl said that can I go out and may I have some money, the father refused!

Laxmi: They don't trust the daughter. They asked for many details like, "Where is all that money that I had given you? What did you spend it on?" And there is no rule like that for boys.

. . .

Teacher: So, why is this so? The structure of family—like the one you just showed; why is it like this?

Preeti: In most of the families you can see that father is the one who is working, and women stay in the house and do household chores, so no value is given to the household chores—that they are not bringing the money home. So women don't have any money and also they can't say things like, "We go out and earn, and we get tired all day, etc." After all, everyone thinks, "What's domestic work? Just cooking, cleaning; that's all." So, fathers have money in their hand, the main thing is money.

. . .

Teacher: And so money is not given to the girls. First we said that "Father earns," and we see that even though the boy is not earning, he still gets money. So why does the boy get it?

Preeti: Because . . . he's the son, so they think he's the one who will do them proud in future, and not their daughter.

. . .

Teacher: So in this system where Father takes all the decisions, and the father is training the son telling him, "You will study and only you will have control over money, you will take the decisions in the house," Father in a way is preparing him—and you used this word also. So this system of training the son, why does it exist?

Laxmi: Because it's happening since the beginning [of time] that girls go to a different house, so property rights are passed down to the son. Daughters don't have a right on it, so boys are considered more important, you know, like, "He will grow up and be my heir and will take care of my family."

The teacher goes on to drill into Laxmi's point, moving the discussion to equal property rights to illuminate the multiple ways in which patrilocality disenfranchises girls. She references a story in the news in which a judge ruled that a girl did not have the right to her father's property, reinforcing the significance of land being registered only to the father's name. The students react to the story:

Preeti: The judge is saying that she will get property from the husband, but husband also says, "You don't own anything here, nothing!" So, where is her right? She is not getting it from the either side. She ultimately ends up on the road. She should somehow get her rights.

. . .

Teacher: So, after a lot of discussion, because women's groups brought up the issue several times, the government also felt that it should happen for agricultural land which can now be held in the name of a woman. So the government has given the right, they have legalized it, but to accept it in society is very difficult. Before 2005, agricultural land could not belong to a woman. Why?

Preeti: Because it's coming down from father to son, from grandfather, great grandfather, etc.

Teacher: Okay, now tell me, how will change come? First, let's think, why is change needed? If patriarchy prevails, then father rules, and father and brother get most of the benefit, so now, what's the harm if mothers and daughters also get the same rights? What's the harm in that? So, there's a group in Kerala, haven't heard of any other—it's a matrilineal society. There after marriage, the groom is sent off to the bride's house. He brings gold and silver in dowry, but those families work well. The daughter's lineage is carried forward, marriages are working well, girls are safe and are also educated. Kerala has the highest literacy rate in India. So, if nothing is wrong there, then why are people afraid that if women gain any control, if they have power, if their decisions are upheld in the house, if they start moving out of the house, then there will be a problem?

Preeti: They fear that the way they are treating women, if women have control, they become heads of the house, they will treat them similarly!

Moni: And it can also happen that they feel that women might just take away their rights over the family property.

Sunita: If women fight over this, then a lot of them are even killed by their own family members. There's a woman who lives near my house; she gets beaten up by her husband on this every day, so out of fear, she doesn't even tell anyone or she will get beaten up more.

Preeti: If we talk about changing all of this, girls who want to have such a law will be considered big criminals, that "Why are you doing this? This is happening in our family from centuries."

Teacher: So now that you know all this, and that this is wrong, so what can we do? Can we change things?

Sunita: I am definitely going to demand my share in my father's land. I will do it, you see.

This excerpt, like the others, illustrates what M. M. Bakhtin thinks of as "ideological becoming" in the process of learning and identity formation.[23] Here, the girls are beginning to name their reality, to question the authoritative patriarchal narrative, to contest the dominant discourses within that narrative, and learn to develop their own voices in opposition to them, despite the fear of serious consequences. Like Sunita, they are coming to an understanding about themselves and a decision to transform their own lives. They are also analyzing unequal power relations and their underlying causes. As Preeti concludes, no value is given to women's work in the home because it is unpaid, whereas men go out and work for money and so have more power.

Guiding this critical dialogue, the teacher plays the role of connecting the girls' very personal improvised play to the larger legal and social structures, as she tells them about the law, the women's movement, and patriarchal and matrilineal societies in a distant state, Kerala, helping them develop a sociological imagination. In other words, she is helping them transgress traditional identities and redefine themselves as citizens with constitutional rights.

Authoring Their Own Disruptive Texts

Our students have also written their own disruptive texts in the form of diaries, essays, and poems. Following the lead of a teacher in a Canadian school, I asked our girls to think of the "doors" in their lives. What did the word mean to them; what did it say to them? Which doors were open and which doors were shut in their lives? We did a word splash where everyone said the words that came instantly to mind when we thought of doors. We came up with these: oppression, protection, privacy, darkness, imprisonment, despair, safety, security, locked, and unfair. We discussed these words and what they meant to us, after which all of us wrote our own poems about these. I wrote with them, so they could see that I was struggling to find words as much as they were. We took them home and edited them, crafted them, and brought them back to read to each other. We gave each other feedback about the poems and discussed the themes that arose.

Following are the English translations of poems written by our students, originally in Hindi:

A door—
Open or shut
An open door reveals a vast, wide world
A closed door shuts out the truth
Offers despair, only despair
Hope beckons through the open door . . .

The door firmly shut
Blocks my path
How shall I come out?
Society closes around me like a prison
No hope for the future
Do I see in this closed space

Nothing to live for
Behind this closed door
Why am I condemned behind it?
What is my fault?
Just this—that I am a girl?
Don't I have a right to know
What lies beyond?

How shall I imagine
The universe of my dreams
Behind this shut door?
Do I not have the right to dream
Do I not have the right to know and
Be my "self"?
  —By Laxmi

Door—a familiar word
What is the reality of its being there?

Somewhere open—somewhere closed
The doors of the mind—
Resistant—not yet open

Confusions, doubts and
The fear of society
Close the doors of my mind

Door—a familiar word

Today
I have smashed all the doors
Doors that confused my mind

Come let us fly away
To a world where
No doors are closed
Ever . . .

Door—a familiar word.
    —By Soni

A closed door hides many secrets
Secrets—hard to conceal
Hard too, to reveal
Secrets that everyone knows about
Feeling Bitter, so bitter
More than their truth
Bitter feelings turning into a maelstrom

All my dreams trapped
Behind closed doors
Dreams that crave free flight
But how shall they fly
I can see no sky
Behind shut doors

Why are the doors locked only for me?
What have I done wrong?
Done wrong
That I am a girl?

We must break the chains
And unlock this locked door
Chains that are strong
But stronger is my determination
It shall break closed doors

Now my dreams can fly
Leaving behind locked doors

Maybe the chains want to be free too?
Maybe they want the open skies too?
   —By Kunti

A door . . . A door . . . A door
Closed or Open
The open door opens out the whole wide world
The closed door hides half truths
The closed door gives only despair
The open door opens me out to hope
Do not close the door
Do not shut out hope
When we saw the open door
Hope flowered in our hearts afresh

I too will grow wings of hope
And leave all despair behind

Even so
I will not forget the space behind the closed door
That kindled in me the desire to break out!
   —By Sunita

The girls have used their poems, in the words of Audre Lorde, to "name the nameless" as they give voice to their feelings. They are using their poems to give legitimacy to their indignation, to protest against their oppression, and to demand the rights and freedoms they have been denied. As I had learned from my own life, feeling angry at injustice is an important first step toward resistance.

The girls immersed themselves completely in writing their poems, fully engaged in the struggle to express their emotions and their experiences through the "heightened language"[24] afforded by poetry. Many of them made poetry writing an extracurricular practice at home, too, because they said it helped them sort their feelings out and gave them direction.

Through activities like the "Doors" project, Prerna is able to stand conventional theories of learning on their heads, by giving emotions primacy over reason, dreams over concepts, feelings over ideas. Allowing sufficient curricular space for feelings and experience to be explored and to gain legitimacy and validity, Prerna students are empowered to produce important self-knowledge and cultural knowledge. Our students not only read disruptive texts, they also create and write their own disruptive texts. In doing so, they learn not only that they can be authors of poems and plays, but, more important, they can be authors of their own lives.

Verbatim Theater

The girls took the metaphor of doors forward, and created and performed the following script for a play using Khushboo's experience. We reconstructed her conversation with her parents in my office almost verbatim, using the same phrases. This abridged version of the script was performed by the students:[25]

Khushboo's character: I want to study, I want to study.
Father: No, that's enough! I don't want to educate you any more.
*Mother:** Yes! No more school for you!
Khushboo: I topped my class! I want to study more.

Mother ties Khushboo's *dupatta* (scarf) around her arms.

Father: Now listen to me carefully—once and for all, I am telling you.
          You are not going back to school! No further studies.
          Do you understand me? Do you hear me?
Mother: We are NOT going to educate you any further.

---

* As mentioned before, Khushboo's mother is a stepmother.

Khushboo:	I will study! I will study!
Father:	Education has made you arrogant and insubordinate!
	You are defying me, talking back, arguing with ME.
	I am not educating you any further.
Khushboo:	I will study! I will study!
Father:	If you want to stay in my house, you will do as I say!
	No studying anymore!
Mother:	Do the housework! Wash the dishes, cook and clean.
	That's what you are meant to do.
	You don't need to study any more.
Khushboo:	I am not refusing to do the work! I will do the housework!
	But I will study too! For sure, I will study!
Father:	Stop this litany! I have to marry you off!
	Where will I find a husband for you if you study so much?
	The more you study, the higher the dowry demand.
	I cannot let you study any more.
Mother:	We need to get you married and out of this house.
	No more education for you.
Khushboo:	Run away I will.
	Maybe die, too.
	But study I surely will.

Teacher (enters):	Why can't Khushboo study? Why is it a crime to study?
	Why is education a crime and a cause for violence?
Father:	Let me marry you off and if your husband chooses,
	he can let you study.
	It will be up to him.
Khushboo:	First your slave, then his?
	And me? Who am I?
	Am I nothing?
	My desires? Nothing?
Teacher:	Yes, what about Khushboo?
	What about her rights as a person?
	What about her aspirations?
	What will happen to Khushboo?
Father:	Rights? Aspirations? Khushboo a person?
	I am her father, her protector! I will decide what happens to her.
	Whatever I wish, she must do.

Mother: Yes! As you wish so she will do.
Khushboo: I want to study! Please let me!
Father: If you want to study, you must leave my house!
                   You cannot live here unless you do as I say.

Khushboo (rising slowly): This house—not a home but a prison now.
                   My family, not protectors but my jailers they be.
                   I want to escape, escape I must, but fearful am I.
                   Will I be able to live, without the protection of my father's roof?
                   Will I be able to take care of my life, all mine, all by myself?
                   Where is my home?

Teacher: Fear not you—this world is yours. Make it yours; for you it is made.
                   And all of us here to help you, support you.
                   To make this world your home!

Sunita played Khushboo; Laxmi, her father; Soni, her mother; and Kunti, the teacher. They performed the play several times, for a variety of audiences, including the parent community. Sunita often cried during her performance. I interviewed them about their experience with this play, and Sunita said she could feel her friend's pain when she spoke her words. She said she could imagine how frightened she must have been, but also how brave.

Aunty, this happens all the time. It's only because of all the support [from her friends, Childline, and the school] that Khushboo was able to stand up to her father and was saved. Otherwise, she might have been married off secretly, or even killed, and no one would even have known or cared.

Khushboo said that every time she watched the play, she remembered that time and marveled at where she found the courage to stand up for herself.

The play also gave voice to the girls' feelings, helping them express themselves through the prism of theater to a parent community in a safe manner, without fear of direct and violent reprisal.[26]

With this disruptive text that they had created, they are accomplishing multiple things: they are developing subversive agency, a "voice," demanding on the basis of equal human dignity better terms of recognition from the powerful others in their lives, in this case their parents.[27] They are practicing their voice and exercising what Appadurai calls their capacity to aspire in a relatively safe space, readying them for the real, potentially hostile public spaces in life.[28] It is also their attempt to build an alternative "consensus" in the broader community regarding better terms of recognition for girls, terms that recognize the rights of girls to equal dignity, respect, and autonomy.

School—Site of Self-Theater

Our girls found school to be what Bond calls a site of self-theater, a safe space where they could theorize, imagine, play, and rehearse possible futures. It was where they learned to resist, to be indignant about their lives, and to understand that their indignity was valid because what was happening was wrong. And they learned that it could be changed and could be different.

By providing sites of resistance, or self-work, Prerna girls found ways of using gaps for transacting the self, negotiating it with others, and thereby creating the self. This is allowing and enabling theorizing, as hooks calls it, and an ideological becoming, as Bakhtin calls it. Imagination is an important mode of knowing and can be developed in all of us, teachers and learners. As these examples show, critical literacy, critical dialogues, and drama offer countless possibilities for this. Drama provides a nonthreatening context for self-work where there is no fear of suffering actual consequences; it is a place to rehearse resistance.

I must sound a cautionary note. The real circumstances in which these girls live are oppressive, limiting, hostile, and often violent. These environments are not easily transcended and, as in Khushboo's case, might become more violent and restrictive when resisted. Yet these girls, and countless others like them, must either fight back or continue to suffer in submissive silence. For example, what were Khushboo's choices? While Prerna teaches resistance, we are careful to provide a strong safety net of supportive peer networks, teachers, and social organizations such as Suraksha, Childline, and the police. The girls learn how to access these networks when they need them. They need everyone's support along with the conceptual tools that a critical education can provide. I agree with Kunti; it is through strong selves that we have any hope of changing our lived worlds.

A Home of Their Own

Though girls have found a self-affirming security, or a sense of home in school, they are now even more acutely aware of their literal homelessness in the world. They have learned they have a right to be at home in the world even though societal norms under patriarchy permit only conditional homes for girls and women. Family residences largely belong to men, and girls are moved from their father's house to their husband's, which often becomes their son's home in old age should they be widowed. While the responsibility to take care of the home, maintain it, and be the homemakers is always theirs, women almost never own a home and can always be cast out if they do not please their men or are disobedient or defiant like Khushboo was. By some reports only 13 percent of the land nationwide is owned by women, as low as 3.3 percent in some states.[29] Most Dalits are landless. Women in India have had an equal right to inheritance since 2005, but very few, including educated middle-class women, feel they can exercise this right. Research shows that ownership of property has huge implications for the lives of women. A study in Kerala, one of India's more progressive states, with a 91.98 percent literacy rate for women, "showed that among the propertyless women (owning neither land nor house) 49 percent experienced physical violence and 84 percent experienced psychological violence. In contrast, those who owned both land and house reported dramatically less physical as well as psychological violence (7 percent and 16 percent respectively)."[30]

Our girls are learning to see and understand very clearly the structural injustice inherent in the patriarchal denial of an unconditional home to girls and have learned to oppose and change this narrative for themselves. Preeti, Sunita, and Aarti are concerned about securing more permanent homes, both for their mothers and themselves. Sunita is determined to get her right to her land from her father so she can sell it and buy a house for her mother, her sister, and herself. Aarti has already invested in a plot and is taking another loan to build very soon.

Khushboo struggled with the idea of having her own home that was neither her father's nor her husband's home in the strongly patriarchal social environment of India. It is a revolutionary idea for girls and women to even think of having a home of their own. But the girls have moved from "wishful thinking to thoughtful wishing" as they plan and take action to secure homes of their own.

9

Empowerment as a Social Act
From Self-Work to Social Work

Laxmi, Khushboo, Preeti, Aarti, Kunti, and Sunita have all made a long journey on the road to empowerment. With the school's support, they have managed to construct themselves as equal persons and, against many odds, are determining the course of their own lives. They have learned to rewrite the narrative of their lives, to reconstruct the ideology that governed their lives. Aarti said to me one day:

> You used to say things like—a girl can become something. Before that I never thought girls can be anything. It was just about eating, sleeping, working and passing time aimlessly, getting married, having children. I never thought education can be useful. I never thought about having a job. It never came to my mind. Then you gave us those diaries. I would write about the questions you would give. Then slowly I started reading, writing, and thinking and talking during our critical dialogues, then I realized that, of course, I am something. I can be something.

Today, Aarti and her friends are more than just something. For example, Preeti won a competitive national scholarship for a year of community college study in the United States. Khushboo and Laxmi successfully resisted their families' efforts to marry them early and have both finished their bachelor's degrees. Khushboo is pursuing her master's in women's studies and aspires to do a Ph.D. and to become a professor. And Laxmi is enrolled in an MBA program sponsored by her employers.

Beyond pursuing further education, Prerna graduates are taking control over their lives as well as their mobility. Both Preeti and Kunti have bought motorized bikes, colloquially called a scooty in India. This, seen as a rebellious thing to do in their communities, was frowned on and invited many unwelcome comments. Nonetheless, they continue to empower themselves with a powered vehicle, fueling their robust sense of self-assurance, self-esteem, and self-efficacy to make concrete plans to start their own businesses. Laxmi, who was promoted to head sales manager at a third-party service provider, Shiva Enterprises, earns a monthly salary of 25,000 rupees ($373). She recently spoke to me of being proud of herself and her capabilities, confidently stating:

> Today I know I am capable of taking care of myself and my family without anyone's help. My employers are very appreciative of my capabilities. I know I can achieve anything.

With increased ownership over their economic lives, all the students have been able to continue contributing to their families, in some cases taking over the household expenses, as Kunti and her sister Rama did, each contributing 2000 rupees ($30) every month. Moni, Kunti, and Laxmi even helped finance renovations or additions to their families' houses. What is noteworthy is how the girls' economic empowerment trickled down to other female members of their household. Priya, another alumna, related how she spends her income:

> I give 3000 rupees [$45] to my mother, for household expenses. Earlier mother used to cook in homes, but now she is not doing that. And then 1000 rupees [$15] goes in my account; then if sisters and all need something, clothes, etc., I get those.

The girls also saw the value of their own lives and investing in their futures. Since graduating, they all have begun to practice saving money for themselves. In Aarti's words:

> So we don't have to depend on others, we can just take it out and do things according to our own wishes.

For example, Rama said she had purchased a life insurance policy and saved the interest in her own account. Similarly, Preeti had saved an impressive sum and was earning interest to enroll in an MBA program. Anjali, another alumna, said:

> I want to go for a nursing course in Chennai. My family doesn't want me to go. They want me to get married, but I am determined to do this. So I am keeping my money for myself. I know they won't support me, because they don't want me to go.

While they carry a strong, confident sense of themselves, they also display a healthy nervousness about their futures. What is truly noteworthy is that they see their lives as their own. They have acquired a strong ownership over their lives, along with a sense of agency, as they thoughtfully make concrete plans for the future. They seem to be well on their way to developing a feminist consciousness. They are aware of having been wronged. They have arrived at an autonomous definition of their goals and strategies for changing their conditions and have made considerable strides there, and have developed alternate visions of their futures. All these steps are important stages in the development of an empowered person.

I like to think of them as personal activists; that is, they have taken conscious, deliberate, and persistent action to transform their personal lives. As a personal activist, Aarti has taken two kinds of action. The first and primary one is forming an identity, or recognizing herself as a person through the dialogical process of conscientization. The second important action was to become an active agent in overcoming the internal forces of oppression, in refusing to accept the dictates of the dominant ideology that had framed her life. Through long and persistent practice of critical literacy, critical thinking, and critical dialogue, she has asserted her personhood, a very important achievement for someone who had been systemically denied it.

Developing Voice and Harnessing the Capacity to Aspire

The girls speak with a strong voice about how their aspirations have grown. Aarti says:

> I wasn't sure I would even finish high school. But now I have a B.A., I am doing my M.A., and I want to do a B.Ed. I want to learn dancing and computers and everything, anything.

Arjun Appadurai, a contemporary social-cultural anthropologist, recognized worldwide as a major theorist in globalization studies, refers to "aspiration as a cultural capacity,"[1] a characteristic that is weakly developed among the poor and other marginalized groups:

> The relatively rich and powerful invariably have a more fully developed capacity to aspire . . . because the better off you are [in terms of power, dignity, and material resources], the more likely you are to be conscious of the links between the more or less immediate objects of aspiration . . . a larger repertoire of more complex life experiences to draw from . . . are in a better position to experiment and try out different things and see their outcomes . . . they not only can express their aspirations better, they also have the language to build a narrative around them, justifying them and explaining them using metaphors and building pathways . . . [They] have a more developed navigational capacity because they have more opportunities and resources to exercise options.[2]

The poor lack precisely these opportunities and resources; therefore, they have poorer "navigational capacity." The capacity to aspire, according to Appadurai, is also reciprocally linked with the faculty of voice: "Each accelerates the nurture of the other." He believes that developing voice and the aspirational capacities of the poor "ought to be a priority concern of any developmental effort and a priority component of any project with other substantive goals." Developing "voice" is vital, because without voice—and without the ability to protest and demand, or to participate in debates concerning their welfare—the poor, the disadvantaged, cannot surmount their oppression.[3]

At Prerna, we realize that our students are marginalized twice over, by poverty and gender. Our educational goals prioritize empowerment, defining it in terms of developing the capacity to aspire, which includes developing a self-aware, strong voice. We are convinced that developing these capacities is key and foundational. In its classrooms and beyond, Prerna tries to provide these opportunities, repeatedly, regularly, and in a multimodal way through reading, writing, critical dialogues, drama, art, career counseling, continuous mentoring, and opening of middle-class networks. Similarly, the continued engagement with parents also attempts to enable them to see that much more is possible for their daughters beyond their current aspirations.

Our educational goal rank orders this knowledge, this capacity, at the top. We are guided by the understanding that once they develop this capacity, our girls can develop other capabilities, including academic learning. The converse is not necessarily true; mere academic learning will not necessarily empower girls. The girls' lives and words vindicate our ideology and practice.

Recognizing "Self" as Equal

Charles Taylor, a Canadian philosopher known for his examination of the modern self, points out the connection between recognition and identity. In his essay, "The Politics of Recognition," he says:

> Our identity is partly shaped by recognition or its absence, often by the *mis*recognition of others, and so a person or group of people can suffer real damage, real distortion, if the people or society around them mirror back to them a confining or demeaning or contemptible picture of themselves. Nonrecognition or misrecognition can inflict harm, can be a form of oppression, imprisoning someone in a false, distorted, and reduced mode of being.[4]

Taylor goes on to discuss women specifically:

> Thus some feminists have argued that women in patriarchal societies have been induced to adopt a depreciatory image of themselves. They have internalized a picture of their own inferiority, so that even when some of the objective obstacles to their advancement fall away, they may be incapable of taking advantage of the new opportunities. And beyond this, they are condemned to suffer the pain of low self-esteem. . . . Their own self-depreciation, on this view, becomes one of the most potent instruments of their own oppression. Their first task ought to be to purge themselves of this imposed and destructive identity.[5]

Through the practice of critical literacy, critical thinking, and critical dialoguing, the students became personal activists taking conscious, deliberate, and persistent action to transform their personal lives. The recognition they received in school from their teachers and peers, along with the tools of "reading, writing, thinking, and talking," seemed to help them change their sense of self into that of capable agents, as a person who "can make plans for her own life."[6] They did not construct this identity alone, but in dialogue with others. As Taylor says, "We define our identity always in dialogue with, sometimes in struggle against, the things others want to see in us."[7]

The girls also became active agents in overcoming the internal forces of oppression, in refusing to accept the dictates of the dominant ideology that had framed their lives. Aarti triumphantly spoke about how she overcame her fear of speaking up at home and how this has made her father stop beating their mother. She speaks with strength about how the knowledge of her rights has given her the power to demand them and assert them:

> Slowly I started voicing my opinion. When the situation demanded, I even raised my voice while talking to him and finally succeeded in getting him to mend his ways.

Yet while the process of becoming capable agents was critical and liberating, there were still moments of struggle and confusion. For example, they resisted efforts to marry them off and were determined to be in control of their lives as they thought of marriage, even entertaining the idea of not marrying. In one conversation two Prerna alumnae, Anjali and Kiran, asked their teacher: "Can't we live without marriage?"

Her response to the question was:

> You can [live without marriage]; marriage is not compulsory. You don't have to, if you don't want to. But what we are saying is that you don't have to be scared of it, as well. Because things have changed for you now. If by your own choice, by your own decision, your own wish, you get married, because you think you are ready, want to be with someone and want children, then it's fine. You feel you want to marry and keep your job, that's okay, too. You can negotiate with your husband about sharing the housework, so that you can manage together. The basic point is that first you should have control over your life, which I feel a lot of you have. . . . And of course you will feel scared, everyone does, especially women and girls, because the world, everyone, keeps telling us that you should not have control over your life. You should stay under someone's control, your brother, your father, and that you aren't safe unless you are married. And you are going against all of that and finding the strength within yourself. It's a difficult task, but you are still doing it. You are earning your own money, fighting to continue your education, moving forward. It's so brave of you.

Given the almost compulsory and inevitable nature of marriage, especially for girls in India, this conversation represents a big leap forward. The narrative of marriage begins very early in girls' lives. As evidenced by the stories told by the teachers, the girls, their mothers, and me, it is clear that marriage is positioned by their families and society as the primary and final goal of their lives. The cultural discourse leaves almost no room for a life outside marriage for girls; their lives are meant to be legitimate only when lived in marriages, abusive or otherwise. Widows, single women, and divorced women are considered tragic aberrations. By contrast, many Prerna alumnae are able to imagine a legitimate life outside marriage, sounding a strong note of resistance and dissent to the dominant patriarchal discourse.

Prerna takes every opportunity to strengthen and support girls' aspirations, supporting and also lauding their intellectual and physical acts of resistance and transgression, as they seek greater control over their lives and attempt to construct more fulfilling lives for themselves. Rakhee, their principal, reassured them in the same discussion:

> I just wanted to tell you all that not everyone's marriage fails. So many of our students have gotten married; we have been to so many weddings. They aren't all bad.

Christina, another alumna, added in support:

> First of all, we have to see that marriage in itself is not bad, like every girl feels scared about marriage, it's not bad! But first we should be independent, and after that you should get married.

I am reminded here of Periyar, the Dalit activist and women's rights champion in South India, who, as early as 1928, conceived of the "Self-Respect Marriage" as part of his Self-Respect Movement, launched in 1925. Periyar rightly recognized the centrality of marriage in producing and perpetuating unequal patriarchal power structures and relations and its major role in keeping women subordinate and under control. The Self-Respect Marriage was a way of providing an alternative personal and social identity to women, as V. Geetha comments:

> Free to remake themselves in whatever manner they desired and tied to men in their lives through ties of mutuality, women acquired a new identity: that of the citizen, the women of civic virtue, and one who could claim and act on an identity which did not subordinate her to men.[8]

Our collective goal at Prerna during our critical dialogues around marriage is to enable our girls to articulate and imagine an alternative view of marriage consistent with their recognition of themselves as equal persons, one that lets them live a life of mutuality, reciprocity, and, of course, one in which they can maintain their self-respect.

Taking Action at Home: Changing Terms of Recognition

Aarti and her friends all struggled against the misrecognition of their families, and they worked hard to reformulate their identities in their own terms. Moni describes how she managed to change her father's perception and treatment of her by discussing it and with support from her teachers:

My father would say, "You are just sitting and laughing. Don't you have any work to do? Go inside and work."

She described the severe restrictions on her mobility:

And my father would say that all of us [sisters] will not go out anywhere, so I asked him what if someday Mother is sick? Then who will take her? Will we just sit around waiting for uncle or brother to come and take her to hospital? So then he started understanding a bit. He used to also come to school for the meetings and the aunties would talk to him. And then one day, there was no one at the home. Father wasn't home and Mother was sick. So, we [she and her sisters] took her to hospital and did everything, so then he understood that what we were saying was right. Because if something had to be bought from the market also, he used to say that you won't go anywhere—brother will go, but now he trusts us enough to send us. Now, he allows me. I travel with my work, sometimes for a week. He doesn't say anything.

Prerna alumnae and students report that as a result of their own changed perceptions of themselves and the transformation in their ways of acting and presenting themselves, their parents' perceptions of them have changed, too. Many report that their parents trust and respect them more and even resist social pressure and opinion in their support for their daughters.

Preeti explains this well:

> The people in the neighborhood haven't changed. They have wrong
> conceptions about Prerna in their minds. They say "girls from Prerna
> think they are very smart, they think they are Rani Laxmi Bai; they are
> always ready to fight and roam around with boys." They say many
> things about us, but my parents ignore them. They say "our daughter is
> not like this."[9]

Poorna reported that her father had learned through the regular parent
meetings that it was wrong to marry a girl at a young age, and he had decided
not to do that to his younger daughters. Priya reported that her mother now
takes her advice on things:

> Yes! On everything, even if someone has to be invited over or some-
> thing, or if clothes or anything needs to be bought for the house. She
> never used to talk to me before; now she consults me.

The students' own sense of self-efficacy, their own belief that they can succeed, seems to have rubbed off on their parents. Sadhana says:

> Now they feel that we can do something. Earlier they used to think we
> can't do anything; now Mother doesn't say no to my studying. I am
> doing my M.A. They say study as much as you want.

Our community survey and focus group discussions with the parents corroborate the girls' statements. Parents say they "trusted" their daughters more,
had "greater hopes from them than their sons," and believed that "boys and
girls both should be educated." One parent said, "We have become smarter
because of our daughter." Another said, "Not only is my daughter learning
very well, she also tells me new interesting things every day."

The girls seem to have succeeded in negotiating better terms of recognition
for themselves. Their parents are now recognizing them as capable, valuable,
equal persons, and are according them more respect, consulting their opinions, trusting them more, granting them more space and opportunities to
grow, and listening more to their "voice." There is a virtuous circle of recognition. Girls recognize themselves as equal, autonomous persons, worthy of respect, give voice to this self-recognition and act from it as equal persons. Their

parents recognize them on new terms, which then feeds back to girls' renewed recognition of themselves as more capable persons.

Changing these terms of recognition is an outcome of Prerna's long and persistent efforts, both with the girls and with their parents. Teachers have used multiple platforms and media to engage with the community, to advocate for their students and their intrinsic value as persons, having rights. The monthly parent meetings, drama presentations at cultural events, counseling interventions, regular critical dialogues with the students, have collectively come together to bring about a transformation in the girls' own self-recognition, consequently transforming their parents' views of them. It has by no means been an easy win, and many parents still resist. As Sadhana said ruefully:

> Aunty, Mother has changed a lot, but Father is still the same. He hasn't come to the school once; he just didn't get involved. Because I am just a daughter! But Mother has started supporting me. And she is doing that even now.

Khushboo's father and stepmother also have firmly resisted change, though Khushboo has managed to enlist her grandmother's support in her journey forward.

In negotiating terms of recognition with powerful and dominant others, Kiran, another Prerna alumna, cautions against using their education to add another layer of inequality—between literate and illiterate:

> I am saying that just because we have studied, we should not stop respecting the elders [our parents]. If we talk properly, and with respect then obviously they will respect us back.

Kiran reminds us that the process of changing terms of recognition is long and difficult, requiring persistence, patience, and respect.

Empowered Daughters Empowering Their Mothers

Daughters are witness to their mothers' lives, as were Sunita, Aarti, Preeti, Kunti, and Laxmi. They saw and suffered the pain their mothers lived as they bore their husbands' abuse and neglect. They worked alongside their mothers from very young ages and were their partners in childcare, housework, and work outside the home. They forged a strong bond with their mothers even as they decided that their lives would be different.

These girls felt deeply responsible for their mothers, protective and determined to take care of them. Sunita said with tears flowing down her face:

> She did so much for us. Once she had chicken pox and yet she went to work on the construction site. She couldn't afford not to work. If she didn't, then what would we eat?

Today Sunita makes plans for her mother, as well:

> I am planning for Mummy. We had bought a [sewing] machine a long while ago. And now she is getting old. It's hard to do this construction site work; it's hard labor climbing the scaffolding. So I am thinking if she does some stitching work at home, it will be easier for her, so someone can train her and she can find work.

Many of the girls report that they were in the habit of taking the critical dialogues home and discussing them with their mothers. Aarti said:

> Whatever would be taught here, we would go back and discuss among us at home. Mother would keep listening to what we were saying. In the beginning she thought it was only words, but then she saw it was very practical what we were saying.

Aarti's sister Nishu, also a Prerna alumna, now in acting school, added that they made sure to discuss the dialogues very loudly, to ensure her attention.

Aarti and Preeti told us how they managed to strengthen their mothers and stop their fathers from abusing their mothers. Aarti described a troubling scenario involving her father:

> At times, he would smash her in the wall, holding the neck. And Mother won't even say anything. When we were small we didn't know what to do; when we would hear his voice, we would hide under the bed. We were so scared of him. Then you [addressing a teacher] once said during our critical dialogue on domestic violence, "If he is hitting, why can't you resist? Why can't you stop him?" So slowly, whatever teachers used to say here, I would go home and tell my mother, and then when next time he raised his hand, all of us stood up—me, Nishu, brothers, everyone—and

Aarti and her mother Manju

said that, "If you will hit now, we'll hit you back, we won't let you hit her." Then I grabbed his neck, same way he used to do to Mother; after drinking he had no strength. He just went limp. We used to be afraid of him for no reason. My mother still defended him but I said, "I am seeing this since childhood. He always beats us, then why can't we resist?" Then he was pleading, "Please leave me, please leave me." Now even Mother is more strong. Now he doesn't say anything. He keeps quiet.

Preeti shared a similar experience where her mother is no longer scared of her father and even defends herself against his physical abuse. When the teacher asked Preeti how her mother gained this strength, she replied:

Because whatever I used to learn here, I would go back and tell my mother. So slowly, she also learned that something wrong was going on [that she was being wronged].

In our focus group discussions, mothers corroborated largely what the girls had reported. It seemed having developed their own "voice" at school, our girls were taking those voices home and lending them to their mothers, demonstrating how strong daughters can make their mothers strong.

Preeti and her mother Rajeshwari

Transforming Brothers and Fathers

Aarti and Laxmi indicate they also have had an impact, a gentling effect, on their brothers. In Aarti's case, she notes:

> My brother does not bully me, because he has been listening to my discussions at home with my mother for a long time, since he was little. Whatever happened at home I used to discuss it at home. I used to tell him that boys are not supposed to do all that they do. They shouldn't be roaming the streets and harassing girls on the street. That this is wrong. Since he was exposed to all this from the beginning, there is a difference between him and other boys.

And she added, smiling, "He doesn't mind cooking and cleaning either."

We wish more brothers had been transformed, and that will be our goal and effort with our Prerna boys school. Several of our girls complain about the bullying attitudes of their brothers, who are raised to believe they are superior to their sisters and have a legitimate right to exercise control even over their older sisters. Both Jyoti and Sandhya tell us how they fight against their brothers' resentment toward their pursuit of higher education, insisting that they, as women, be recognized as persons entitled to the same right to education afforded to their brothers, as men.

The girls also helped shape their mothers' perceptions about having daughters. Sunita, who does not have a brother, says her mother has stopped wishing she had had a son. "She told me I am son-enough for her." It would be even more fitting, of course, if Sunita were "daughter-enough" for her mother, yet this is a significant shift in attitude, given the widespread prevalence of preferences for sons in Indian society.

In a recent study on son-preference attitudes, it was reported that, among the states, Uttar Pradesh had the largest proportion of men and women, close to 50 percent, who had strong son-preferring attitudes.[10] Although Rakhee reports that parents have told her that they are very proud of their daughters, sometimes more than of their sons, and that their daughters are now taking on more responsibilities than their sons, it would be a stretch to say that a majority of the parents have given up this preference, given how firmly entrenched it is in the patriarchal ideology that structures their feelings and behavior. It will take much work, perseverance, and patience to alter these norms. We can only be encouraged that Prerna is trying to change these age-old patriarchal norms, attitudes, and feelings—one life at a time.

Prerna Girls Take Social Action

For those of us who have been activists struggling to overcome socially structured challenges in our personal lives and guided by the awareness that the problem is systemic, we are almost naturally propelled to the next step: to take social action, our self-work moving seamlessly into social work. In her book *Making a Difference*, feminist activist and writer Ritu Menon has compiled personal memoirs from 21 women who made significant contributions to the women's movement in India. She writes that for each of them, it was a decisive moment in their own lives—"An experience—of discrimination in girlhood or adolescence, dimly understood then, that suddenly fell into place as unfairly and humiliatingly gendered; . . . an understanding, that patriarchal privilege cuts across class, as well as caste"—that led them to become social and political activists.[11]

My own experience bears this out. Similarly, for all the girls in my story and many of their friends, once their consciousness is stirred, they make tentative moves from personal activism to social action. Aarti relates an incident where she was moved to take social action[12]:

My own village is in a very remote area. There are no [education] facilities. Not even a single girl is going to school. This is the situation there. They talk very badly to women. If anyone is beating up a poor woman, they say that she deserves to be beaten, because she has done some wrong. I went there this winter. A woman used to come and fill water from the hand pump outside my uncle's house. He is a very arrogant man. He took away her bucket and threw it in the pond. He said, "You come and show your stupid face here every morning. Don't come here when we are using the hand pump." I was standing there and watching everything. Then even some other women supported my uncle. Then the poor woman asked for her bucket back—she just said that—"Please can I have my bucket back?" Just this much and my uncle slapped her.

Detecting a caste conflict here, I asked Aarti: "Who was the woman?"

Aarti: "The woman is from a family of potters. They are very poor and the potter caste is supposed to be a lower caste. So, I went there and said that there is no such thing as a higher or upper caste. I used to be scared of my uncle. That day also he was giving me a look. I told him that I, too, understand what is wrong and what is right. I told him, "You can't beat this woman. If I complain to the police, you will be in jail. And then you will understand. And this hand pump belongs to [the] government and is meant for everybody's use. You do not own this." And then more women came and began to justify the beating. So I asked them why they were taking his side instead of telling the man to stop. This all happens because they are from an upper caste. They think that they can do anything to the people from lower caste. Then the women told me that I am not allowed to talk to my uncle like this because he is elder to me. They said, "Is this what you have learned from your education?" And they said that just because I am living in a city should not mean that I disrespect my elders. I said that "for a wrong act, I would speak up. And you are no one to tell me otherwise. And if this woman doesn't complain to the police, I will do so. If he tries to slap her again, I will file a complaint." And I asked him to pick up her bucket and give it back to her. And then he picked up the bucket and gave it back.

Teacher: So didn't he scold you later?

Aarti: He was giving me a look. But I didn't care.

This was a very brave act. As Aarti had begun to act against oppression in her own life by pushing against its oppressive gendered boundaries, she became more aware and sensitive to other forms of oppression. She learned to speak up for injustice wherever she saw it. In this incident, the attack on the poor lower-caste woman arose from an unholy nexus of poverty, caste, and gender. Aarti's response was instinctive, but her argument was insightful. She challenged her family and the other women of the community for their caste-related violence, argued against caste discrimination, and strengthened her argument by invoking the law to challenge their traditional beliefs and practices. She also defied the cultural codes of deference to elders by challenging her uncle. Her insubordination to her elders was criticized by her family, who attributed it to an arrogance born out of her urban, educated status. Aarti was able to give an appropriate response and, indeed, restore some justice in that particular case: "I said for a wrong act I would speak up, and you are no one to tell me otherwise." Aarti is using her voice to assert her right to use it not for her own welfare alone but for that of others, as well. She is trying to change people's minds about their cultural attitudes or mind-sets.

Aarti is questioning the "cultural consensus" around existing terms of recognition prevalent in her home community that favor the dominant caste.[13] According to Appadurai, cultural norms, rules, and customs are formed and held together by a cultural consensus that determines, among other things, the terms of recognition between groups, which, in turn, determine power relations, hierarchies of status, and social boundaries. These terms of recognition become fairly fixed over time so that even the groups adversely affected by them, for example, the lower-caste potter woman in this case, comply with rules that disadvantage them, thus maintaining the superiority and hegemonic control of the dominant groups. As a result, social movements hoping to transform power relations must focus on changing the cultural consensus.

Aarti, even though she herself belongs to the upper-caste group, is fighting on behalf of the lower-caste woman, demanding from her community that they recognize that she deserves equal human dignity despite her caste membership. Aarti is taking social action by sounding a dissenting note and hopefully creating a fissure in the existing consensus.

There have been several similar cases where our girls have taken action individually in their communities and neighborhoods. Khushboo narrated an incident at her university recently. As part of their affirmative action program, Dalit girls and boys are refunded tuition fees in state universities. Khushboo and her classmate Sandeep, also Dalit, were at the university office to complete the paperwork for the refund.

> The clerk was a Brahmin—His last name was Dubey—[and] he knew from Sandeep's last name that he was Dalit, but insisted on hearing him say it, telling him to confirm his caste status out loud, asking him to say, "I am a Chamar."[14] Sandeep was silent. I spoke up and told the clerk that he was being casteist. I told him, "You know who he is, but you just want to humiliate him. See, I am a Chamar and I am not ashamed of it. You may be a Brahmin, but there's no difference between you and me. We are both the same." He didn't like it and told me not to be rude and complained to my department that I was talking back to him. But I told my professor, when she questioned me, that I will speak up if anyone is being unfair to me or my friends.

Getting Organized: Veerangana

When Laxmi's cohort was in the eleventh grade, the students said to me during one of our critical dialogue sessions:

> We want to do something. We think we should share with other girls and women what we have got from our education. We have become strong and can resist, fight, but the others can't. They haven't learned to think like us. So what can we do?

After much discussion we decided the girls would form a group and conduct similar critical dialogues with groups of women and girls in their community. All our dialogues had been filmed and were on DVDs, and they decided they would take the DVDs and play them on televisions, so they were supported while conducting the discussions. They called this group Veerangana, which means "brave woman."[15]

They began to meet regularly in homes every week, conducting critical dialogues with women from the community. The girls worked in a group of six, and while one of them led the discussion, they all participated actively, each advocating for girls' right to education, to personal integrity, greater mobility, against child marriage, and for a life free of violence and humiliation. The meetings were well attended and the women participated actively in the discussion. Many of the women were veiled and came only after much persuasion. It is noteworthy that the women, all older than the girls, accepted their leadership. The women sometimes agreed and endorsed their views, and disagreed and argued their own position at other times. One woman said child marriage was not such a bad thing, and even though her daughter was only 13, she was looking for a groom, and if she found a good one she would go ahead and marry her off. The girls argued that the daughter should be allowed to have an education with a chance at a better life, saying, for example, "If she is educated, then when she has problems in her marriage, she has an option to fend for herself." The woman replied, "If she is going to have problems she will have them in any case. Education or no education, and early or late, it doesn't make a difference." The girls were very persuasive. This transcript gives us a flavor of the discussion:

Laxmi: Some people get their daughters married off early [child marriage], why do you think this happens? Like making sure they don't go wrong [become sexually promiscuous] is one reason.

Woman 1: Some people just like to get their daughters married early, so that they can marry their sons and bring a daughter-in-law, who they can boss over. My daughter herself says that she wants to get married. My daughter is 13 and I have started to think about getting her married.

Laxmi: Aunty, they are kids; they do not understand the meaning of marriage or of what they are saying. But you are older and more mature. It is your duty to make them understand about such things. Please don't get your 13-year-old daughter married just because she likes the idea of getting married for new clothes and jewelry and things like that.

Woman 1: But we also got married at the age of 16.

Khushboo: Aunty, that was a different period. If you get your daughter married at 13, when they are not ready physically, mentally, and socially to handle the burden of a married life, then they will face a lot of problems later.

Woman 1: If she has to suffer, she will suffer irrespective of age. It depends on what kind of house she gets married into. If she doesn't get a good family, then her life will be hell, whatever her age is.

Woman 2: But if this is the case, and if you marry your daughter after getting her educated, then she would at least be able to earn for herself and live.

Khushboo: Yes, she doesn't necessarily have to suffer.

Preeti: And we are not asking you to not get your girls married. But you should get her married only after a certain age.

Anjali: Aunty, all of us know about the [high] suicide rates among the girls [and young women].[16] Why do you think it is so high? They are married off at an early age, then she has to face so many difficulties and is burdened so heavily that she gives up.

Khushboo: If she is educated, she can live according to her wishes; she can go anywhere.

Woman 1: Yes, but then she will also have to understand her responsibilities.

Anjali: This will only happen if you educate her.

Woman nods in agreement.

Preeti: Are you sending her to school?

Woman: No.

Anjali: We just want to say that you should send them to school; whichever school you want to, but send them.

Laxmi: We just want everyone, all the people in this neighborhood, to educate their children and also make sure that children, especially daughters, are not beaten at home.

Anjali: We also don't think cases like these [of physical abuse] should be kept a private affair of the family. You have the right to interfere in these cases and stop the abuse. When someone says "it is my husband, my brother, and you cannot interfere," you should say, "No, this is not a private affair. Since it is a case of domestic violence, stopping this is my duty."

Preeti: This is because you all are a part of the same society. Men, they have a lot of solidarity among themselves. But we women need to understand the importance of unity among us. See, when we make our homes and families better, only then can society improve. That's why we have made this Veerangana group, so that we can work at making our society better. And we want you to work with us. Let's stop this violence at home and early marriage.

The transcript illustrates how, despite the limitations and exigencies of their lives, the girls—who were working and studying and had very little free time and, of course, no money—recognized the need to take social action in their communities. They seem to realize that because women's lives are lived and created in social spaces, it is important to align their personal and social worlds.

They are seeking to raise the feminist consciousness of the women, and working to help them understand the unfairness and wrongness of the social norms that leave them at such a disadvantage. They are urging the women to aspire to better lives for themselves and better futures for their daughters. They are also trying to empower the older women, as they had been empowered, and to encourage dissent against the dominant ideology. The women they are addressing have given their consent to this ideology and internalized it, accepting and complying even though the terms are grossly unfavorable and unjust. Our students encourage them to resist and reject these terms, saying, for example, "You have the right to say no," and "She doesn't necessarily have to suffer." They are working hard to build a new narrative, one that offers a place of respect and safety to women and their daughters.

As part of the community, the girls understand the particulars of the cultural norms that keep women and girls oppressed, along with the social rule of keeping family matters within the family to safeguard the family's honor. They try to share with the women their own important learning, that the oppressions they suffer in private spaces should be shared and held up for public scrutiny, thus affording women more safety.

The transcript above also shows how well the girls support each other through the dialogue, strengthening each other's argument, working persuasively together. It is a good example of "dissensus" within a cultural community, trying to give different shape to the existing cultural consensus.[17] All social movements against dominant forces attempt to do this, to transform the cultural consensus by raising social awareness regarding some injustice or oppression, changing conceptual and emotional maps or mind-sets, and moving the collective consciousness to a fairer place. Doing this is the lynchpin, the key to social transformational change.

Motivated by the same goal, they also conducted dialogues on child marriage. They led meetings and interviewed individual women and men, informing them of the law.

Following is a transcript of an interview Laxmi conducted with Sunanda, her friend Nandini's mother, about Nandini's sudden early marriage. Sunanda had been almost belligerent in her insistence to get Nandini married and resented our intervention, ignoring it completely. This interview took place a year after the wedding:[18]

Sunanda: We are regretting getting Nandini married. I haven't spoken to her in months. They [her in-laws] don't even let her telephone me.
Laxmi: How old was Nandini when you married her off?
Sunanda: She wasn't very old, 16?
Laxmi: Why did you marry her off at such a young age?

Sunanda: I don't know (shaking her head), the circumstances were such, I was having problems, health issues.

Laxmi: What problems? Was there any societal pressure?

Sunanda: Yes, that is always there, but mostly it was my wrong decision; only married her off because I felt I had to. It was my mistake. I regret it now. I won't marry Gayatri, my younger daughter, so young.

Laxmi and her friends conducted several similar interviews with girls and women, trying to get them to reflect on their situations.

Khushboo similarly interviewed a man in the community:

Man: Child marriage is not what you think it is. What do you consider child marriage? If a girl is 12 or 13 that is child marriage; 16, 17 is a fair age to marry girls off. I don't think that is child marriage.

Khushboo: But sir, then why is the legal definition of marriage 18 years for a girl?

Man: Oh that. That doesn't matter. I agree that at 16 the girl is a minor, but I don't think marrying a girl at 16 or 17 is child marriage! After all parents have to get rid of their responsibilities and if they move the age by a few years for that, I don't think that is wrong.

Khushboo gently persists in her line of questioning, trying to convince this man otherwise, also trying to assert that girls are citizens with legal rights. The older man dismisses this impatiently, illustrating the general societal insistence on maintaining traditional social definitions and, in a sense, refusing to grant women and girls their constitutional rights of citizenship. We don't know if he changed his mind, but both Khushboo and Laxmi persisted, trying to move him and others to change the terms of recognition accorded to girls as "burdens" to be "rid of" as soon as possible.

Given the codes of deference in India, where girls, especially if they are younger, should only be seen and not heard, it was particularly risky for the girls to engage in these conversations with elders in the community because they were trying to challenge the dominant discourse around girls and women. It speaks to their self-assurance, the conviction of their beliefs, and their faith in their own voice that they were able to stand their ground. Getting Nandini's mother to accept that perhaps she had been unfair to her daughter was not easy, but Laxmi's interview helped move her in that direction. As a result of efforts by Laxmi and teachers at the school, Nandini's younger sister was spared an early forced marriage. The girls took their critical dialogues into the community, engaging in the same cultural prodding they had received in their empowerment classes.

Public Campaign to Change Social Consensus

Helped by their teachers, the girls embarked upon a public awareness campaign against child marriage and domestic violence. They went house-to-house getting people to sign a pledge saying that domestic violence was against the law and committing to honor the law. Those who pledged said they would neither engage in domestic violence nor tolerate it. They made banners with slogans, and, together with the teachers, they marched in their community, chanted slogans, sang empowerment songs, and wrote and enacted a street play on violence in the square in their neighborhood. They brought in a police inspector to talk to the people about domestic violence being a cognizable offense. Their goal was to enlist the commitment and support of the local police and to make women aware that the law was on their side. They also enlisted the support of women's organizations like Suraksha working against domestic violence, which joined in the march.

They were rallying all the social forces they could muster, understanding, perhaps, that it would need a critical mass of dissenters to change the prevailing cultural consensus or collective consciousness.

The girls report that they found this campaign extremely empowering. As Sunita explained:

> This really made me feel my voice counts. I count. People in Guari Gaon have taken note of this movement; they have taken note of us. They think of us as persons who they can turn to for help and persons who can effect change. No one, especially not schoolgirls, have done this before, asked them these kinds of questions, or listened to them.[19]

Our girls had developed their voice in the spaces and opportunities afforded to them by their school, in the classroom, on the stage, in their community, and in dialogue with others. Their individual empowerment was not just individual; it was a collective achievement. Freire says that "liberation is a social act. Liberating education is a social process of illumination."[20] Their voice, developed in critical dialogues, was strengthened further when they used it in public social spaces and felt it was heard and that it counted.

Protesting against domestic violence

Including Social Action in the Curriculum

Encouraged by the impact on the girls of the Veerangana group and its activities, and seeing its potential effect on the community, Prerna continued the group activity initiated by Laxmi's cohort. It has acquired a more formal structure as an official part of the school's activities. Prerna has included social action in its curriculum as an important foundation for leadership training for girls. All the girls from eighth grade onward, 140 in all in 2016, are enrolled in the group. Guided by alumnae and teachers, they engage in a number of activities inside the school and in the community, including conducting two campaigns against child marriage, following a format similar to that previously described.

The Veerangana group also had a discussion with other girls in their neighborhood who were not in school because they were compelled by their circumstances to work. They gave those girls their own examples and encouraged them to come to school, saying that it was possible to fit their studies into their work schedule. They emphasized the importance of a high school education for better long-term prospects for the girls' lives. Similarly, they have held discussions with women, raising awareness on a number of themes, including their right to equal wages. They have been mobilizing them to demand equal wages in their work places and to resist exploitation, including sexual harassment. They have also made it their business collectively to educate women and girls in their communities about the laws made for their protection, including the laws against domestic violence, early child marriage, dowry demand, and harassment. Recently the girls in the group had two discussions with the Prerna boys school on gender discrimination at home and sexual harassment on the streets. Their goal is to engage boys in dialogue regarding systemic discrimination and to make them their allies in their effort to effect structural change.

Moving Beyond "Educated Girls Become Educated Mothers"

One of the arguments made in favor of educating girls is that they become more educated mothers, which means better health for themselves and their children and advantages for families and the community. I have argued against taking this kind of instrumental view of girls and girls' education. The reason for promoting education for girls, or, indeed, education for anybody, is that it is essential for their own development; it is their right to be educated for their own full functioning as a human being. That they become more productive economically and develop as good "human resources" should also be a secondary consideration.

Girls' education has for too long been argued as a way of developing potentially healthier, better mothers. Our work with Prerna shows that educating the girls did, indeed, impact the community and their families, but in a different manner. In their own families they made their mothers stronger women, more aware of their intrinsic right to personal integrity, dignity, and respect. They went out into the community and tried to raise a similar feminist consciousness in other women and girls. They also tried to raise the consciousness of men and make them allies in the effort to achieve gender justice for girls and women.

The girls were supported by their school and teachers, who worked alongside them and their communities to shift the collective perception of girls and women from one that valued them for their domestic, sexual, and reproductive labor to one that focused on the girls' intrinsic worth and their right to lives of their own choosing, lived freely and equally.

Education enabled the girls to try to effect change in the dominant discourse of patriarchal ideology as they advocated for gender justice. The narrative of better-educated girls making better future mothers neither does enough for girls themselves nor does it help build a new, gender-just, democratic social order. It does not recognize, and in fact denies, women and girls the right to self-determination, to define their social roles in their own terms, and to chart out their future life plans accordingly. As far back as 1928, the Dalit activist Periyar recognized that identifying women primarily with their reproductive functions restricted them from laying claim to complete autonomy; he, instead, advocated reproductive choice for women.[21] Prerna and its students pick up this refrain and show how they advocate for girls' education as a way to help girls and women achieve their intrinsic right to equal dignity and to full lives as human beings.

10

Learning Outcomes and Beyond

As I reflect on Prerna's 14-year journey, I ask myself what we have we achieved. The standard parameters of a school's success are enrollment, attendance, retention, completion, and achievement scores. Girls should come to school, attend regularly, and complete the program, and they should demonstrate grade-level learning of the official curriculum. The global and national discourse and efforts surrounding girls' education are focused on these parameters, and it is assumed that by achieving them we will have solved the problem of girls' education and gender equality.

Prerna's definition of a high-quality education, however, takes a different, broader approach. We believe that while girls should come, attend regularly, stay, complete, and learn, these necessary goals are by no means sufficient to ensure better life outcomes for girls or achieve the larger societal objective of gender equality. We believe a high-quality education for girls must include—and perhaps prioritize—a strong focus on their empowerment. It must enable them to develop self-esteem and to see themselves as equal persons, worthy of respect, possessing human dignity and the right to equal participation in society. Prerna focuses on developing girls' capacity to aspire, to speak up for themselves with a strong voice, to challenge discriminatory structures, and to be capable agents and drivers of their own lives. These are Prerna's parameters of a successful education for girls.

TABLE 10-1. *Growth of Prerna*

Year	Number of students	Number of teachers
2003	80	4
2004	160	6
2005	200	6
2006	250	8
2007	335	10
2008	435	12
2009	451	16
2010	480	18
2011	510	20
2012	587	22
2013	697	25
2014	711	28
2015	800	35
2016	880	37

Source: Prerna Girls School Records.

Girls Come to School

Prerna's openly and unapologetically declared feminist approach runs counter to the social norms and values practiced by the communities, and there have been a few confrontations between the school administrators, teachers, and parents. Despite that, our enrollment has grown steadily each year since its inception in 2003, as shown in table 10-1. We began with 30 girls, and 80 had joined by the end of the first year. By 2016 the student body was 880.

Attendance Rates

As mentioned in chapter 6, the school's average student attendance is 83.6 percent, compared to a state average of 54.7 percent (at elementary level) and a national average of 71.1 percent.[1] The state and national average student attendance rates have been taken from the ASER Centre report of 2014, which assesses attendance in rural schools and is based on one visit per school in the largest government primary school in a sample district. The ASER data are not strictly comparable with data from Prerna, given that Prerna is an urban school and the attendance averages reported are over a three-year period. However, the data from Prerna do demonstrate consistently high attendance over a long period.

All the reasons for poor attendance of girls in government schools also apply to Prerna's student population—poverty, uneducated parents, perceived low value of girls' education—but Prerna manages to show high attendance averages. Still, attendance remains one of our major challenges, requiring persistent effort. Teachers' attendance is even higher, averaging 96.48 percent, when compared against state averages of 85.6 percent and a national average of 85.8 percent.[2] According to a World Bank study based on unannounced visits to government schools, 25 percent of teachers were absent from school, and only about half were teaching.[3] I believe students' high attendance at Prerna is partly inspired by the high teacher attendance. Prerna teachers demonstrate their seriousness by tracking students' attendance carefully and aggressively.

Girls Stay: Retention and Completion

The national dropout rate for girls, as recorded by the Ministry of Human Resource Development, from grades 1 to 10 was 46.7 percent in 2014.[4]

Between 2014 and 2016, for all grades from pre-school to grade 12, Prerna recorded an average attrition rate of 8.14 percent. Nearly one-third of those leaving moved residence and transferred to other schools, sometimes even fee-paying schools, according to our records. Because it is uncertain whether the remaining two-thirds have continued in other schools, they are counted as having dropped out.

Many of the girls' parents are migrant laborers. They move wherever their work takes them, and when there is no work, they move back to their native villages. The majority of the clear dropouts include girls who have migrated from the neighborhood with their parents, either back to the village or to distant construction sites. Some have rejoined Prerna when their parents found work in Lucknow and returned.

A very small number of the students dropped out because of marriage, sickness in the family, personal health issues, and family problems. For instance, one girl has been compelled to take on her mother's job full-time because the mother became seriously ill and was unable to work. Another girl has tuberculosis. In

TABLE 10-2. *Transition Rates (Percent)*

Level	Prerna	Uttar Pradesh	India
Primary – Upper Primary	90.44	78.5	89.7
Elementary – Secondary	90.11	93.82	92.62
Secondary – Higher Secondary	95.03	80.45	68.35

Source: Prerna Girls School Records; Uttar Pradesh and India figures are from District Information System for Education (DISE), 2014–15.

the last three years, Prerna has lost six girls to marriage, though all of them were 18 or older. One student dropped out of school because she eloped with a boy, but she has since returned to school.

The average transition rate from Primary to Upper Primary for the last three years has been 90.44 percent (see table 10-2); from Elementary to Secondary the rate was 90.11 percent; and from Secondary to Higher Secondary, 95.03 percent. Our completion rate from grade 8 to 12 is 87 percent. While we do not have similar figures disaggregated by sex for Uttar Pradesh or India, table 10-2 presents the combined figures for boys and girls.

Girls Learn: Achievement Scores

Table 10-3 gives Secondary and Senior Secondary Certification (pass percentages) comparison for Prerna Girls School and National Open School national averages.[5]

Except for the 2010–11 cohort, when the senior secondary pass percentage was only 60 percent, and the 2015–16 cohort, when it was 95 percent, all other Prerna cohorts have demonstrated a shining 100 percent pass percentage. Accounting for the lower pass percentage of the 2010–11 cohort, Rakhee, Prerna's principal, says five girls failed their English exam and had to take it again six months later. She says they failed because these particular girls had enrolled in Prerna only in the ninth grade. They found it hard to perform at the required standard for twelfth grade, even though they managed to pass in tenth grade. She added, additionally, that they were insufficiently supported by the English teacher, who was changed after that year. The pass percentage in 2015–16 recorded a slight dip when commerce was introduced as a subject

TABLE 10-3. *Students' Completion of Secondary and Senior Secondary Education: Prerna Girls School versus NIOS (Percent)*

		2010– 11	2011– 12	2012– 13	2013– 14	2014– 15	2015– 16
Prerna Girls School	Secondary	100	100	100	100	100	100
	Senior Secondary	62.5	100	100	100	100	95
NIOS Average	Secondary	42.41	40.27	47.81	56.28	54.81	n.a.
	Senior Secondary	40.13	36.93	43.17	42.83	44.55	n.a.

Source: Prerna Girls School Records; National Institute of Open Schooling, "Statistical Report," 2016 (www.nos.org/stastical-report.aspx).

for the first time in 2015, as according to Rakhee both students and teachers were still finding their way in this unfamiliar terrain.

Even though Prerna's assessments for all grades up to tenth grade are internal, the goal of these assessments is to evaluate grade-level learning by the students. Prerna's records demonstrate that on average 96.9 percent of our students achieve grade-level learning, move successfully to the next grade level, and are able to cope, though at varying levels of proficiency.[6]

Students' achievement scores are tracked with as much zeal as their attendance rates, and parents are kept abreast of these at regular parent-teacher meetings. Parents are called at the end of each summative assessment to collect their daughters' report cards, which are discussed at length with them. The school wants parents to know that they care deeply about their girls learning and invites parents to care as well.

Those who are poor are acutely aware of their diminished bargaining power, leading them to believe they cannot make demands or hold more powerful entities, such as schools, accountable. But parents' experience at Prerna is different. We have found that parents, especially mothers, even when unschooled, attend these meetings with great enthusiasm, eager to learn about their daughters' performance and progress. Parent involvement, particularly that of fathers, in their daughters' education has increased over the years. Their motivation has a direct, positive effect on their daughters' performance in school. "The girls are so happy when their parents appreciate their good grades," Rakhee commented.

As the *Public Report on Basic Education* points out:

> Some parents simply feel that the schooling system is "not for them."
> The teachers may treat them with indifference, contempt, or even hostility. Their children may be discriminated against at school.[7]

During my own research in a rural government school, I found that many parents sense and resent the culturally patronizing and disrespectful stance of the teacher. They said that the teacher talked down to them and disrespected them because of their poverty, illiteracy, and their lower-caste rural status. School administrators are positioned in a seat of power and often not held accountable, either to the children or parents, blaming parents and their children, their poverty, and ignorance for poor performance.[8] Prerna does the opposite, holding itself accountable to parents and encouraging parental involvement.

Community Perceptions

In our parents' survey, all 80 respondents rated Prerna as a good school, with 90 percent pointing to the quality education as the reason. In addition, 80 percent cited overall development, which includes self-confidence, good communication and negotiation skills, and decisionmaking and problem-solving skills, along with academic proficiency, as a key factor; 78.75 percent valued the low fee; and 65 percent mentioned the midday meal as important. Figure 10-1 summarizes parents' responses. Other factors mentioned by parents included the safety of the girls, suitable time of instruction, and the fact that it is an all-girls school.

Some, though critical of it, do not seem overly concerned by the subversive effect of the critical feminist education their daughters are getting in school. Khushboo's father, for instance, despite some concerns, has not pulled his other six daughters from Prerna. This might be because he does not fully grasp the powerful way in which their education subverts the patriarchal conditioning of girls into silent submission and acceptance of discriminatory social norms, impacting thereby their daughters' way of thinking of themselves and, consequently, their ways of acting in the world.

Khushboo's father is probably typical of many. He sees education of girls as benignly adding to the girls' value but not as something that has the potential of subverting the social structure. In his view, even educated girls must accept their "proper" place and traditional role at home and in society;

Figure 10.1. *Why Parents Think Prerna Is a Good School?*

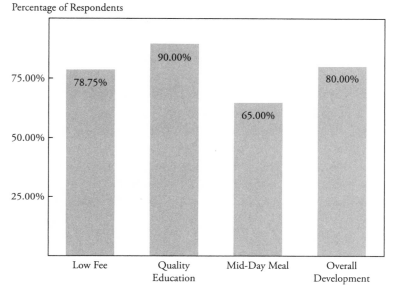

Percentage of Respondents

Source: Prerna Community Survey conducted in 2016.

education for girls is not meant to transform their unequal status or give them aspirations for equality. In short, according to him, this is not the proper role of education in school. He may feel he can keep traditional values and belief systems in place, because of his strong patriarchal control at home.

A majority of the mothers and an increasing number of fathers, however, recognize the empowering and transformational potential of education and are secretly glad for the support. They want their daughters to get away from poverty and advance their lives. Said one mother:

> Now my daughter is moving ahead. I am very happy. My husband is also slowly understanding.

In response to the question of whether they agreed with the school's empowerment program, which included teaching girls to speak up for their rights and to oppose early marriage and domestic violence, 79 of 80 parents agreed; 28 strongly agreed.

In response to the question, "Has Prerna affected any change in you, your family, and your community?" only seven of the 80 respondents said they perceived no change. All the others agreed that change was evident, with more than half saying that substantial change had been felt in their communities' way of thinking and in the treatment of daughters.

One mother responded: "I am learning to oppose injustice." Another said, "There is change. We are learning to break the silence." Yet another said, "We have learned to speak up against violence. The atmosphere of my house has changed." One mother specifically referred to "critical thinking," saying, "There is a lot of change. Girls have developed critical thinking, and they want to have better lives. It's all because of what they are learning in school."

One father responded:

Because of Prerna, I have seen change in my family and in my neighborhood. People's mentality has changed. This school encourages girls. That is good.

Another father, disagreeing a little, said:

Though I can't say for sure there is a change in the whole community, I know I have changed. Daughters in my family were married at a very early age, but I won't do that. I will let my daughters study and make something of their lives. I will think about their marriage later. This is the most substantial change in me.

Other parents spoke appreciatively of the development of "courage" and "confidence" in their daughters.

During the focus group discussions, I asked the parents:

We speak against many practices in society, like child marriage; we also teach your children to protest against them, so people ask us, how is it that parents don't pull out their daughters?

Not addressing the question directly, one of the mothers responded thoughtfully and simply: "Yes, but everything good is happening here—children are studying nicely."

Parents seem to value the culture of care at the school and feel their daughters are safe, happy in school, learning well, and flourishing. They want better futures for their daughters, even though many cannot get beyond the belief that marriage is a daughter's final destiny.

Even though the traditional indicators of performance—enrollment, attendance, retention, completion, and achievement scores—are not our sole focus, Prerna manages to outperform state and national averages on all these. More girls are coming to school, and most of them are staying, learning, and completing. The focus of our education, however, is a more holistic one, which I believe is the secret of Prerna's success. Girls strive hard to achieve academic success because they feel empowered, with a growing sense of self-confidence, self-esteem, and self-efficacy, while they also grow in academic learning. Prerna looks at learning outcomes from the prism of the girls' lives and measures success or failure by the girls' life outcomes, to which we now turn.

What Life Outcomes Does Prerna Enable?

Prerna's main goal is to educate its students so they develop a feminist consciousness and grow into emancipated women with a perception of themselves as equal, autonomous persons having the right to equal participation and to develop aspirations and skills for such equal participation. To this end, girls must:

+ Learn to perceive themselves as equal persons.

+ Emerge with a sense of agency and control over their lives, aspirations for the future, and the confidence and the skills to realize these things.

+ Gain a critical understanding of the patriarchal social and political structures that frame their lives and restrict possibilities, using this knowledge to push the boundaries and to reconstruct their world.

+ Learn to read, write, and successfully complete the government-mandated syllabus up to grade 12.

As shown by tables 10-4 and 10-5, a majority of the girls achieve this last goal, but while completing the twelfth grade may be important, even essential, it is only one part of Prerna's comprehensive educational goals. Inspired by Paulo Freire, we believe that becoming empowered, becoming free, is a serious educational outcome, demanding the same rigor and intellectual attention by the educational institution as is typically reserved for academic study.[9] Prerna works assiduously and persistently to enable this space for learning.

TABLE 10-4. *Life Outcomes of Seven Cohorts of Prerna Graduates*

Cohort[a]	No. of Students	Transitioned to higher education (percent)	Married as of 2016	Average age at marriage	Employed (percent)
2008–09	9	100	5	23.4	45
2010–11	15	93.3	4	23.5	60
2011–12	15	93.3	1	18	73.3
2012–13	18	100	1	21	55.6
2013–14	21	95.2	5	20.5	24
2014–15	18	100	1	18	55.6
2015–16	19	100	1[b]	17	57.9
All cohorts	115	97.4	18	21.5	52.2

Source: Prerna Girls School Records.

a. Year 2009–10 is missing as there were no students in that cohort.

b. Neetu was married at 17 years of age, when in grade 9. She left school and returned five years later.

Since its founding in 2003, through 2015, Prerna has graduated 115 students, whose life outcomes are very encouraging. Most of the students were first-generation graduates. Of the students who completed tenth grade, 88.1 percent went on to graduate from the twelfth grade, resisting, with the school's support, societal "pull out" pressures. Of our twelfth grade graduates, 97.4 percent have progressed to higher education and are studying for, or have completed, a bachelor's degree, either through the Indira Gandhi National Open University (IGNOU), a well-regarded distance learning national university, or local colleges.[10] Table 10-4 gives a comprehensive picture of the girls' life outcomes to date—their transition to higher education, employment status, and marital status. The data demonstrate quite clearly that our girls have developed aspirations for themselves. Nine percent have also progressed to the master's level academically (see figure 10-2).

Figure 10.2. *Higher Education Status of Prerna's Alumnae*

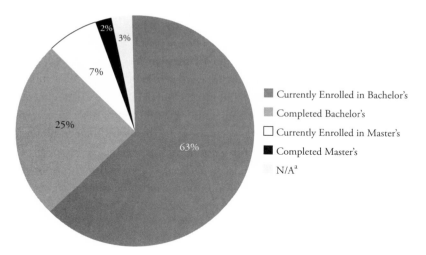

■ Currently Enrolled in Bachelor's

▨ Completed Bachelor's

□ Currently Enrolled in Master's

■ Completed Master's

▨ N/A[a]

Source: Prerna Girls School Records. Data compiled for 96 students in the year 2016.

a. The data on current status of remaining 3 percent were unavailable and thus they were assumed to have not transitioned.

Over 52 percent of Prerna graduates are employed, most part-time and some full-time, while studying simultaneously for their higher degrees. They have progressed from working as housemaids to better-paid, higher-status jobs, with 25 percent working as teachers or teacher assistants, 38 percent working in administrative jobs, 15 percent as managers in sales and market-ing of goods and services, 18 percent in manufacturing and distribution in the food and clothing sectors, and 4 percent employed in the technology sec-tor. All are earning monthly salaries ranging from 4000 to 25,000 rupees ($60 to $300). Only 15.65 percent of the Prerna alumnae are married—all of them after age 18. Prerna graduates' average age at marriage is 21.5 years.

Making Gains in Girls' Empowerment

The empowerment literature identifies agency, voice, and the capacity to as-pire as key components of empowerment for marginalized groups.[11] Agency involves perception of oneself as an equal person with rights, a critical analyti-cal understanding of society and one's place in it, and the capability to take control, make decisions, and take action in one's life. Yogendra Shakya and Katharine N. Rankin also mention a subversive agency; that is, the ability to resist, quietly or overtly.[12] Voice is the ability to speak up, to protest, and to demand one's rights, and the capacity to aspire is the capability to imagine possibilities beyond those immediately visible in one's circumstances and work toward actualizing them.

It is important to bear in mind that agency—and voice and the capacity to aspire—does not alone create an empowered individual; it must come together with supportive relations and structural change in society.[13] Supportive relations are key to providing marginalized people the strength to resist, negotiate power, and become agents of change in their own lives and in their communities.[14] Structural change is enabled by challenging structures, which involves gaining a critical understanding of the social and political structures, the power relations of the social order that define lives, thus enabling persons to challenge the routine, conventional norms and the stereotypical definitions of roles and responsibilities and other taken-for-granted behaviors that shape their lives.[15] Together these components are like interconnected wheels, each interdependent on and mutually enforcing the development and strength of the other.

Given this framework for thinking about empowerment, it has been difficult to construct a measurement tool that makes an accurate quantitative assessment of girls' empowerment without reducing the complexity of the capacity being measured or the environment on which it is mutually dependent. As such, the school attempts to assess the students' development of agency, voice, and critical understanding of structures through a holistic set of proxy indicators measured by observing their behavior, for example, their ability to resist child marriage; to transition successfully to high school and onward to tertiary education; to mentor junior students; to speak out against discriminatory social norms; to advocate in their communities against domestic violence and child marriage; to find employment outside the home; and to participate in decisions regarding their marriage. Other programs around the world have adopted similar modes of assessing empowerment through proxies. For example, the Tuseme Project, which works on developing girls' empowerment through drama in 13 countries in sub-Saharan Africa, assesses student empowerment by observing students' participation and behavior in the classroom.[16] The project has not yet developed formal measurement tools.

In 2012 Prerna administered a one-time questionnaire to 85 girls from the ninth through twelfth grades using a number of these proxy indicators to gain a sense of whether the school has made any noticeable, quantitative impact on girls' empowerment (see table 10-5). Responses confirmed that a large majority

TABLE 10-5. **Are Prerna Girls Empowered?**

Agency

75% believe they have the right to choose their own husband.

65% said they have the right to as much free mobility as their brothers.

88% said they had the right to be as educated as their brothers.

Knowledge of Law

85% knew the legal age for marriage in India, for both girls and boys.

76% knew there was a law against child marriage.

59% said they had an equal right as their brothers to the family wealth and property.

Ability to Resist

67% said society was not fair to girls and women.

56% said they would resist if their parents force them to marry before 18 years.

79% said their father did not have the right to beat their mother.

Aspirations

91% specified ages when they would like to get married, averaging 23 years.

95% said education was important for girls and that they would complete grade 12.

86% said they had plans to go on to college.

80% said they had plans for future careers.

Source: Survey conducted in Prerna Girls School in 2012.

Moni

had a good sense of their rights and expressed a willingness to act if their rights were violated.

Because of the highly subjective and progressional nature of empowerment, researchers like Gita Sen and Naila Kabeer recommend the process of empowerment be self-assessed and validated by the agents themselves.[17] Borrowing this idea, I asked the graduates of Prerna to write retrospective self-narratives. As noted in an earlier chapter, the students are encouraged to write self-reflective journals regularly, which they share with their teachers, helping their teachers assess their empowerment outcomes. Responses from three students not featured earlier in this book follow.

Moni comes from a family of four sisters. Her parents are Dalit and wash people's clothes (a caste-related occupation) for a living; her family's total monthly income is about 20,000 rupees ($300). She earned her bachelor's degree in 2015. She was an apprentice photographer for a year and went on to become the lead photographer in Digital Study Hall, with two other girls on her team. She wants to be a professional photographer. She applied for a postgraduate program in a very prestigious university in Delhi (Jamia Millia Islamia, reputed to have the best photography program in the country) and made it to the waitlist. She did not clear the waitlist, however, and is determined to apply again in 2017.

Meena

I feel I can now become someone, anyone I want to be. I have learned I can fight for my rights. . . . I learned in school that I have the right to take decisions about my life. Today I have convinced my parents that I can make my own decisions. Now they discuss things with me. Society is like a wall for girls. It does not let us do anything, doesn't let us grow. I know now that this is unfair and society should change, let us progress, hear us. I have learned that I can speak up when I see something wrong and I have the confidence to do that.

Meena is a 20-year-old Dalit woman, a graduate of the 2014–15 Prerna cohort. Her parents are illiterate, do other people's laundry for a living, and together have a total monthly income of approximately 8000 rupees ($120). She is the youngest of six siblings: three girls and three boys. She is in her second year of an undergraduate law program at Lucknow University. One of her sisters, who married early, is going through a very exploitative and contentious divorce. Meena is managing all the interactions with the lawyer and the courts.

I joined Prerna in 2007. The teachers here had faith in me, which gave me the confidence that I can do something. I got the opportunity to partici-pate in sports, drama, public speaking, many things. It is because of my education here that I learned to dream and decided to become a lawyer. I am now studying for law against many odds. I have to walk long distances to go to college, and paying the fee is a challenge. My teachers from Prerna have helped me find scholarships, which is why I am able to continue. . . . I am determined to be a lawyer and defend the innocent.

She mentioned in her interview that one of the reasons she wants to be a lawyer is because she wants to defend women like her sister, as well as her father, who was unfairly implicated in a crime and suffered because he could not afford competent defense.

Fatima, a Muslim girl, is in eleventh grade and has been in Prerna since pre-school. Her father is a chauffeur and her mother is a housemaid. Both parents are illiterate and, together, they earn approximately 9000 rupees ($134) per month. She is one of three sisters. Her elder sister was married very early and has a child, while her younger sister is in Prerna. She says her father had refused to send her to school, saying he had no money, but her mother fought for their education and succeeded in sending her and her sister to Prerna.

They all wanted to marry me off, but I resisted. I explained to them, in a very calm voice, that they had ruined Didi's life by marrying her early. So shouldn't they learn from that? It took some time, but I succeeded in getting them to agree, though I had to promise that I would not do anything "wrong." They refused to send me to Delhi for the school trip, saying I would wear jeans in Delhi. But I argued and fought and managed to go and I wore jeans, too! I have learned not to be afraid. I can argue for my rights and I am confident that I can face any situation. I know I can also help other girls with their problems and I have done so. My friend was being harassed by a boy on the street, and she was very scared to do anything about it. Then I took her with me and we complained to this boy's mother and said that if she didn't say something to her son, we would make noise publicly. Then she did scold her son and my friend is more confident now. I want to be a bank manager, which is why I have taken commerce.

These retrospective self-narratives show that the students have learned that they are equal persons, and they are beginning to assert this identity and resist practices at home that would work against this recognition. They have made a

Fatima

conceptual shift, a structural change, in how they look at themselves and their lives. All three girls display agency and higher aspirations, and have made specific plans for acquiring the skills needed to lead successful lives of their own choosing.

The girls also display an understanding of an unequal social structure, knowing that it is not permanent and can be altered with effort. Several mention that they have been able to negotiate a better place for themselves in the family. And they all mention that they have learned these skills in their school. They make an important point: quality education is about learning to live, about changing our lives, about taking action in our worlds. Education is incomplete and sterile unless it touches our lives and teaches us to live effectively.

Kunti describes what Prerna has meant to her:

Prerna is focused [on its goal to empower girls]. Like the aim with which we started, we are achieving it. The changes we want, the aim for which Prerna stands, to change girls' lives, it is actually happening. Girls are changing. So when you do something with a purpose and it succeeds, then your strength increases more.

And she goes on to explain Prerna's impact beyond the school:

Like we are motivated, we will guide others, we will advise. That will impact others. Then others will also think like this. . . . More girls will come and they, too, will change, like us. Teachers are very supportive; they know how to deal with children like us, and they know how to enable actual learning, because most of them are well qualified and talented. So there's good teaching. But apart from the [academic] curriculum, other skills are getting developed. . . . That's the main thing—learning practically about living matters and that happens here.

11

Scaling Prerna

Prerna has successfully addressed the compelling challenges of educating girls in Lucknow, India, including access to and achieving quality learning, transition to and completion of secondary education, safety, school-to-work transition, and empowerment of girls and women through education.[1] The question arises: Can this work be adapted to a larger scale? And if so, how? Cynthia Coburn, professor at Northwestern University, aptly noted that scaling is not just about numbers reached but about "simultaneously ensuring the depth of change necessary to support and sustain a lasting educational improvement."[2]

At Prerna we have been particularly cautious about scaling. We did not begin our program with the aim of scaling and were focused for the first several years only on developing it for the girls we were working with. We believe in our idea, our philosophy, and pedagogy, which is now supported by a great deal of research on girls' education and by the growing attention to life outcomes—variously called social learning outcomes, life skills, and so on.[3] We also believe that lessons from models like Prerna can be scaled, or in Sunita's words: "There should be many more Prernas. The world will change if we can have more Prernas."

Prerna's approach is one way to empower girls and help them achieve better life outcomes through education, but many other methods can be adopted in other contexts. Scaling cannot, and in my opinion should not, involve an exact replication of any model. However successful, a model is particular to the social, cultural, and political context in which it has emerged. Successfully using any given model requires adapting to local contexts, cultures, and challenges, while keeping the central idea, or theory of change, intact.

Our Early Efforts to Scale

Prerna emerged from and is supported by a complex, fairly elaborate ecosystem created by the Study Hall Educational Foundation (SHEF) over three decades. It uses the Study Hall School's infrastructure, that is, a secure, well-equipped building; its midday meal is supported by DiDi's, which also developed from the school; and SHEF enterprises—Study Hall School and Digital Study Hall—along with DiDi's, provide training and employment opportunities for Prerna alumnae. It might be argued that to achieve Prerna-like results, this entire ecosystem must be replicated. That is a challenging but possible option, but I argue that even without SHEF, the Prerna model offers many avenues for scale and replicability. Prerna's theory of change certainly can be articulated concisely this way: girls come, stay, learn, complete, and are empowered when a school:

- ⟶ Adopts an expanded educational goal, which includes learning and life outcomes, with girls' empowerment as the central focus.

- ⟶ Builds a school culture that is safe, caring, and supportive of students, their parents, and teachers with the interests of girls at the center.

- ⟶ Is responsive to students' lives and needs.

- ⟶ Engages proactively with students and their parents to ensure that girls stay and complete.

- ⟶ Has a life-enriched curriculum that includes critical dialogues and strong classroom delivery by trained teachers who not only teach girls to become self-advocates but also advocate for girls' rights themselves.

These central ideas have already made their modest way beyond the walls of our school. We have made early efforts at formally scaling our ideas, our theory of change, and our delivery innovations to other schools in the states of Uttar Pradesh and Rajasthan.

In February 2012 we were invited by UNICEF Lucknow to share our empowerment curriculum and pedagogy with 38 Kasturba Gandhi Balika

Girls at a KGBV

Vidyalayas (KGBVs) in three districts of Uttar Pradesh. KGBVs are all-girls residential schools, sixth through eighth grade, run by the government of Uttar Pradesh in educationally underserved areas for girls from very low-income, lower-caste groups. Mostly located in remote regions and free, the schools are often understaffed, and classes held in inadequate buildings. Teachers come ill-prepared for their roles to bridge girls' learning and are not supported sufficiently by training and resources to do so.

A national evaluation of the KGBV program in 12 states ("National Report of KGBV Evaluation 2007"), commissioned by the Indian government, reported that while, by and large, the retention rate was good, the teaching methodology was outdated and inadequate to meet the learning needs of girls from challenging backgrounds. The report especially recommended that the program needed to integrate gender sensitization and development of life skills, including self-esteem and confidence, with a balance of academic and nonacademic learning. It recommended "more thought/planning needs to go into the special training and ongoing academic support needs of KGBV teachers."[4] So the ground seemed fertile and ready for our intervention.

In response to the request from UNICEF Lucknow, we developed an empowerment tool kit, distilled from the good practices of our several years of experience, and a scale-up plan.[5] We called our program Aarohini, which in English means "girl/woman on the ascendant," or "girl rising," and implemented it in the 38 schools, impacting over 3500 adolescent girls. Given the success of our program, we entered the second phase of our scale-up activity. Partnering with UNICEF again, we broadened our program to 52 additional schools, and in 2016 we entered the third phase and expanded it independently to the remaining 646 schools, in partnership with the Uttar Pradesh government. Our scale-up activity is still in process and we will cover all the KGBVs in 2018. We have also extended our program to Rajasthan in collaboration with UNICEF, the government of Rajasthan, and other nongovernmental organizations. Currently we are spreading Prerna's ideas and delivery innovations to over 1000 schools, with the hope of impacting 100,000 adolescent girls.

Aarohini: The Prerna Empowerment Program

SHEF's empowerment tool kit used to adapt elements of Prerna's model into the KGBV schools was developed in consultation with Prerna teachers and consists of:

+ Teacher training modules and manuals for an initial two-day teacher-training workshop and for another follow-up two-day community mobilization teacher-training workshop.

+ A teachers' handbook with a detailed grade-wise curriculum for grades 6 through 8.

+ A set of DVDs with video recordings of the critical dialogue classes at Prerna, also offered on a flash drive where teachers find it a more convenient delivery mechanism. Each dialogue focuses on a theme; for example, domestic violence, patriarchy, child marriage, sexual abuse, menstrual hygiene, and the issue of honor. DVDs also include the plays and short films made by the students of Prerna on these themes and video recordings of teacher trainings for on-site support.

+ These resources are supplemented by a series of posters on critical issues of gender-based violence, girls' rights, and related laws.

The scale-up program includes the following steps and goals:

1. *A two-day training workshop with two teachers from each KGBV:* The overarching goal of this workshop is to enable the teachers at the KGBVs, 99 percent of whom are women, to critically examine and understand how gender has constructed and impacted their own lives; to understand the Prerna theory of change; to expand an understanding of their role as teachers; and to understand the theory and practice of critical feminist pedagogy.

2. *On-site and long-distance coaching and support:* We understand the complexity of the task ahead for the teachers and the brevity of the training we are able to provide. Our support materials, in the form of the videos, are designed to provide dynamic on-site support. Teachers can view the training video to refresh their conceptual knowledge and can view the critical dialogue videos, alone or with their peers, to review the pedagogy, or view with the students to help facilitate discussions. In addition, we provide off-site support and coaching from our office, where a dedicated Aarohini team manages a helpline, providing mentoring support. Their telephone sessions range from 10 to 30 minutes, with records maintained for every call. Teachers use this helpline freely, often seeking counseling for personal matters as well.

Through these calls, the team provides teachers the following types of support:

→ Identify and plan the sequence and flow of critical dialogues for the month.

→ Co-create solutions to address situations of conflict or sensitivities that may have arisen with students and teachers in the critical dialogue process.

→ Support teachers as they walk through their own journey of self-discovery.

→ Equip the KGBV staff with additional information on specific issues, laws, policies, and so on.

→ Link the school to other allied support providers in the district/block, such as child protection services, NGOs, and women's organizations, to fast track a solution or an idea.

→ Plan and detail campaigns and other cultural events around gender issues.

SHEF also uses social media, like Whatsapp groups, to facilitate peer-networking among the teachers. Our goal is to demonstrate responsive care with this helpline, believing that all teachers, on-site and off-site, need to feel cared for, responded to, and addressed if they are expected to provide the same care and respect for their students. This is our way of building a supportive network of relationships.[6]

3. *A two-day follow-up refresher workshop for teachers on mobilizing a community:* Our goal here is to assess the use of critical dialogues with the students and to give teachers additional skills and tools.[7] Most important, this training aims to help them see their role as not only helping girls become self-advocates but also them becoming advocates for their students with the parent community, with the goal of eventually making parents allies in the common endeavor to educate and empower their daughters. Teachers learn ways to successfully engage with the community and increase the community's interaction with the school. They learn to include parents in the network of critical dialogues, getting them to reflect on the imperative of completing secondary education for girls and their inviolable right to live a life of their own choosing as a free equal person. Specifically, teachers are taught:

- ❖ How to plan, organize, and conduct effective meetings with parents.

- ❖ How to invite parents to parent-teacher meetings in a respectful way.

- ❖ What issues to raise and how to do so sensitively at these meetings.

- ❖ How to promote a girl's right to a complete education and a life of dignity.

4. *Creation of Local Support Network of Allied Institutions for Teachers:* By including members of the district police, child welfare services, local NGOs, and child protection services in these workshops and facilitating an interface with the KGBV teachers, a web of local support is created. Teachers can reach out to this network for local support when needed. An example of how this works in practice follows.

Karishma (age 15), a KGBV alumna from Badaun district, was studying in tenth grade when she learned that her parents had arranged her marriage. She and her friend decided to approach the head teacher of their KGBV for help, who then contacted the Aarohini helpline while also simultaneously trying to counsel the mother. Karishma's mother claimed helplessness in the face of severe pressure from her community. SHEF staff then contacted Suraksha, who, with the staff of Childline Badaun and the local police officer, went to Karishma's house to talk to the mother and the community. Together they ensured that the early forced marriage was canceled. As of now, Karishma is continuing her studies and has completed her tenth grade in 2016.[8]

5. *Scholarships for Continuing Education:* The KGBVs in Uttar Pradesh cover only through the eighth grade, and since the schools cater to girls from the poorest and most marginalized families, many of the girls are in danger of dropping out of school after eighth grade because families are unable to afford the fees and transportation costs of sending their daughters to secondary school. One of the head teachers asked us if we could help fund the secondary education of some of the most deserving girls who could simply not afford to go to secondary school without help. Poonam was the first girl who reached out for support and the reason we scaled our scholarship program. Her story (see box 11-1) illustrates the far-reaching impact of expanding Prerna's empowerment program.

Impact of Scaling Up

After more than a year of work with teachers of the first 38 KGBVs, we felt that scale-up of Prerna's model was having significant impact on the teachers and the culture of KGBVs. An evaluation of this first scale-up effort, conducted by an agency in Delhi called START Up!, confirmed that our intervention caused "a behavior change in all the stakeholders. Several have also stepped out of their limiting boundaries to take action." The evaluation by START Up! reported:

> At the institutional level, KGBVs now see high attendance levels—an outcome that the wardens and teachers attribute to the SHEF-Prerna intervention. Students now return to school immediately after the end of their vacations. Parents are better tuned in to the academic needs of their daughters. KGBVs have built greater community credibility as "caring organizations." The result: eight of the ten schools that we visited, no longer find it daunting to fill up the stipulated numbers of new admissions. The trigger for these advancements has been the cementing of positive parent-teacher relationships—an outcome of the Jan Jagriti (community mobilization) program. Parents, in turn, have begun to champion KGBVs in their villages.

BOX 11-1. *Empowering Girls beyond Prerna:*
Poonam from KGBV Malihabad

Poonam

Poonam, a young Dalit woman living in Shankarpur, a village 45 kilometers from Lucknow, was pulled out of school at six years old. Her father told her he did not see the point of educating a girl. Undaunted, she continued to read her brother's books. An alcoholic, Poonam's father passed away when she was 10. At the urging of a family friend who suggested she attend a KGBV school, which was free and gave special preference to girls who have dropped out, she enrolled.

At the KGBV school, her teachers often showed critical dialogue videos. These videos showed girls discussing topics such as a dowry, the right to education, and child marriage. After playing each of the critical dialogues, the KGBV teacher would pause the video and discuss the topic with the girls, getting them to think about the issues. This, Poonam said, was a very different and unique kind of a class. It was during the course of these dialogues, Poonam says, that she decided she wanted to study further and live an independent life—a life free from poverty, subordination, and exploitation.

Poonam topped her grade each year and she wanted more, but after the eighth grade, her tenure at the KGBV was over. When she returned to her village she found herself in the same situation as before. Her family could not afford to send her to secondary school. For help she turned to her KGBV head teacher, Neelima, who appealed to SHEF for a scholarship for Poonam. This call for help initiated SHEF's KGBV scholarship program.

Today, Poonam is in her second year of a bachelor's degree program and teaching out-of-school children at an informal education center in her village with the goal of transitioning them to formal school. The students' parents respect and admire her, while their children love and idolize her. Poonam explains:

[My students] will become doctors, they will become teachers. . . . They say, "Ma'am, I will grow up and be just like you," so I say to them, "You will have to keep studying hard to be like me," and they reply, "We will." I like to teach because at first I, too, was not able to study. These children are like me in the village, and they are unable to get an education. I feel very sad when I see they are not going to school. If I can teach them, then my village will grow. My village will become a Post, from a Post it will grow to a Block, from a Block it will become a City, and from a City the whole Country. When the entire country has educated citizens, then how wonderful it would be!

In 2014, SHEF applied for funding and expanded its KGBV scholarship program, calling it the Mona Scholarship program, named after our most consistent funding partner, the Mona Foundation.[9] We instituted a 5000 rupees scholarship for two of the most meritorious and needy girls in the 38 KGBV schools with which Prerna was already working. In the third year of the scholarship program, the entire first cohort of 60 students transitioned to grade 11. The second and third cohorts are all enrolled in grades 10 and 9, respectively, demonstrating the value of these scholarships in helping girls transition to high school. The third phase of our scale-up plan, which would extend the scholarship program to the remaining 646 KGBV schools in the state of Uttar Pradesh, is contingent on the availability of funds or the adoption of this idea by the state government.

At the staff level, KGBV wardens and teachers have moved beyond their roles as teachers to catalyze change within their students' extended communities. Consider the following milestones achieved:

→ Three of the 10 KGBVs interviewed by us have mobilized all parents to sign a pledge to not marry their daughters before they turn 18 years of age.

→ In one KGBV, where parents' alcoholism had caused much anguish among students, the warden and teachers succeeded in mobilizing parents to sign a *shartnama* (a version of a pledge) to refrain from substance abuse.

→ Wardens of some KGBVs have developed a tracking mechanism to follow up and exert positive pressure on parents for continuing their daughters' education after they leave the KGBV. The warden of the Dharampuram KGBV told us,

> We maintain a register and before handing over the transfer certificate to the parents we collect information on where they are planning to get their ward admitted for Class 9 onwards. It is a good way to keep a check and track students—that way we know if they have discontinued their studies.

→ In the KGBV at Rajgarh in Mirzapur district, the empowerment counseling has been extended by teachers to not just the community of mothers, but to the sisters of the students, as well. Once, a mother who had one daughter in school complained that she was not getting a marital match for her other daughter, who was 15 years old. The entire staff explained to her the merit of a marriage after a girl is 18 years old.

→ In the KGBV of Muftiganj in Jaunpur district, almost 90 percent of the parents who participated in the community mobilization programs now refrain from engaging their daughters in child labor.

→ One KGBV has made an active attempt to enroll mothers in their school management committee. The committee is charged with the mandate of ensuring that students receive all-round education and "life-coaching."

→ Some of the schools are looking to hold a districtwide rally in the coming year to spread awareness on the right to education for girls.[10]

The teacher training had a considerable impact on the teachers' perception of their roles, their own sense of self-worth, their skills, and their increased status in the local communities. All the teachers interviewed by START Up! reported a dramatic gain in four areas:

Knowledge Capital or the acquiring of information, data and theoretical and technical knowledge of human rights and gender equality; Skill Capital or the development of new pedagogies, facilitation skills and tools; Developmental Capital, or the build-up of confidence, agency and self-esteem that spurred the teachers to take several developmental decisions for themselves and their students; Social Capital or the high social net worth of teachers, resulting from increased goodwill and credibility from parents and other allied partners.

Many of the teachers reported how they have taken intervening action to help their students, which they would not have considered before the program. One noted particularly:

Previously, we did not enquire much about girls' personal problems. There was a clear demarcation between what they could share in school and their personal life. Now we are like life coaches to them. The students are no longer scared of us.

Another teacher remarked:

For us, the entire SHEF intervention has been one of tremendous capacity building—we see an improvement in every aspect of our work—from articulation to language, energy, and enthusiasm levels.

Teachers said that implementing the lessons from the training resulted in an improved relationship with parents and their greater involvement in school. Some schools reported that parents' attendance at these meetings was up by more than 50 percent. One of the KGBV teachers said:

At our PTMs [parent-teacher meetings], we tried out several exercises and games that we played in trainings. Immediately the atmosphere changed and everybody began to have fun, and got to know each other. We realized that we and the parents are one—we have a common goal. We are not on opposite sides.[11]

Multiple Pathways to Scale

In the process of scaling Prerna's model vertically to government-run KGBVs across Uttar Pradesh and horizontally to the state of Rajasthan, Prerna has demonstrated the importance of continuously engaging supportive partners over the long term. We have been working closely with state and national governments to effect policy change in girls' education and to strengthen governments' institutional capacity to deliver quality and empowering learning opportunities to marginalized girls, with the goal of mainstreaming key elements of Prerna's model into policy. In the "National Evaluation of KGBVs 2013," we were able to make the following recommendation, which made its way to the final government report:

> Gender training, education about their rights, adolescent sexual and reproductive health education, life skills, and self-defence should form part of the enriched and regular curriculum. The girls require a definite focus on gender training and leadership development, development of "voice," in order to achieve a holistic development of the girls and to attain the goal of the KGBV programme, which has the definitely stated goal of empowering girls through education. The teachers should be trained in critical feminist pedagogy so that they may be made aware of their social, economic and political realities along with their systemic causes, learn to question these and develop the capacity to transform their own lives and their communities. This will empower them to become change makers. . . . Materials already developed by experienced and credible NGOs can be adapted to the local culture and used.[12]

We also work as advocates of the KGBV staff to the government for better infrastructure, a speedy redress of their grievances, and better access to the funds and goods allocated to the schools. We have made every effort to keep our scale-up activity cost-effective and simple, though we must guard continuously against a dilution of the program as we do so. Prerna's teachers, like Chetna, and an increasing number of our Prerna alumnae, are engaged in our scaling efforts. Our biggest challenge is the complexity and the size of the problem in terms of sheer numbers just in India, and the financial and human resources that we need. This challenge is made more difficult by the many gaps in governance of the schools by what can only be described as an uncaring, demoralizing system.

This book is part of our effort to scale and replicate, by offering our ideas and practice for adoption by others similarly engaged in promoting girls' education and empowerment. I have attempted to describe how one school took a feminist perspective on girls' education with the goal of raising the feminist consciousness of a particular group of girls in a particular part of the world. Prerna's experience is a replicable example of an empowering education for girls. It is our modest offering in the hope that our experience might be helpful and useful. We also invite discussion and suggestions for how we might do this better by others who have done it in other contexts.

12

Reframing Girls' Education

When we look at the lives of all the girls featured in this book—Laxmi, Khushboo, Aarti, Sunita, Kunti, and Preeti—and the several other Prerna students and alumnae included, what do we see? These were girls who had been kept from or had been pulled out of school by their parents to help support the family through paid work, to take care of their younger siblings, to stand in for their dead mothers, to marry them young, or out of fear for their safety in an inhospitable world. Families, especially fathers, governed their daughters by the belief that the home, and not school, was a girl's proper place and that silence, service, unquestioning acceptance of socially prescribed rules, and subservience were girls' appropriate modes of behavior. These were the messages they received from their families, their culture, and society, which framed their perception of themselves, their rights, and their competencies.

However, we saw a dramatic shift in the girls' biographies while they attended Prerna and beyond. They not only stayed the course, resisted all efforts to pull them out of school, and finished, but more important, they learned they were equal persons worthy of everyone's respect, including their own. They developed strong selves, found strong voices, nurtured a sense of self-efficacy, deconstructed the social definitions of who they should be and what they should do with their lives, and redefined these in empowering ways.

217

The girls challenged, reframed, and staked out new positions for themselves within their domestic spheres and in the world. They resisted early forced marriages, stood up to abuse and unfair discrimination, and made sure their siblings went to school. They constructed new roles for themselves at home, often strong decisionmaking roles; they supported, strengthened, and empowered their families, particularly their mothers, and left the confines of the home, literally and figuratively, expanding their horizons of possibility. They stepped into a world where they are striving to feel at home, strengthened and propelled by the newfound conviction that they have the right to stake a claim and be at home in it and to live a life of their choice.

They are establishing economic independence, pursuing college degrees, planning professional careers, moving toward buying their own homes, and gaining increasing control of their lives. They are unafraid now, feeling capable of facing many of the challenges that still face them. They are questioning the inevitability of marriage and beginning to look beyond the definition of home as either parental or marital. Given the ideology that governed their lives, these are large strides, indeed. They have been successful personal activists, having taken action in their own lives. They have begun to expand their freedoms, to eliminate their un-freedoms, to lay claim to human dignities, and to imagine and seize possibilities to live freely chosen lives.[1]

Furthermore, they have taken the knowledge they gained at school beyond its walls—taking social action in their own families and communities. Supported by the school, students and alumnae from Prerna are also acting together, taking their hard-won agency to others, advocating against child marriage and domestic violence in their communities and raising the feminist consciousness of men, women, and girls by advocating for girls' rights to education, freedom, safety at home and outside, and to a full human experience.

Key Features of Prerna's Success

Though there are several reasons for Prerna's success in empowering girls' lives, what follows is a set of aspects considered most important.

Expanded Vision of Education

Prerna adopts an expanded vision of education, recognizing that the goal of education is to learn to live and to understand who you are and how you are related to others in the world. As Kunti says: "That's the main thing, learning practically about living matters." Prerna focuses on making the girls' lives better, on their life outcomes, and keeps their empowerment at the center of the program as the main educational goal. Everyone in the school is aligned with this goal and committed to keeping all the girls in school by actively devising strategies to enable them to counter societal obstacles and challenges.

Network of Supportive Relationships

Prerna has constructed a strong network of supportive relationships: between the teachers and students, among student peers, and between the school and the community. Teachers are mentored and trained to take a gender perspective and to be caring about and sensitive to students' needs and home backgrounds.

Teachers have faith that the girls can learn, and they communicate that faith to them, thereby helping them acquire a similar trust in their own abilities. Teachers care about how students feel about themselves and help them build a strong self-image, self-esteem, a sense of self-efficacy, and a strong voice and agency. They help them develop a capacity to aspire by helping them envision possibilities and plan careers, and by showing them how they might equip themselves to achieve their goals.

Similarly, the teachers feel equally cared for, respected, and affirmed by a supportive, sympathetic, nurturing, and consultative school leadership. Together they have turned the school into a universe of care.

Responsive to Students' Lives and Needs

Prerna has constructed an enabling web of supports, visible and invisible. The teachers listen to students and address them as whole persons and view their learning holistically in the social and cultural context of their lives. They care enough and take the trouble to get to know their students and their lives. They understand the constraints of their lives—hunger, ill health, and poverty—and they care enough to provide appropriate supports in school. The school administration is sensitive and responsive, as well. The school adjusts to students' needs, rather than the opposite.

Engagement with the Community

Prerna engages continuously with the parent community. The school communicates clearly to the girls and their parents that they care about the girls, their lives, and their education. Teachers advocate for their students' rights and demonstrate to parents that they are their partners in the common endeavor to educate and empower their daughters. Prerna is guided by the belief that while girls can come to understand and fight discrimination through a process of "conscientization," their communities must also be prepared to welcome them as equal persons, as complete human beings. The school works hard at moving parents to see the possibilities of their daughters' lives, both present and future, and to convince them that growing up to be strong, educated, independent women is good for the girls themselves, their families, and the community.

Enriched Curriculum, Strong Classroom Delivery, Democratic Classrooms
The school has an enriched curriculum balancing study of the arts, mathematics, sciences, social studies, sports, and social action; an equal focus on cognitive, social, political, and emotional learning; and a team of well-qualified, competent, committed, and caring teachers who are trained regularly in the use of an engaging, participatory, interactive, activity-based critical pedagogy. The democratic participant structures in the classrooms, the non-hierarchical organizational structure of the school, and the consultative leadership paradigm together convey the same message of equality, freedom,

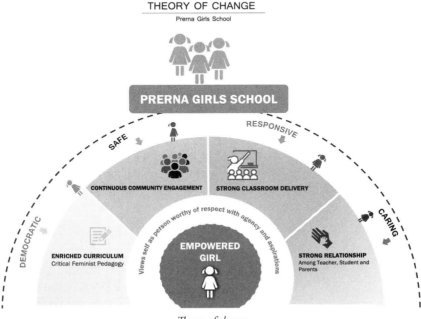

Theory of change

and fraternity. This ensures that the official curriculum—the academic and nonacademic subjects taught inside and outside the classroom—will be consistent with the structures and processes in which it is transacted. As a result, the students get a consistent message of equality, from their official curriculum and from the culture of the school, which forms the underlying curriculum.

Critical Feminist Pedagogy

While a strong focus on gender equality and justice permeates all the curricular and extracurricular activities, weekly special empowerment classes are included as part of the official curriculum. During these classes girls learn to examine the systemic discrimination and oppression they face and are empowered, or learn to act individually and collectively, to become self-advocates and to challenge unfair social structures. We believe girls must acquire this important knowledge if their education is to succeed in helping them achieve better life outcomes.

All these features are relevant and work in tandem to realize the main educational goal of the school, which is to empower girls to be the drivers of change in their own lives; to help them emerge as women with a perception of themselves as equal persons deserving and demanding respect—with strong voices, agency, and raised aspirations—convinced of their right to equal participation in society, aspiring to this, and equipped intellectually and emotionally for full democratic citizenship.

Going Forward

Even though now 14 years old, Prerna is very much a work in progress because we think of the model as an emergent one and our school as a learning organization. We are considering and discussing the possibilities of moving in several directions.

Should Prerna Become Coeducational?

While we agree that a campus with both boys and girls would provide a more "natural" environment in which both could work out the power dynamic underlying gender relations and also be a move toward desegregation of a strictly segregated society, we have several reservations. First, girls have been at such a disadvantage for so long that we would like to concentrate all our attention and resources on them. Second, all the parents we have consulted on this matter have responded overwhelmingly and unequivocally that they do not want Prerna to become a coeducational school. This is especially the case for girls after grade 5, whose safety becomes an object of concern for parents. We are, however, considering merging our Prerna boys with the girls' school in the primary grades as a first step, while we will continue to find spaces for the older Prerna boys and girls to interact and work together. We believe it is important for them to become friends, and to learn that girls and boys are equal human beings while dialoguing with each other in a safe, neutral, and mediated setting. Becoming friends across social boundaries is an important equalizing step.

More Inclusion of Fathers in Community Engagement Programs
We have focused on mothers more than fathers because they have been more forthcoming and have shown greater interest in their daughters and have, therefore, been easier to reach. This is probably because child rearing, which includes the education of children, falls to a mother's lot, according to traditionally prescribed gender roles. Fathers have formed a small percentage of the parents at our monthly meetings and other community events, though that number is increasing encouragingly. Unfortunately, our interactions with them have been limited so far to problem situations, cases of abuse, early marriages, and similar issues. This has led to a gap in our own understanding of their perspective. We believe it is important to engage more actively with them, perhaps with the help of supportive fathers and by having separate fathers' meetings.

We believe it is important for our girls to understand their fathers more to communicate better with them. Recently, 80 of the older girls were asked to interview their fathers so they could better understand their fathers' dreams, struggles, and aspirations for themselves and their daughters. Approximately 30 percent of the girls failed to get their fathers to agree to be interviewed. This is not surprising, given the traditional distance between fathers and their children, daughters in particular. Some of them had their mothers answer the questions as proxy for the fathers. The fathers' responses from these interviews have been illuminating, however. They described their struggles and sacrifices to provide for their families. While most said they never had any dreams, a few acknowledged they had once aspired to different outcomes—becoming a football player, a policeman, a doctor, for instance—but could not find a way to realize these dreams because of a lack of education and opportunities. They did have aspirations for their children, and though they all said marriage was the final destination for their daughters, they wanted them to pursue higher education, get jobs, and be independent. The girls say they have gained a new understanding of their fathers as a result of this exercise. We plan to include more such learning activities in the future.

Critical Dialogues

Though our girls' lives are challenged by gender, caste, and class, our critical dialogues have focused predominantly on gender because we believed gender was the biggest barrier to their education. Gender also cuts across caste and class boundaries, so that all women experience sexist oppression. We believe this has been a successful strategy. The teachers have related to gender more easily despite their caste and class differences with the students and have adopted the critical pedagogical approach more readily. They are now ready to move on to other issues, like caste and class, which we plan to focus on directly in our critical dialogues. Even though we have not discussed caste directly, our students have contested challenges to their equality in terms of class and caste, too. For examples, Khushboo and Aarti have challenged caste discrimination more directly, while Kunti and Sadhana have broken caste barriers by embarking on intercaste marriages. Several of our students have challenged their employers' exploitative practices. Together with Prerna alumnae, we are also exploring culturally acceptable ways to discuss issues of sexuality, sexual freedom, and sexual rights in these dialogue sessions.[2]

Reflections and Larger Implications

Prerna's story gives us reason to pause and reflect and offers some larger implications for girls' education, empowerment, and gender equality.

Girls Need Not Drop Out Because They Are Girls

Anugula Reddy and Shantha Sinha point out that:

> Providing access to schools in areas of high dropout rates, [with] large numbers of working children and large numbers of illiterate parents, requires more effort. The rules, procedures and administrative set up need to be sensitive to the requirements of illiterate parents and first generation learners.[3]

They argue that there is too much focus on social factors and too little on the role of schools in the "push out" of girls.

Reform or reorganization in procedures and rules in schools and the wider education system can do a great deal to reduce the number of children who drop out or are pushed out of school. Innovative programs include *Escuela Nueva* in Colombia, the RIVER program in Andhra Pradesh, the *Bodh Shiksha Samiti* in Rajasthan, the *Mahila Shikshan Kendra* in Jharkhand, and the *Sahajani Shikshan Kendra* in Lalitpur. These programs and others demonstrate that reorganizing schools by keeping students' needs, social context, and challenges at the center, as well as building the organizational structure, curricula, and teaching methodology around these needs, with a strong community outreach, can have a powerful, positive impact on both learning and the reduction of dropout rates.[4]

Prerna demonstrates how girls need not drop out because they are girls. Schools can, indeed, defeat the social obstacles to girls' education provided they are committed and engage actively to counter the gender-based factors that keep girls out of school. For example, just in terms of responsive school timings, government schools could offer two shifts, if that is cost-effective, or, as at Prerna, conduct school in the afternoon, if that is more convenient for girls who are compelled by poverty to work. Of course, community involvement in these decisions is essential.

Similarly, none of Prerna's strategies are ones that large government school systems cannot also do, provided there is a serious commitment to girls' education and to gender equality and the willingness to transform structures and perspective. These strategies include:

* Keep girls' lives front and center and focus on an education that helps them achieve better life outcomes.

* Train teachers to learn about their students' lives and to be sensitive and responsive to them.

* Have teachers track attendance regularly, with follow-up and timely intervention to arrest drop out.

* Train teachers to engage effectively with the community and be more responsive, respectful, and inclusive of parents, demonstrating that they are partners in a common undertaking.

* Train teachers to expand their roles and become advocates of girls' rights in the communities.

→ Make school management structures, at the school and education department levels, respectful, participatory, and responsive to all the stakeholders in the system—teachers, parents, and students.

→ Establish flexible assessment systems and tutoring programs in school to ensure that girls are supported and not discouraged from completing coursework.

A Cost-Effective Program

Prerna offers a very cost-effective program at $350 per child per year. The figure is low, however, because Study Hall School covers infrastructure costs such as rent and maintenance.[5] A private organization would need to factor in these costs if it were starting fresh and could not find a school to partner with. This amount is comparable to the per child/per year cost spent by the Indian government in public schools. As much as $367 per child/per year might be allocated in some states, most of it spent on teacher salaries. As has been detailed elsewhere, government schools often do not provide the extra resources teachers need, such as adequate training and materials, adequate equipment, safe buildings, and a caring, respectful, responsive, supportive management structure. Such a structure supports teachers, giving them autonomy to think and act creatively and proactively in their classrooms and communities.[6]

We have kept Prerna costs low by design; innovative programs must be kept cost-effective if they are to become models for individuals, organizations, the government, or even the community itself. In addition, by being economical the Prerna model demonstrates that more money is not always the best solution to a problem. The school's success lies in the features already described, none of which can be bought or necessarily requires additional financial resources. Rather, the Prerna model requires a change in perspective and a judicious use of resources.

Including Gender Studies in the Official Curriculum

Prerna demonstrates that, to achieve gender justice, it is important to ensure that girls are empowered by their education—that they acquire power within themselves, power to act alone and with others to challenge discriminatory structures.[7]

The unique aspect of the Prerna program is that empowerment is part of the official curriculum. Empowerment is not an extracurricular or after-school activity. Furthermore, it demonstrates how a formal K-12 school can success-fully incorporate gender study alongside other more traditional curricular subjects like math and science. Nelly Stromquist, in her address at a 1999 conference on gender and education, acknowledged that several countries had attempted to do a gender scan of their textbooks, revise them, and develop new gender-sensitive educational materials, but she regretted that no country had developed a gradually graded curriculum of gender knowledge that ap-propriately deals with gender issues across the levels of schooling and ages of students. Some scholars in India also call for a similar movement toward cur-ricular and organizational reform in the mainstream education system.[8] Pre-rna has recognized this as an important part of providing an empowering education for girls and has attempted to construct just such a pedagogy and curricular framework.

Other projects and programs around the world have also demonstrated the value of focusing on girls' empowerment directly. The *Sistema de Apren-dizaje* Tutorial in Latin America offers a nontraditional secondary school experience for both adolescent boys and girls (as well as adults). Its interdisci-plinary curriculum sets it apart as a unique model of gender-responsive design and pedagogy.[9]

In Tanzania the Tuseme project is a theater-based empowerment process begun in 1996 and has since spread to 13 countries in sub-Saharan Africa through facilitation by the Forum for African Women Educationalists, or FAWE. The schools that adopted the program report higher achievement scores and reduced dropout rates and pregnancies, along with an attitudinal change.[10]

Tostan is another program, located in Senegal, which began as a women's literacy project but went on to shift its focus to include human rights and de-mocracy in response to the needs of the women. It has shown amazing results, both educational and social. It describes its new educational approach as a holistic, human rights–based program of nonformal education.[11]

In India the Gender Equity Movement in Schools (GEMS) program, jointly developed by the International Center for Research on Women and the Committee of Resource Organizations for Literacy and the Tata Institute of Social Sciences, sponsors a school-based program for students in grades 6 and 7. Its goal is to promote gender equality by encouraging equal relationships between girls and boys, examining gendered social norms, and questioning the use of violence. After being piloted in Mumbai, the state government of Maharashtra has taken elements of the program for implementation in a large number of its public schools. The evaluation results show improved attitudes toward equitable gender roles, gender violence, and early marriage.[12]

The Mahila Shikshan Kendra program in India is an 11-month residential program for poor, illiterate girls and women between the ages of 15 and 35. It is an accelerated learning program, covering course content up to grade 5, with the intention of mainstreaming girls into upper primary public schools. The curriculum focuses on teaching life skills, vocational training, computer training, and gender training. It is learner-centered, holistic, and feminist in its approach.[13]

The Better Life Options program, based in rural Uttar Pradesh, includes group-based learning strategies and opportunities that provide girls a safe space to meet and develop peer networks along with life skills education, all focused on developing girls' agency and awareness about reproductive and sexual health and rights, while fostering egalitarian gender role attitudes.[14]

Udaan is a learning program in India designed for girls age 10 to 14, with a focus on adolescent girls who have either dropped out of school or never been to one. It has an innovative bridge program that enables girls to complete their primary education within 11 months at a residential camp managed by CARE India in association with local nongovernmental organizations at Hardoi district in Uttar Pradesh and, more recently, at Mayurbhanj district in Odisha, Mewat district in Haryana, and Madhubani district in Bihar. It also focuses on empowering girls to become better citizens and live a more independent and informed life.[15]

The programs outlined here, along with many others, have a central focus on girls' empowerment. Their students experience an educational plan that addresses their needs through a gender-based approach to education. Except for the GEMS project, they differ from Prerna in that most are short-term, informal programs, or are after-school or extracurricular. Most do not include gender studies as part of the official curriculum in a formal school, like Prerna does.

As Prerna shows, post-primary students, both boys and girls, benefit from gender studies, which contribute to greater understanding of one's culture and awareness. While it is important to develop mathematical and scientific thinking in students, it is equally, if not more, important for them to develop egalitarian thinking through gender studies and the incorporation of a critical feminist pedagogy.

In a democracy it is imperative that we have an open discourse on power, engaging both boys and girls. Gender equality is an important developmental goal. According to the *World Development Report 2012*, the "stickiest" obstacles to achieving gender equality are social norms maintained at home and in school. Nelly Stromquist makes the point that educators and feminists have not paid enough attention to formal school education as a site where gender is constructed.[16] The ideological underpinnings of primary and post-primary schools and teacher-training institutions should be scrutinized. Processes, structures, and content of education need to be reexamined from a feminist point of view, and necessary changes made. Indian feminist writers repeatedly emphasize that though the women's movement in India has worked hard to promote women's rights as human rights, including advocating for the inclusion of girls and women in education, most of its energy has been directed at the empowerment of adult women and at higher education, to the exclusion of girls and school education.[17] This needs to change. We need to start earlier and take feminist goals and perspectives into schools.

Reflecting on "Quality Learning"

Educational discourse around the world is making a welcome move away from mere enrollment and toward "learning." There is a growing awareness internationally and in India that there is a crisis in learning. Despite increased enrollment in schools, report after report tells us that a majority of children, especially in developing countries, are not learning at grade level.[18]

The focus now is on "quality education" and "equitable learning for all."[19] In my view the idea of "quality learning" needs to be examined, too. Global and national discussions centered around concern for quality of learning are almost always focused on reading and math in the primary schools, adding science in the secondary grades. Consider the Annual Status of Education Report (ASER) in India; its results are used for advocacy of better-quality education. While it cannot be denied that competency in reading, math, and science and the acquisition of cognitive skills are all good things and necessary components of a high-quality education, this is by no means sufficient. It is interesting that while we lay an enormous burden on education to solve the ills of the world, we continue to define and treat education as narrowly as we do.

There are welcome movements to expand and broaden the definition of learning. A task force set up by the Center for Universal Education at Brookings Institution included a large global consultation aimed at defining a globally acceptable metrics for learning.[20] The report issued identified seven domains of learning, including social and emotional learning, and listed as subdomains the development of social awareness, leadership, civil engagement, positive view of self and others, resilience "grit," and moral and ethical values. The Learning Metrics Task Force and, more recently, the Center for University Education's Skills for a Changing World project have furthered the call on the global community to include opportunities to build a wider breadth of skills in schools. This is a welcome progressive movement, which opens the door to thinking about learning in a broader way.

Even more recently, in their book, *What Works in Girls' Education*, Gene Sperling, Rebecca Winthrop, and Christina Kwauk discuss a "high-quality education," mentioning three main dimensions:

+ Inputs, such as textbooks, well-resourced schools with materials and well-qualified teachers, and good infrastructure like buildings, water, and sanitation facilities

+ Learning outcomes; that is, students' mastery of grade-level educational content

+ Social learning outcomes, which "include things such as young people's beliefs about themselves and others, attitudes toward gender equality and gender-based violence, and their ability to communicate effectively with others"

The authors go on to comment that:

This third dimension is not as widely used as the first two but is very important for understanding the full ways in which education can empower girls and women. After all, a girl could be taught in a well-resourced classroom and excel in core subjects but still learn and believe that she is less valued in society than her male peers. Paying special attention to social learning outcomes means focusing on educational processes inside the classroom as well as outside in the school and community environments. Most important, it means that gender equality is built into definitions and measurements of educational quality.[21]

Prerna has focused, with encouraging results, on all three of these dimensions, with a special focus on the last one, which we call "life outcomes." We believe it is a crucial dimension, requiring special attention. Prerna welcomes the move that the academic community is making to develop curricula and frameworks for this and lends its voice and experience to this effort. We believe learning must include social, emotional, and political learning.

While discussions of learning always include calls to ensure equity, they normally do not go far enough. Providing equal access and equal opportunity is an important necessary condition for social equality, but it is not sufficient. So long as political and social structures remain hierarchical and structurally unequal, they limit the extent to which education can work its magic. Equal opportunity in inherently unequal social structures is hard to realize. Unequal structures in terms of class, caste, race, and gender create invisible barriers to equality that are hard to surmount even when access and opportunity are equalized. When patriarchal structures are firmly in place, gender equality will continue to be a receding chimera. I propose that students—both boys and girls—learn to look critically at social and political structures and the underlying ideology and become aware of how inequality is constructed. This knowledge can lead to the development of a social and political consciousness, enabling them to find ways of deconstructing inequality and constructing in its place a fairer and equal world. Such an education, which aims at developing a democratic consciousness, is more likely to be transformative and liberating.

As educators, we need to think hard about our definition of relevant knowledge. What in these times do our children need to learn? They do not only need more technology and more science. They need more critical thinking, with subject matter more connected to real lives, the real world, and urgent social issues. We need a liberating education, which Freire reminds us is "a democratic education, an unveiling education, a challenging education, a critical act of knowing, of reading reality, of understanding how society works."[22]

Girls' Education as Political Commitment

Any activity that claims to be for gender justice is a political activity, requiring a clear political commitment. The movement to abolish slavery, the civil rights movement in the United States, independence struggles in India and elsewhere, the movement against racial apartheid in South Africa—all dealing with unequal power relations—are political struggles, clearly stated and recognized to be such. The struggle for gender justice, also dealing with unequal power relations, is also a political struggle, requiring a clear political commitment. Women and girls' rights are, after all, human rights! Education is one important pathway, among others, to achieving gender justice and it should also be recognized as such. We at Prerna understood this and made no pretense of being anything else. We openly declared our commitment to gender equality and democracy, to equality and freedom for girls and women, guaranteed to them by the constitution of their country.

Nelly Stromquist points out:

> Education is seen by most national governments and international development institutions as creating democratic values and an informed citizenry. . . . Democracy cannot exist until women are equal citizens; yet, a democratic citizenship calls for more than voting at elections and having political representation. Democracy (and gender equality) requires open discourse on power.[23]

Schools must teach their students, both boys and girls, to engage in an open discourse on power. If girls are people who should take their place as equal democratic citizens, then their education should prepare them by engaging them in critical thinking and analysis of power, especially in the context of gender. Can we talk about gender equality and empowerment without discussing power? Education that focuses on empowerment is essentially political, seeking to change unequal power relations in society.[24] Perhaps a lack of focus on power is the key missing element and the reason why, despite greater participation of girls in education, gender equality is still far from being a reality.[25] A distinct radical feminist perspective of girls' education and of women's equality is needed, with a focus on discussions around the distribution and location of power in social structures.

In Conclusion

This place called school is potentially a powerful site for social change and transformation, provided we recognize this and are able to organize structures within schools, develop pedagogies, train teachers, construct curricula, and redefine "quality education" in ways that will empower students to realize their full humanity. Giving girls access to school education equal with boys is an important first step toward gender equality, but more important, we must pay attention to what we teach in school, why we teach it, how we teach it, how our schools are organized, and what kind of ethic and philosophy inform teaching and learning in schools. It is high time we expanded our vision of education and move it from a narrow focus on learning outcomes to a more holistic one of life outcomes.

Yes, students must learn to read. But as Freire, Dewey, Tagore, and many other educators from across the world taught us many decades ago, for their education to be meaningful and transformative, students should learn to read "their worlds" and in doing so learn to transform their worlds. Education, to be transformative, needs to be transformed.

Epilogue

Educating Boys for Gender Justice

In response to requests from the parents of girls in Prerna, the Study Hall Educational Foundation launched a parallel Prerna Boys' School in July 2009, starting with a primary school and expanding it to high school in 2015. The school is housed in a separate SHEF building and also holds classes in the afternoon. We were motivated by the belief that to achieve a gender-just society, boys and girls both must receive an education that teaches them to critically examine the construction of gender in patriarchal societies and learn how to deconstruct a patriarchal conception of masculinity and reconstruct an egalitarian one in its place. As such, the Prerna Boys' School was founded to provide boys with a quality education with a strong critical feminist perspective. The same educational goals for the girls' school were adopted for the boys. The boys must:

→ Learn to read, write, and successfully complete the government-mandated syllabus up to grade 12.

→ Learn to recognize themselves as equal persons.

→ Develop a sense of agency and control over their lives, aspirations for a future for themselves, and the confidence and skills to realize it.

→ Develop a critical understanding of the social and political structures that frame their lives and determine the limits and possibilities.

→ Develop a critical feminist consciousness.

Prerna boys

Currently 100 students are in the primary section and 50 in the senior section of the school, with nine teachers, three of them male and six female. Three of the teachers are part-time, while the others are dedicated to boys' school full-time. All the teachers in the primary school section are female. The teachers are recruited for the boys' school via the same procedure as for the girls' school and are given similar continuous mentoring and training, which includes ongoing workshops and critical dialogues around care, masculinity, poverty, patriarchy, social structures, and gender equality.

The boys range from age four to 19. Thirty-nine percent are brothers of Prerna girls. The social profile of the boys is fairly similar to that of the girls. All are from poor families, with 66.7 percent belonging to the historically disadvantaged OBC and SC castes. The average family income is approximately 9000 rupees ($135), and the average family size is 5.6. One-fourth of the boys are either working or have worked before at some point in their lives; five of our students had run away from another state and were taken in by an organization called Ehsaas, which rescues boys from the streets. Forty-one percent of fathers and 62.8 percent of mothers are illiterate.

In 2016, one year after we began the senior section of Prerna boys' school, we began to engage in critical dialogues with the senior boys. These dialogues will form part of a curriculum for boys on gender justice, which is still emerging from our interactions with them. The dialogues are part of the official curriculum, which includes the typical subjects of reading, math, and science. The critical dialogue classes are conducted by the teachers once each week, mostly in parallel but sometimes together with the girls.

The boys' school follows the same ethic of care that characterizes Prerna girls' school and is governed by the same pedagogy and philosophy. Like Prerna girls' school, the boys' school also focuses on the students' lives and on achieving high outcomes for both learning and life in general. They follow the same curriculum and take the NIOS exam, just like the girls. For the present, the boys' school is segregated from the girls' school in response to parents' concern for the safety of their daughters, both physical and moral. However, the boys and girls meet regularly for critical dialogues and for some activities and classes. This interaction is encouraged with the motive of helping boys and girls gain a better understanding of each other, to become friends, and to learn to negotiate cross-sex relationships in a safe, mediated setting. We might consider amalgamating the schools in the future if resources and parents permit.

Deconstructing Masculinity in the Context of Domestic Violence

Patriarchal societies promote and foster conceptions of masculinity that are sexist, which are further reproduced in insidious ways by social, political, economic, and religious institutions, so that both men and women are persuaded to believe that dominant conceptions of masculinity are normal, natural, and right. Hegemonic masculinity makes everyone complicit in its construction and maintenance. Even though this concept of masculinity promotes the dominance of men over women, it does so with the cooperation of women, because they also see it as "right."

An excerpt of a critical dialogue conducted with the boys, with the goal of denaturalizing conceptions of masculinity, patriarchy, and unequal gender power relations by encouraging the boys to develop a feminist consciousness follows. The dialogue revolves around violence against women at home and on the streets, because this issue confronts their sisters and co-students; such real events provide stark illustrations of destructive ways in which masculinity often manifests itself. At the time of the dialogue, the boys had been discussing this issue for the previous three weeks and had engaged in one discussion with the girls.

Teacher: Okay, boys, like he said, we talk here about general awareness, so can I ask a question? He was talking about domestic violence; what is that?

Bhaskar: Ma'am, violence that happens in homes.[1]

Teacher: What is this violence?

Rahul: Oh, when people fight it's called violence, like when someone beats a person, that's violence.

Vishal: Like when the father comes home drunk, he starts showing his masculinity.

Teacher: So what is this "masculinity"?

Vishal: He bullies his wife trying to show how powerful he is.

Teacher: And what about how he used to beat you; what's that?

Students: That's also violence.

Teacher: Yes, that's also domestic violence, like he [your father] used to beat you? What about when brothers hit their sisters? . . . Is that not domestic violence?

Students: Yes, that's also domestic violence.

Suraj: Aunty, discrimination. They discriminate between girls and boys, like when a girl gets married she isn't asked what job she has. A boy is asked how much his salary is and what he does. But parents teach their daughters, right from childhood, that they have to eventually go to a different house, so there's no need to study. So even the mother is responsible.

In discussing domestic violence, the boys are beginning to talk about "masculinity"—actually the literal translation would be "manhood," or *mardanagi* in Hindi, which seems to connote a show of brute strength and dominance. With great insight, Suraj points out that discrimination against girls is also a form of domestic violence, going on to say that mothers are just as complicit in discriminatory socialization as are men: "Even the mother is responsible."

Teacher: Okay, so tell me, why are parents afraid of letting their daughters go outside? Why do they stop them, forbid them to go anywhere?

Rahul: They don't let them go outside because they're afraid that boys might follow her and harass her.

Suraj: Parents are afraid that their daughter is alone and that some boy might do something improper.

Teacher: Okay, I understand. . . . So how many times have you heard about a boy being harassed on the streets?

Vishnu: Never.

Teacher: Why? Why don't girls harass boys? Why do boys harass girls?

Rahul: Just to have fun.

Teacher: So girls don't want to have fun?

Arif: Ma'am, some boys are wicked, who just stand on the roads. They don't know how to behave with someone's sister; they are the ones who do this.

The teacher leads boys to name and examine the ways in which public spaces and private spaces like their homes are unsafe for girls, and the implications of that for them. She also tries to denaturalize accepted differences with the statement, "So girls don't want to have fun?"

Suraj: Ma'am, the jobless boys who stand on roads, who just do wrong things, so if a girl even resists a boy then the other friend persuades him to retaliate, so the friend forces him to go and hit her, so he will either harass her or hit her.

Teacher: What does he get from harassing the girl? They must be getting something out of it. That is why they do it.

Santosh: A boy just fulfills his desire. Or maybe he's just taking up someone's challenge, proving that he can do all this.

The boys describe the kinds of peer pressure they face to prove their manhood, and Santosh makes the point that some of the harassment is driven by (sexual) "desire." This should be read in the context of a sexually segregated society like India where there are very few outlets for romance-driven sexual encounters between boys and girls, as there is no practice of dating, except among middle-class youth in large, urban cities. The teacher continues to move the boys to think of sexual harassment on the street from the girls' perspective.

Teacher: Do you think that the girls like it when boys harass them on the road?

Students: No, Ma'am.

Teacher: They don't like it, right? Do you know how many restrictions are imposed on them because of this? What if you're prevented from going outside because someone might tease you on your way; would you feel good about that?

Suraj: No, Ma'am. It would be like being a prisoner in your own home.

Teacher: So girls are prisoners, indeed, right? Your own sisters, have you ever thought how they feel about that? When I was a kid I had three brothers. I wasn't allowed to go anywhere, and my brothers would go out. . . .

The teacher continues to explore issues of safety and sexism with the boys, pointing out how girls' insecurity leads to severe restrictions on their mobility.

Suraj insists that it is "jobless" boys who engage in this behavior, linking poverty with sexism. The teacher acknowledges that poverty is a bad thing for everybody, but goes on to help them see that sexism often transcends class and differing levels of education.

Teacher: But even boys from well-to-do homes also do such things. They study in good schools; even then they do such things. Why is that?

Santosh: Ma'am, they are not told about these things at home. Whatever he does no one in his family stops him because they think that they are rich so their son can do anything and no one can hold him accountable.

Teacher: Tell me something . . . so why is it—this I never understood—that even though both the daughter and the son have the same parents, yet the boys loaf around creating all kinds of trouble, harassing girls and doing many other things, like gambling, drinking, etc. But girls aren't doing that, although they are from the same home. Why is that?

Rohit: Ma'am, the thing is that man has been the dominant one since forever. A man has more say in anything than a woman in the house. So the father and the son are the same, so whatever the father does, it is passed on to the son. The mother was always suppressed and that is passed on to the daughter. If the father is intelligent then he would treat his son and daughter the same way. My home is in the village and I have four sisters. One of them wants to study and she goes to a school which is 24 kilometers away. Right now her exams are on, and every day my father drops her and picks her up from school. My father is making sure that she carries on with her studies even when he struggles to provide enough food for everyone. But she wants to study so he supports her.

Teacher: Oh, good for him! [Then, addressing the whole group:] What is Rohit trying to say here?

Raj: In a society with male dominance, a change can take place only when there is a change in the thinking of men. Otherwise, the son will learn from his father whatever his father learned from his own father and the same goes for mother and daughter.

This dialogue demonstrates that both boys and girls are socialized by their parents into different gender norms and roles, leading to the dominance of men and boys. From this dialogue, it is evident that the boys are developing an awareness that the social norms promoting unequal power relations in families and society are responsible for the violence against girls and women. They also conclude that society can change if "there is a change in the thinking of men." They seem to be conceding the possibility of changing men's thinking and that since men hold the power, the pathway to change lies in getting them to change their perceptions.

This is the primary goal of the critical dialogues, to move boys to the understanding that unequal structures are human constructions, are unfair, and can be changed—and they, as boys, can play a role in bringing about this transformation. The teacher is trying to get them to name the injustice in widely prevalent practices, which is the first step in developing a feminist consciousness. She goes on to discuss the voicelessness of girls, with the goal of building an empathetic understanding of girls' feelings of fear and repression at home.

Teacher: Why don't daughters speak up? Why don't they say something? They couldn't be liking all that, right?

Santosh: Ma'am, because they are taught [not to speak up], to be like that right from the beginning.

Teacher: What if they start to speak up?

Santosh: Yes. If they speak up then it's possible that someone could listen to their problems and help the girls find solutions.

Teacher: So what are the girls afraid of?

Rohit: In this patriarchal system when the father beats his son then the mother tries to stop it, but when the mother is being beaten up then no one can stop that. . . . That is how girls get scared.

The boys describe the power structure at home and how even their masculine power at home is limited by their fathers, the patriarchs reigning supreme. They explain how girls and women learn, by instruction and fearful example, to remain silent. They refer to the "patriarchal system" as the culprit, in the process of developing an understanding that sexism is systemic, even when individuals are the ones who practice it.

Empowering Boys to Be Part of the Solution

Our goal is to help boys become aware of the injustice of discrimination even when they are not at the receiving end of it. Our aim is to help them denaturalize firmly entrenched social norms and practices in their social imagination. The critical dialogue classes also aim at developing empathy with girls—"Can you imagine how they feel?"—through role-playing exercises and writing. The long-term goal is to enable boys to construct a more egalitarian conception of masculinity in place of the hegemonic masculinity they know from home.

There have been some heated arguments between the boys and girls during the mixed dialogue class, as sometimes the girls accused the boys of being sexist and the boys placed responsibility on the girls for provoking and tempting boys with inappropriate clothing and mixed signals. Despite these arguments, the boys have collaborated with the Veerangana group (see chapter 9) and staged a street play together with the girls against gender-based violence at home and on the streets. The boys also took social action when a 12-year-old girl from Prerna was nearly raped in a neighborhood close by. The teachers discussed the case with the boys, who got together and held a meeting with a group of boys in that community, calling on them to take responsibility for the violence against girls in their neighborhood, urging them to mend their predatory ways and work, instead, to protect the girls. Though still adopting a patriarchal perspective of the issue, the boys are moving toward taking responsibility, which is a good first step.

In subsequent dialogues, the boys have often raised issues of poverty and class, and recently we have introduced the issue of caste. The curriculum will continue to develop around the issues deemed important by the boys and their teachers. By engaging boys in discussions around gender justice, we hope to empower boys to realize how they can contribute to changing unequal power relations or an unequal social structure by building solidarity with girls and working together to create a more gender-just world.

Appendix A

Caste in India
A Brief Note

Caste is an institution uniquely associated with the Indian subcontinent.[1] Although originating within Hindu society, the concept of caste has spread to the Muslim, Christian, and Sikh communities. *Caste* is a Portuguese word that conflates two Indian words: *jati*, the endogamous group one is born into, and *varna*, the place that a group occupies in the system of social stratification mandated by Hindu scripture. There are four varnas—*brahmana*, *kshatriya*, *vaishya*, and *shudra*—with the dalits (formerly known as the "untouchables") constituting a fifth (and lowest) strata outside of the caste hierarchy. Members of the four varnas are collectively referred to as Savarna. Into these varnas fit the 3000 and more jatis.[2] It is generally agreed, although opinions differ, that the four-varna classification is roughly 3000 years old.

The most commonly cited defining features of caste are:

1. Caste is determined by birth.
2. Caste groups are endogamous, with strict rules about marriage within the caste.
3. Caste membership involves rules about food that can be consumed and with whom food can be shared.
4. Castes are arranged in a hierarchy of rank and status.

5. Castes are traditionally linked to occupations. A person born into a caste could practice only the occupation associated with that caste. Members of other castes could not enter that occupation.

As noted, the "untouchable" castes are outside the caste hierarchy. They are considered to be so impure that their mere touch severely pollutes members of all other castes. Members of these castes are confined to menial and despised jobs. After India became independent from British rule in 1947, a new constitution was adopted, which abolished untouchability and prohibited discrimination in public places and offices. The ex-untouchable communities and their leaders chose to use *Dalit* to describe themselves and this is now the generally accepted term for referring to these groups. In Indian languages, the word *dalit* literally means "downtrodden" and expresses the sense of an oppressed people.

Tribe is a modern term in India used for communities that are among the oldest inhabitants of the subcontinent. Tribes, or *adivasis,* were communities that did not practice a religion with a written text; did not have a state or political government; did not have sharp class divisions; and, most important, did not have caste. Like the term *dalit, adivasi* (literally meaning "original inhabitants") connotes political awareness and the assertion of rights.

The Indian state has had special programs for the Scheduled Castes (SCs, also known as Dalits) and Scheduled Tribes (STs) since before independence. In 1935 the British Indian government recognized them as deserving special treatment because of the massive discrimination practiced against them. After independence, the same policies were continued and many new ones added. The most important state initiative attempting to compensate for past and present caste discrimination is the one popularly known as "reservations." This involves the setting aside of some places or "seats" for SC/ST groups in different spheres of public life. These include reservation of seats in the state and central legislatures; reservation of jobs in government service across all departments and public sector companies; and reservation of seats in educational institutions.

Though untouchability was the most visible and comprehensive form of social discrimination, the constitution of India recognizes the possibility that there may be groups other than the ST/SC who suffer from social disadvantages. These groups, which need not be based on caste alone, were described as the "socially and educationally backward classes." This is the constitutional basis of the popular term Other Backward Classes (OBCs), in common use today.

Like the SC/STs, OBCs also have reservations in different spheres of public life.

Despite the government's efforts, positions of administrative, economic, and political power are still controlled by Savarnas due to centuries of social advantage. Today, Dalits make up 16.6 percent of the total Indian population, but their control over resources of the country is marginal—less than 5 percent.[3] Close to half of the Dalit population lives under the poverty line, and even more (62 percent) are illiterate.[4] Less than 10 percent of Dalit households can afford safe drinking water, electricity, and toilets, indicative of their deplorable social condition.[5] Studies show that in India's rural areas, and more subtly in urban areas, negative attitudes and behaviors toward Dalits still prevail, including when they attempt to exercise their rights.[6]

Appendix B

Methodology

1. Formal and informal student and teacher interviews: I conducted in-depth interviews with the six focal students and three teachers, which were audio recorded and transcribed, following up with shorter, more informal ones, unrecorded, when I needed more information. Information gleaned from the interviews with the students has been used to understand how they view learning in school and what impact it has had on their lives. Interviews of the six focal students were conducted in 2015–16, four to six years after they had finished their schooling at Prerna. The majority of the dialogues mentioned in the book have been conducted by me, when I was teaching their cohorts during 2007–09.

2. Focus group discussions (FGDs) with 20 students and alumnae, 15 teachers, and 10 parents of Prerna alumnae were conducted, recorded, and transcribed. Teachers were selected based on the number of years they had taught at Prerna. Only teachers who had been at Prerna for five years or more were selected. No special criteria for selecting students or parents were used. The alumnae who were still in touch with Prerna were invited for the focus group sessions, and parents who were willing to participate were included.

3. A community survey: A survey of 10 percent of the parent community was conducted to understand their perceptions of the Prerna School and its impact on them and the community. Parents were selected based only on their willingness to participate and whether a daughter or daughters were enrolled in the school, but we made an effort to include those who had been with us for at least five years. The survey was conducted by two Prerna alumnae, one of whom was enrolled in a master's program in women's studies in Lucknow University. There were 80 respondents in the community survey: 58 respondents were women, 17 were men, three did not respond, and one form was filled out by both parents. Despite repeated attempts, the representation of fathers was inadequate, which leaves a gap in a much-needed male perspective of our program.

4. Data on socioeconomic status of girls' families were collected using a structured questionnaire administered on a stratified random sample of 10 percent of the student population. For boys' families, data were compiled from 80 percent of the students due to a relatively small population size; 20 percent couldn't be taken into account due to non-availability of students during survey days or provision of incomplete information.

5. School records and staff reports: The school principal, vice principal, and teachers provided a detailed description of the school, its daily schedule, curriculum and assessment methodology, and enrollment process. School records were studied for achievement scores, attendance data, enrollment numbers, and college placement information. The quantitative data include enrollment and dropout figures, completion and transition rates, along with student and teacher attendance averages for the last three years. These were derived from school records and used to evaluate the school's performance as compared with national and state averages.

6. Self-reflexive narrative reports derived from in-depth interviews and several informal conversations with the focal students have been used to understand how the school has impacted their lives. What life outcomes have come from their education? Have they been empowered by their education, and what, according to them, was the most empowering component of their education? This along with data that provide information regarding the current life status of 90 percent of the seven cohorts graduated by Prerna, 115 girls in total, in terms of their current educational

status, marital status, employment, and income levels, was obtained to evaluate life outcomes.

Ethnographic methods of participant observation were used, combined with review, transcription, and analysis of several hours of audio and video tapes of the interviews, FGDs, various classes, and events in the school, along with an analytical review of written texts produced by the students, including poems, essays, and scripts, to understand, discuss, and describe the pedagogical practices and the culture of the school. I have examined and described the empowerment curriculum, especially the critical pedagogy, including critical dialogues, critical literacy, and critical drama as it is practiced in the school, in greater detail, as it is the distinctive focus of the school program.

All the interviews, the FGDs, and the community survey were conducted in Hindi and translated into English, with minor edits for better readability, for the purpose of this book. Since English and Hindi have different syntax structures, a literal translation has not been possible, but the translation has tried to capture the meaning as closely as possible.

Appendix C

Historical Backdrop of Girls' Education

T he movement for girls' education is more than 200 years old, led globally by women's rights activists all over the world. These activists include Mary Wollstonecraft in London, Savitribai Phule, and Pandita Ramabai Saraswati in India, Raden Ajeng Kartini in Indonesia, and Charlotte Maxeke and Olive Schreiner in South Africa, among others.[1] The nineteenth century saw the opening of schools for girls and campaigning for girls' education as a way to further women's right to equality.

It was in the twentieth century, however, that the principles driving women's movements were translated into global declarations, including the Convention on the Elimination of All Forms of Discrimination against Women (1979),[2] the Convention on the Rights of the Child (1989),[3] the Jomtien Summit (1990),[4] the Beijing Declaration for the Education and Training of Women (1995),[5] and the Dakar Education for All (EFA) Platform for Action (2000).[6] Each of these declarations emphasized universalizing primary education and pledged to gradually work at achieving gender parity in education. Though the more recent treaties made references to secondary education and to the quality of learning, the focus has been primarily on equal access to primary education.

The focus on gender parity in educational access has begun to shift only in the last decade, both in India and abroad. While there is still discussion of

TABLE C-1. *Literacy Rates in Post-Independence India (Percent)*

	Rural			Urban			Combined		
Year	Female	Male	Total	Female	Male	Total	Female	Male	Total
1951	4.87	19.02	12.1	22.33	45.6	34.59	8.86	27.15	18.32
1961	10.1	34.3	22.5	40.5	66	54.4	15.35	40.4	28.31
1971	15.5	48.6	27.9	48.8	69.8	60.2	29.97	45.96	34.45
1981	21.7	49.6	36	56.3	76.7	67.2	29.76	56.38	43.57
1991	30.17	56.96	36	64.05	81.09	67.2	39.29	64.13	52.21
2001	46.7	71.4	59.4	73.2	86.7	80.3	53.67	75.26	64.83
2011	57.93	77.15	67.8	79.11	88.76	84.1	64.64	80.89	72.99

Source: Census of India 2011 (New Delhi: Government of India, 2011).

access, girls' completion of secondary education has become a new focal point, along with a strong push for raising the quality of girls' education and their learning outcomes.[7]

Educating India's Daughters

Among all the developing countries, India is recognized by some as having one of the most complex patriarchal systems, structured as it is by the multiple and diverse forces of religion, caste, region, language, class, and gender.[8] This has strong implications for the education of girls in India. Historically, women of all castes and classes, and particularly poor Dalit rural women, have been excluded from education. Table C-1 shows that though literacy rates for men and women both have risen considerably over the decades, there remains a glaring difference in the literacy rates of men and women in post-independence India, in both rural and urban regions. According to Census 2011, women are still less literate than men nationally (see table C-1), and rural women are behind urban women. More than 75 percent of India's Dalits live in rural areas,[9] and 62 percent of this population is illiterate, compared to the national illiteracy rate of 26 percent.[10]

The Women's Movement in India

India has the most burgeoning contemporary women's movement among all developing countries, which has contributed significantly to the progress made in girls' education in India.[11] Beginning in the early nineteenth century, alongside national movements for independence and social reform, the condition of women began to receive attention first from Hindu religious groups. Many of these initial actors were men—including Raja Ram Mohan Roy, Ishwar Chandra Vidyasagar, Keshav Chandra Sen, and Jyotiba Phule—who challenged the subordination of Hindu women and fought to give them some degree of dignity and status. Their efforts resulted in the ban of *sati*, or widow immolation, child marriage, and the custom of disfiguring widows, among other traditions.

While the outcomes of the social reform movement promoted girls' access to schooling, it was focused on upper caste Savarna girls and the movement did not carry the goal of liberating girls and women or of equipping them to play a larger role in social life. Nonetheless the efforts of social reformers and British missionaries did pave the way for the establishment of three main women's organizations and the vanguard of India's women's movement—though it was dominated by the interests of Savarna women.[12]

After independence, several committees and commissions were established to promote girls' education and to close the gender gap in schools, which still yawned large.[13] In 1974, the Committee on the Status of Women produced a landmark study called "Towards Equality," with Vina Mazumdar as the chief author.[14] This study gave a detailed and shocking description of women's status in India, on all indicators of human development.

The report set women's literacy in the age group 15 to 19 years at 36.9 percent and in the age group of 25 to 34 years at an alarming 18.8 percent. It also reported that a large number of girls were out of school, as many as one in three in the age group six to 11 years, and four in five in the age group 11 to 14 years, with dropout rates at 70 percent in primary school. Furthermore, the study highlighted that the educational system, especially its curriculum, had contributed to the perpetuation of traditional ideas of women's subordination.[15]

The 1980s were marked by several positive developments by policymakers and women's activists in the direction of increasing girls' enrollment in primary school.[16] The government made the inclusion of girls in education a priority of its sixth five-year plan, 1980–85, which recognized the alarming gender inequities in education. Motivated by the belief that the inclusion of girls will lead to gender equity, the government has worked in a multi-pronged way through the District Primary Education Program in 1994 and, later, the Sarva Shiksha Abhiyan (SSA) in 2000.[17] The SSA focused on enhancing access and retention of all children, with a special focus on girls, by ensuring a school at every kilometer of habitation, by giving free textbooks to all girls up to grade 8, by providing girls-only schools at the upper primary level and separate toilets for girls, by recruiting 50 percent women teachers, and by gender-sensitizing textbooks. In addition, two focused interventions especially for girls—the National Programme for Education of Girls at Elementary Level (NPEGEL) and the Kasturba Gandhi Balika Vidyalaya (KGBV)—were launched to reach girls from extremely marginalized social groups.[18]

In 2009, the historic Right to Education Act made free and compulsory education a constitutional right for all children, male and female, between the ages of six and 14.

While these policy achievements deserve much credit, implementation has fallen significantly short. Government education programs in India have suffered because of a lack of serious political will, insufficiently thought-out management structures, inadequate infrastructure, and poor training, monitoring, and support. The education girls receive does not focus sufficiently on the gendered conditions, constraints, and challenges faced by girls; nor does it make their empowerment and gender equality its central goal. The programs seem to be guided by an unstated belief that getting girls into schools is a sufficient condition for their empowerment.[19]

Consequently, though enrollment of girls grew steadily—from 24.8 percent at the primary level in 1951 to 93.3 percent in 2013–14—the problem of girls' education and women's marginalization and disempowerment remains deeply entrenched.[20] More girls have gained access to primary, secondary, and tertiary education, though their numbers at the last two levels are still far from satisfactory. Continuing high rates of child marriage, gender-based violence at home and on the streets, high rates of son preference resulting in large numbers of sex-selective abortions of female fetuses all show that more education has not transformed girls' lives.

Notes

Preface

1. Kathryn Moeller, "Proving 'The Girl Effect': Corporate Knowledge Production and Educational Intervention," *International Journal of Educational Development*, vol. 33 (2013), pp. 612–21.

2. Ibid., p. 614.

3. Gene B. Sperling, Rebecca Winthrop, and Christina Kwauk, *What Works in Girls' Education* (Brookings Institution, 2016), p. 96.

4. The interviews and FGDs were conducted by the author.

5. For more details of methodology, see appendix B.

Chapter One

1. *Dalit* is a self-chosen political name of castes in India that were historically deemed "untouchable," officially known as Scheduled Castes (SC). They are the poorest and one of the most oppressed and marginalized groups in India. For more information on the caste system in India, see appendix A.

2. To view a short video about Laxmi's life, go to www.youtube.com/watch?v=Xe8VD vVSzT8. All her quotes in this chapter come from a personal interview conducted with her on April 8, 2015.

3. A bachelor's degree in India is an undergraduate degree awarded on the completion of a course of study lasting three to five years, depending on the area of study.

4. Ministry of Women and Child Development, Government of India, *Study on Child Abuse: INDIA 2007* (New Delhi: Kriti, 2007), p. 114.

5. *Savarna* is used to refer to Hindus who are not Dalits. See appendix A.

6. The former number is from Population Research Institute, "Sex-Selective Abortion" (www.pop.org/content/sex-selective-abortion). The latter is from Rita Banerji, "Female Genocide in India: And the 50 Million Missing Campaign," *Intersections: Journal of Gender and Sexuality in Asia and The Pacific*, vol. 22 (2009).

7. International Institute for Population Sciences, *India National Family Health Survey (NFHS-3), 2005–06*, vol. 1 (Mumbai: International Institute for Population Sciences, 2007), p. xxxv.

8. Plan International, "Creating Safer Cities" (https://plan-international.org/because-i-am-a-girl/creating-safer-cities).

9. Quoted in Indrani Basu, "848 Indian Women Are Harassed, Raped, Killed Every Day," *Huffington Post,* December 16, 2014 (www.huffingtonpost.in/2014/12/16/crime-against-women-india_n_6330736.html).

10. United Nations Children's Fund, *Ending Child Marriage: Progress and Prospects* (New York: UNICEF, 2014), p. 1.

11. International Institute for Population Sciences, *India National Family Health Survey*, p. 163.

12. Plan International, *Because I am a Girl: The State of the World's Girls 2012—Learning for Life* (Oxford: New Internationalist Publications, 2012), p. 56.

13. Plan International, *Because I am a Girl*, p. 41.

14. See appendix A.

15. UNESCO, *Education for All: Global Monitoring Report 2012* (Paris: UNESCO, 2012), p. 122.

16. Ibid.

17. Gene B. Sperling, Rebecca Winthrop, and Christina Kwauk, *What Works in Girls' Education: Evidence for the World's Best Investment* (Brookings Institution Press, 2016), p. 65.

18. Ibid., p. 72.

19. Ibid., p. 7.

20. Plan International, *Because I am a Girl*, 2012, p. 110; UNICEF, *The State of the World's Children 2004* (New York: UNICEF, 2004).

21. Barbara Herz and Gene B. Sperling, *What Works in Girls' Education: Evidence and Policies from the Developing World* (New York: Council on Foreign Relations, 2004).

22. Millennium Development Goal 3: *Promote Gender Equality and Empower Women* (www.unmillenniumproject.org/goals).

23. Government of India, Ministry of Human Resource and Development, "National Policy on Education," 1986 (mhrd.gov.in/sites/upload_files/mhrd/files/upload_document/npe.pdf).

24. Anil Bordia Committee, *Right to Education Sarva Shiksha Abhiyan Final Report* (New Delhi: Ministry of Human Resource Development, Government of India), p. 17.

25. Ila Patel, "The Contemporary Women's Movement and Women's Education in India," *International Review of Education*, vol. 44, issue 2–3 (1998), p. 160.

26. Naila Kabeer, "Resources, Agency, Achievements: Reflections on the Measurement of Women's Empowerment," *Development and Change*, vol. 30, issue 3 (1999), pp. 435–64.

27. Payal P. Shah, "Partnerships and Appropriation: Translating Discourses of Access and Empowerment in Girls' Education in India," *International Journal of Educational Development*, vol. 49 (February 2016), pp. 11–21.

28. World Bank, *Empowerment and Poverty Reduction: A Sourcebook* (Washington: World Bank, 2002), p. 11.

29. Kabeer, "Resources, Agency, Achievements," p. 437.

30. Karen Oppenheim Mason, "Measuring Women's Empowerment: Learning from Cross-National Research," in *Measuring Empowerment: Cross-Disciplinary Perspectives*, edited by Deepa Narayan (Washington: World Bank, 2005), pp. 89–102.

31. Arjun Appadurai, "The Capacity to Aspire: Culture and Terms of Recognition," in *Cultural Politics in a Global Age: Uncertainty, Solidarity and Innovation*, edited by David Held and Henrietta L. Moore (England: Oneworld Publications, 2007), pp. 29–35.

32. Jo Rowlands, *Questioning Empowerment: Working with Women in Honduras* (Oxford: Oxfam, 1997), p. 12.

33. Yogendra B. Shakya and Katharine N. Rankin, "The Politics of Subversion in Development Practice: An Exploration of Microfinance in Nepal and Vietnam," *Journal of Development Studies*, vol. 44, no. 8 (September 2008), p. 1230.

34. Patel, "The Contemporary Women's Movement," p. 157.

35. Heidi A. Ross, Payal P. Shah, and Lei Wang, "Situating Empowerment for Millennial School Girls in Gujarat, India, and Shaanxi, China," *Feminist Formations*, vol. 23, issue 3 (Fall 2011), p. 26.

36. See CARE (www.care.org); Room to Read (www.roomtoread.org); Erin Murphy-Graham and Cynthia Lloyd, "Empowering Adolescent Girls in Developing Countries: The Potential Role of Education," *Policy Futures in Education*, vol. 14, no. 5 (2016), pp. 556–77.

37. Ross, Shah, and Wang, "Situating Empowerment for Millennial School Girls."

38. Erin Murphy-Graham, "Opening the Black Box: Women's Empowerment and Innovative Secondary Education in Honduras," *Gender and Education*, vol. 20.1 (2008), pp. 31–50; Nelly P. Stromquist and Gustavo Fischman, "Introduction–From Denouncing Gender Inequities to Undoing Gender in Education: Practices and Programmes Toward Change in the Social Relations of Gender," *International Review of Education*, vol. 55, no. 5 (October 28, 2009), pp. 463–82; Ross, Shah, and Wang, "Situating Empowerment for Millennial School Girls."

39. World Bank, *World Development Report 2012: Gender Equality and Development* (Washington: World Bank, 2011), p. 150.

40. Plan International, *Because I am a Girl*, 2012, p. 96.

41. United Nations Girls' Education Initiative, *Dakar Declaration on Accelerating Girls' Education and Gender Equality* (UNGEI, 2010). For a detailed global and Indian historical background, see appendix C.

Chapter Two

1. Children in Prerna call their teachers "auntie" or "aunty," a common term of reference for women, family friends, and relatives close to the speaker's mother's age.

2. She has visited her village once, accompanied by her friend Laxmi, in an attempt to find out the status of their land.

3. DiDi's is a sister nonprofit organization of Study Hall Educational Foundation (SHEF) engaged in catering and tailoring, which trains and employs mothers of Prerna students and alumnae.

4. At the time of writing, one U.S. dollar was equal to approximately 67 Indian rupees.

5. Community College Initiative Program, 2016–17.

Chapter Three

1. *Pitaji* means father in Hindi.

2. *di* is short for *didi*, meaning elder sister.

3. bell hooks, *Feminist Theory: From Margin to Center* (London: Pluto Press, 2000), p. 35.

4. Urvashi Sahni, "Building Circles of Mutuality: A Sociocultural Analysis of Literacy in a Rural Classroom in India," Ph.D. thesis, University of California, Berkeley, 1994.

5. Ibid.

Chapter Four

1. For more about SHEF, see box 4-1.

2. Terri Thompson and Charles Ungerleider, "Single Sex Schooling: Final Report" (Canadian Centre for Knowledge Mobilisation, 2004), p. 16.

3. The first figure is from Census of India 2011, "Population Enumeration Data (Final Population)," 2011 (www.censusindia.gov.in/2011census/population_enumeration.html), the second from Government of India Planning commission, *Press Note on Poverty Estimates 2011–12* (New Delhi: Government of India, 2013), p. 6.

4. Gender ratio is from Census of India 2011, "Population Enumeration Data (Final Population)," 2011 (www.censusindia.gov.in/2011census/population_enumeration.html), while the death rate is from Government of Uttar Pradesh, *Second Human Development Report of Uttar Pradesh* (Lucknow: Government of Uttar Pradesh, 2008), p. 55.

5. ASER Centre, *Annual Status of Education Report (Rural) 2014* (New Delhi: ASER Centre, 2014), p. 81.

6. International Institute for Population Sciences, *India National Family Health Survey (NFHS-3), 2005–06*, vol. 1 (Mumbai: International Institute for Population Sciences, 2007).

7. Urvashi Sahni, "From Learning Outcomes to Life Outcomes: What Can You Do and Who Can You Be? A Case Study in Girls' Education in India," Working Paper (Center for Universal Education at Brookings, November 2012), p. 11.

8. To know more about children's life at school, see Peter Earth, "Prerna Means Inspiration: Girls Refuse Forced Marriages to Gain an Education," June 14, 2010 (http://pierreterre.org/video/prerna-means-inspiration).

9. For more on castes and OBCs, see appendix A.

10. Anamika, the eldest of the six, joined completely unschooled at age 15 and left after finishing tenth grade at 22, when she married. Poorna, the next eldest, graduated from twelfth grade in 2013 and has completed her bachelor's. Durgesh, next in line, graduated in 2014 and is in the final year of her B.A. Navratri graduated in 2016 and is enrolling in a bachelor's program. The younger two, Panchkumari and Jyoti, are in the eleventh grade.

11. Gerda Lerner, *The Creation of Patriarchy* (Oxford University Press, 1986), p. 223.

12. Martha C. Nussbaum, *Women and Human Development: The Capabilities Approach* (Cambridge University Press, 2000).

13. Karen Oppenheim Mason, "Measuring Women's Empowerment: Learning from Cross-National Research," in *Measuring Empowerment: Cross-Disciplinary Perspectives*, edited by Deepa Narayan (Washington: World Bank, 2005), p. 90.

Chapter Five

1. See appendix A.

2. Urvashi Sahni, "Building Circles of Mutuality: A Sociocultural Analysis of Literacy in a Rural Classroom in India," Ph.D. thesis, University of California, Berkeley, 1994.

3. Nel Noddings, "Caring in Education," *The Encyclopedia of Informal Education*, vol. 935250-1 (2005), p. 2.

4. Ibid., p. 1.

5. Noddings, "Caring in Education," p. 3.

6. Ibid.

7. Ibid.

8. Richard Stanley Peters, *Ethics of Education* (London: Allen and Unwin, 1966).

9. Sahni, "Building Circles of Mutuality: A Sociocultural Analysis of Literacy in a Rural Classroom in India."

10. bell hooks, *Teaching to Transgress: Education as the Practice of Freedom* (New York: Routledge, 1994), p. 41.

11. Noddings, "Caring in Education," p. 6.

Chapter Six

1. For more on castes, see appendix A. These castes have historically been excluded from education, consequences of which continue through today. See Sarva Shiksha Abhiyan, "Coverage of Special Focus Groups," 2009 (http://ssa.nic.in/ssa-framework/coverage-of-special-focus-groups).

2. Plan International, *Because I am a Girl: The State of the World's Girls 2009—Girls in the Global Economy* (Plan International, 2009).

3. The PROBE Team, *Public Report on Basic Education in India* (Oxford University Press, 1999), p. 8. This comprehensive evaluation is based on an extensive survey of 200 villages in five states: Bihar, Madhya Pradesh, Uttar Pradesh, Himachal Pradesh, and Rajasthan.

4. The PROBE Team, *Public Report on Basic Education in India*, p. 29.

5. Sarva Shiksha Abhiyan, *Study of Students' Attendance in Primary and Upper Primary Schools* (New Delhi: Government of India, 2006).

6. Vimala Ramachandran, "Fostering Opportunities to Learn at an Accelerated Pace: Why Do Girls Benefit Enormously?" Working Paper (New Delhi: UNICEF, 2004), p. 5.

7. Recently 15 of our senior students and one teacher have been selected as power angels by this helpline. Power angels are trained to be community advocates, expected to alert the police about cases of gender-based violence in their communities in a timely manner. Parents are also encouraged to support each other in case of violations in the community.

8. The Prohibition of Child Marriage Act of 2006 came into effect to address and fix the shortcomings of the Child Marriage Restraint Act of 1929. Quoted in Neeta Lal, "India, Home to One in Three Child Brides," *The Citizen*, August 21, 2014 (www.thecitizen.in/index.php/OldNewsPage/?Id=209).

9. Azad India Foundation, "Child Marriage in India—Latest Data" (www.azadindia.org/social-issues/child-marriage-in-india.html).

10. *DiDi's—Empower, Encourage and Equip Women to Build Sustainable Livelihoods* (www.youtube.com/watch?v=T0RRkn71BY4) is a short video giving an account of DiDi's work, growth, and impact on the community over the years (http://mydidis.org).

11. Goldman Sachs launched "10,000 Women" in 2008 to provide women entrepreneurs around the world with business management education, mentoring and networking, and access to capital. To date, the initiative has reached more than 10,000 women from across 56 countries.

12. The PROBE Team, *Public Report on Basic Education in India*, p. 88.

13. Ibid., p. 27.

14. Lev S. Vygotsky, *Mind in Society: The Development of Higher Psychological Processes* (Harvard University Press, 1978); Barbara Rogoff, *Apprenticeship in Thinking: Cognitive Development in Social Context* (Oxford University Press, 1990).

15. Urvashi Sahni, "Building Circles of Mutuality: A Sociocultural Analysis of Literacy in a Rural Classroom in India," Ph.D. thesis, University of California, Berkeley, 1994, p. 35.

16. CHILDLINE India Foundation, "Girl Child Protection and Rights" (www.childlineindia.org.in/girl-child-rights-protection.htm).

17. Plan International, *Because I am a Girl: The State of the World's Girls 2012—Learning for Life* (Oxford: New Internationalist Publications, 2012).

18. The PROBE Team, *Public Report on Basic Education in India*, p. 28.

19. Glynda A. Hull, Amy Stornaiuolo, and Urvashi Sahni, "Cultural Citizenship and Cosmopolitan Practice: Global Youth Communicate Online," *English Education* 42, no. 4 (July 2010), pp. 331–67.

Chapter 7

1. Gerda Lerner, *The Creation of Patriarchy* (Oxford University Press, 1986), p. 11.

2. bell hooks, *Teaching to Transgress: Education as the Practice of Freedom* (New York: Routledge, 1994), pp. 62, 70.

3. Paulo Freire, *Pedagogy of the Oppressed: 30th Anniversary Edition* (New York: Continuum International Publishing Group, 2005).

4. Lerner, *The Creation of Patriarchy*, p. 6.

5. Nivedita Menon, *Seeing Like a Feminist* (London: Penguin, 2012), p. 43.

6. Ibid., p. 31.

7. Critical Dialogue—Striving for an Independent Life, Prerna Girls School, Lucknow, 2007 (www.youtube.com/watch?v=_QhOkOhrZKk).

8. In India, sometimes girls are married officially quite young and sent to their husband's home only after reaching puberty or older. The official sending off is called *gauna*.

9. Lerner, *The Creation of Patriarchy*, p. 220.

10. Critical Dialogue—Problems Faced by Women after Marriage: Part 2, Prerna Girls School, Lucknow, 2007 (www.youtube.com/watch?v=PFlBUC1wBLc).

11. Urvashi Sahni, "Building Circles of Mutuality: A Sociocultural Analysis of Literacy in a Rural Classroom in India," Ph.D. thesis, University of California, Berkeley, 1994.

12. Ibid.

13. She clearly demonstrated this understanding in action when, at the age of 23, she exercised her choice in a very brave, independent decision. In opposition to her parental and societal upbringing, she eloped with a young man from a different caste. She had tried to broach the matter with her parents and gain their consent, respecting her relationship with them. They, however, refused even to discuss the matter, so unacceptable was he to them because of his caste affiliation. They had been ready to cast her out of the family, but since have been persuaded by Prerna to look at the matter from her point of view.

14. Critical Dialogue—Deconstruction and Reconstruction of Masculinity and Femininity, Prerna Girls School, Lucknow, 2007 (www.youtube.com/watch?v=kMzOoaeOsWM).

15. hooks, *Teaching to Transgress*, p. 47.

16. bell hooks, *Feminism Is for Everybody: Passionate Politics* (London: Pluto Press, 2000), p. 27.

17. hooks, *Teaching to Transgress*, p. 41.

18. Martin Buber, *I and Thou* (New York: Scribner, 1958).

19. Critical Dialogue—Domestic Violence and How to Counter It, Prerna Girls School, Lucknow, 2010 (www.youtube.com/watch?v=kGkZYBd0fb0&index=18&list=PLgTaUODN 5z97578CGAp3vcJaY4Z4OgI-a).

20. hooks, *Teaching to Transgress*, p. 12.

Chapter 8

1. This project is also described in Urvashi Sahni, "KEYNOTE: Drama in Education: Finding Self, Finding 'Home,'" *Caribbean Quarterly*, vol. 53, issue 1–2 (2007).

2. David Davis, *Edward Bond and the Dramatic Child: Edward Bond's Plays for Young People* (Stoke-on-Trent: Trentham Books, 2005), p. 142.

3. Ibid., p. 128.

4. Ibid., p. 135.

5. Kathleen Weiler, "Freire and a Feminist Pedagogy of Difference," in *Politics of Liberation: Paths from Freire*, edited by Peter L. McLaren and Colin Lankshear (London: Routledge, 1994), p. 27.

6. Audre Lorde, *Sister Outsider: Essays and Speeches by Audre Lorde* (New York: Crossing Press, 1984), p. 58.

7. David Best, *The Rationality of Feeling: Learning from the Arts* (New York: Routledge, 1992).

8. Davis, *Edward Bond and the Dramatic Child*, p. 144.

9. Paulo Freire, *The Politics of Education: Culture, Power, and Liberation* (Westport, Conn.: Greenwood Publishing Group, 1985).

10. Davis, *Edward Bond and the Dramatic Child*; Freire, *The Politics of Education*.

11. The dialogues related to the play *Rani of Jhansi* are from my memory, as the rehearsals were not recorded.

12. Elizabeth Yeoman, "'How Does It Get into My Imagination?': Elementary School Children's Intertextual Knowledge and Gendered Storylines," *Gender and Education*, vol. 11, issue 4 (1999), p. 428.

13. Lilijana Burcar, "Why Feminist Critical Literacy Matters: The Reorganisation of Capitalist Economies and the Significance of Socially Engaged Literature for Young Adults," *Gender Studies*, vol. 11, issue 1 (2012), p. 206.

14. Rabindranath Tagore, *A Wife's Letter* (www.parabaas.com/translation/database/translations/stories/gStreerPatra1.html).

15. All italicized portions are quotations from *A Wife's Letter*; "I" refers to Mrinal herself.

16. Kathleen Gallagher, *Why Theatre Matters: Urban Youth, Engagement, and a Pedagogy of the Real* (University of Toronto Press, 2014), p. 235.

17. Ibid., p. 220.

18. Lorde, *Sister Outsider*, p. 58.

19. Paulo Freire, *Pedagogy of the Oppressed: 30th Anniversary Edition* (New York: Continuum International Publishing Group, 2005), p. 99.

20. Critical Dialogue—Patriarchy, Prerna Girls School, Lucknow, 2012 (www.youtube.com/watch?v=HrmJg3eyQIA).

21. Gallagher, *Why Theatre Matters*, p. 79.

22. Ibid., p. 78.

23. M. M. Bakhtin, *The Dialogic Imagination: Four Essays* (University of Texas Press, 1981), p. 342.

24. Gallagher, *Why Theatre Matters*, p. 212.

25. The play is in two acts. The first act shows Khushboo's (played by Sunita) struggle for education. The second act is the enactment of poems written by Sunita, Laxmi, Soni, and Kunti. To view the final performance of *Darwaze* (*Doors*), go to www.youtube.com/watch?v=Q5I3hM4_Cvo.

26. Khushboo's case had become public before the staging of this play because of the police action and NGO intervention. Also, one of our goals is to shame violations of girls' rights publicly. In this case there was no response from her parents about the play. All her six sisters continue to be in Prerna. One has just completed grade 12.

27. Charles Taylor, "The Politics of Recognition," in *New Contexts of Canadian Criticism*, edited by Ajay Heble, Donna Palmateer Pennee, and J. R. Struthers (Peterborough, Ont.: Broadview Press, 1997), pp. 98–131.

28. Arjun Appadurai, "The Capacity to Aspire: Culture and the Terms of Recognition," in *Culture and Public Action: A Cross-Disciplinary Dialogue on Development Policy*, edited by Vijayendra Rao and Michael Walton (Stanford University Press, 2004).

29. Quoted in Express News Service, "Only 3.3 Percent Land Owned by Women: Study," *New Indian Express*, August 6, 2015 (www.newindianexpress.com/states/odisha/Only-3.3 -Percent-Land-Owned-by-Women-Study/2015/08/06/article2960007.ece).

30. Pradeep Panda and Bina Agarwal, "Marital Violence, Human Development and Women's Property Status in India," *World Development*, vol. 33, no. 5 (May 2005), p. 836.

Chapter 9

1. Arjun Appadurai, "The Capacity to Aspire: Culture and the Terms of Recognition," in *Culture and Public Action: A Cross-Disciplinary Dialogue on Development Policy*, edited by Vijayendra Rao and Michael Walton (Stanford University Press, 2004), p. 62.

2. Ibid., p. 68.

3. Ibid., pp. 69, 70, 82.

4. Charles Taylor, "The Politics of Recognition," in *New Contexts of Canadian Criticism*, edited by Ajay Heble, Donna Palmateer Pennee, and J. R. Struthers (Peterborough, Ont.: Broadview Press, 1997), p. 98.

5. Ibid.

6. Charles Taylor, *Philosophical Papers Volume 1: Human Agency and Language* (Cambridge University Press, 1985), p. 257.

7. Ibid., p. 102.

8. V. Geetha, "Periyar, Women and an Ethic of Citizenship," *Economic and Political Weekly*, vol. 33, no. 17 (April 1998), p. 14.

9. Rani Laxmi Bai was a legendary woman warrior and one of the leading figures of the Indian Rebellion of 1857.

10. Priya Nanda and others, *Study on Masculinity, Intimate Partner Violence and Son Preference in India* (New Delhi: International Center for Research on Women, 2014).

11. Ritu Menon, ed., *Making a Difference: Memoirs from the Women's Movement in India* (Delhi: Women Unlimited, 2011), p. xii.

12. As mentioned earlier, Aarti belongs to a Savarna caste.

13. Appadurai, "The Capacity to Aspire," p. 64.

14. A Dalit subcaste.

15. A short video capturing the girls organizing and engaging critically with their communities as part of Veerangana can be seen at www.youtube.com/watch?v=OsaNraLt3tw. The video features Laxmi's and Sunita's cohort conducting dialogues with women, performing street plays, and running the signature campaign against child marriage.

16. Suicide is the leading cause of death among young women in India, with self-harm replacing maternal disorders as the leading cause of death among women between the ages of 15 and 49. Quoted in Liat Clark, "Suicide Is Number One Cause of Death among Young Women in India," *Wired*, March 27, 2013 (www.wired.co.uk/article/suicide-women-india).

17. Appadurai, "The Capacity to Aspire," p. 61.

18. The discussion with Nandini's mother can be found in *Prerna Diaries* (www.youtube .com/watch?v=ArTeU8H2sHA), a participatory documentary focusing on issues in girls' lives, critical dialogues in school, and the interventions done by the girls in their community in the form of dialogues and interviews.

19. Guari Gaon is the local low-income neighborhood where the campaign was conducted. Many of the Prerna girls live here.

20. Ira Shor and Paulo Freire, *A Pedagogy for Liberation: Dialogues on Transforming Education* (Westport, Conn.: Greenwood Publishing Group, 1987), p. 109.

21. Geetha, "Periyar, Women and an Ethic of Citizenship."

Chapter 10

1. First through twelfth grade, three-year average, 2012–15; state and national figures from ASER Centre, *Annual Status of Education Report (Rural) 2014* (New Delhi: ASER Centre, 2014), pp. 265, 90.

2. Prerna three-year average, 2012–15; national and state figures from ASER Centre, *Annual Status of Education Report (Rural) 2014*, pp. 265, 90.

3. Nazmul Chaudhury and others, "Missing in Action: Teacher and Health Worker Absence in Developing Countries," *Journal of Economic Perspectives*, vol. 20, issue 1 (2006), p. 2.

4. Ministry of Human Resource Development, *Educational Statistics at a Glance* (New Delhi: Government of India, 2014), p. 8.

5. Prerna students take the same national examination.

6. The school average of pass percentages for 2015–16 for all classes, calculating pass at 40 percent.

7. The PROBE Team, *Public Report on Basic Education in India* (Oxford University Press, 1999), p. 33.

8. Urvashi Sahni, "Building Circles of Mutuality: A Sociocultural Analysis of Literacy in a Rural Classroom in India," Ph.D. dissertation, University of California, Berkeley, 1994.

9. Ira Shor and Paulo Freire, *A Pedagogy for Liberation: Dialogues on Transforming Education* (Westport, Conn.: Greenwood Publishing Group, 1987).

10. The Indira Gandhi National Open University (IGNOU) is a distance learning national university, established in 1985. IGNOU is the largest university in the world, with over 4 million students.

11. Karen Oppenheim Mason, "Measuring Women's Empowerment: Learning from Cross-National Research," in *Measuring Empowerment: Cross-Disciplinary Perspectives*, edited by Deepa Narayan (Washington: World Bank, 2005), pp. 89–102; Naila Kabeer, "Resources, Agency, Achievements: Reflections on the Measurement of Women's Empowerment," *Development and Change*, vol. 30, no. 3 (1999), pp. 435–64.

12. Yogendra B. Shakya and Katharine N. Rankin, "The Politics of Subversion in Development Practice: An Exploration of Microfinance in Nepal and Vietnam," *Journal of Development Studies*, vol. 44, issue 8 (September 2008), p. 1230.

13. CARE USA, *Promoting Leaders, Empowering Youth (ITSPLEY): Final Evaluation Report for CARE USA* (Saint Paul, Minn.: Miske Witt and Associates, USAID, and CARE, 2011), p. 8.

14. The Mahila Samakhya Program (Education for Women's Equality), Tuseme (Let Us Speak Out) Empowerment Program and the Grameen Bank of Bangladesh, famous for ushering in a new era of women's empowerment through micro-credit programs.

15. CARE USA, *Promoting Leaders, Empowering Youth (ITSPLEY)*, p. 11.

16. The Tuseme Project began in Tanzania as part of FAWE (Forum for African Women Educationalists), based in Kenya.

17. Gita Sen, "Women's Empowerment and Human Rights: The Challenge to Policy," in *Population, The Complex Reality: A Report of the Population Summit of the World's Scientific Academies*, edited by Francis Graham-Smith (Golden, Colo.: Fulcrum, 1994); Naila Kabeer, "Women, Wages and Intra-Household Power Relations in Urban Bangladesh," *Development and Change*, vol. 28, issue 2 (1997), pp. 261–302.

Chapter 11

1. Gene Sperling, Rebecca Winthrop, and Christina Kwauk, *What Works in Girls' Education* (Brookings Institution Press, 2015), p. 8.

2. Jenny Perlman Robinson, Rebecca Winthrop, and Eileen McGivney, *Millions Learning: Scaling up Quality Education in Developing Countries* (Center for Universal Education at Brookings, 2016), p. 35.

3. Sperling, Winthrop, and Kwauk, *What Works in Girls' Education*.

4. Sarva Shiksha Abhiyan, *National Report of KGBV Evaluation 2007* (New Delhi: Government of India, 2007), p. 16.

5. For more details of the scaling process and impact of this program, see START Up!, "Classrooms of Empowerment, The Prerna-SHEF Intervention in KGBVs," a third-party process evaluation report, 2013–14. START Up! is a company based out of Delhi that offers incubation, impact acceleration, and management consulting services to social ventures.

6. In six months ending June 2016, we made over 4600 calls to teachers and head teachers of KGBVs and received over 1500 phone calls. The impact evaluation showed that our attempt did bear fruit.

7. We have included elements of community mobilization in our trainings in the current phase of our scale-up program.

8. Personal communication from Swati Tripathi, Program Manager, Aarohini.

9. *A Little Goes A Long Way* (www.youtube.com/watch?v-gxznKfCaeIY) is a short video about the impact of our KGBV scholarship program featuring Poonam and her community.

10. START Up!, "Classrooms of Empowerment, The Prerna-SHEF Intervention in KGBVs," 2013–14.

11. Ibid.

12. Ministry of Human Resource Development, Government of India, *National Report: Second National Evaluation of KGBV Programme of GOI November-December 2013* (New Delhi: Government of India, 2013), p. 28. The author was also part of the evaluation and the core group that wrote the report.

Chapter 12

1. Glynda A. Hull, M. Jury, and Urvashi Sahni, "'Son Enough': Developing Girls' Agency through Feminist Media Practice," in *Becoming Political in the Digital Age*, edited by Ben Kirschner and Ellen Middaugh (Charlotte, N.C.: Information Age Publishing, 2015).

2. View the video of Prerna girls performing *Izzat* (*Honor*) at Indra Congress, Plymouth University, UK, 2015 (www.youtube.com/watch?v=wgNZHDFXPpg). The video starts with the screening of excerpts from a few critical dialogues on issues relevant to the play; this is followed by the actual performance.

3. Anugula N. Reddy and Shantha Sinha, *School Dropouts or Pushouts?: Overcoming Barriers for the Right to Education* (Sussex, UK: Consortium for Research on Educational Access, Transitions and Equity, 2010), p. 19.

4. Nicole Blum and Rashmi Diwan, *Small, Multigrade Schools and Increasing Access to Primary Education in India: National Context and NGO Initiatives* (Sussex, UK: Consortium for Research on Educational Access, Transitions and Equity, 2007); Ernesto Schiefelbein, *In Search of the School of the XXI Century: Is the Colombian Escuela Nueva the Right Pathfinder?* (Santiago, Chile: UNESCO, 1991); Kameshwari Jandhyala, "Empowering Education: The Mahila Samakhya Experience," Background Paper for *Education for all Global Monitoring Report* 4 (UNESCO, 2003).

5. See details of how the school is funded in chapter 6.

6. Accountability Initiative, *PAISA National Report 2014* (New Delhi: Centre for Policy Research, 2015).

7. Gene B. Sperling, Rebecca Winthrop, and Christina Kwauk, *What Works in Girls' Education: Evidence for the World's Best Investment* (Brookings Institution Press, 2016), p. 252.

8. Ila Patel, "The Contemporary Women's Movement and Women's Education in India," *International Review of Education*, vol. 44, no. 2–3 (1998).

9. Erin Murphy-Graham, "Opening the Black Box: Women's Empowerment and Innovative Secondary Education in Honduras," *Gender and Education*, vol. 20, no. 1 (January 2008), pp. 31–50. The program is used in rural areas of Brazil, Colombia, Ecuador, Honduras, and Nicaragua.

10. Forum for African Women Educationalists, "Tuseme Youth Empowerment," September 2016 (www.fawe.org/activities/interventions/tuseme/index.php).

11. Nafissatou J. Diop and others, *The TOSTAN Program Evaluation of a Community Based Education Program in Senegal* (Washington: Tostan, 2004).

12. International Center for Research on Women, "Gender Equity Movement in Schools," 2016 (www.icrw.org/research-programs/gender-equity-movement-in-schools-gems).

13. Urvashi Sahni, "From Learning Outcomes to Life Outcomes: What Can You Do and Who Can You Be? A Case Study in Girls' Education in India," Working Paper (Center for Universal Education at Brookings, November 2012), p. 39.

14. Rajib Acharya and others, *Broadening Girls' Horizons: Effects of a Life Skills Education Programme in Rural Uttar Pradesh* (New Delhi: Population Council, 2009).

15. See Sperling, Winthrop, and Kwauk, *What Works in Girls' Education*, for descriptions of more programs with the goal of empowering girls.

16. Nelly P. Stromquist, "Romancing the State: Gender and Power in Education," *Comparative Education Review*, vol. 39, issue 4 (November 1995), p. 445.

17. Patel, "The Contemporary Women's Movement," p. 171.

18. ASER Centre, *Annual Status of Education Report (Rural) 2014* (New Delhi: ASER Centre, 2014); UNESCO, *The Global Learning Crisis* (Paris: UNESCO, 2013); UNESCO, *Education for All: Global Monitoring Report* (Paris: UNESCO, 2012).

19. Sperling, Winthrop, and Kwauk, *What Works in Girls' Education*, p. 160.

20. Brookings Institution, "Learning Metrics Task Force 2.0," September 2013 (www.brookings.edu/learning-metrics-task-force-2-0).

21. Sperling, Winthrop, and Kwauk, *What Works in Girls' Education*, p. 253.

22. Ira Shor and Paulo Freire, *A Pedagogy for Liberation: Dialogues on Transforming Education* (Westport, Conn.: Greenwood Publishing Group, 1987), p. 38.

23. Personal communication, Nelly P. Stromquist, 2012.

24. Patel, "The Contemporary Women's Movement," p. 169.

25. Plan International, *Because I am a Girl: The State of the World's Girls 2015—The Unfinished Business of Girls' Rights* (Oxford, UK: New Internationalist Publications, 2015).

Epilogue

1. The boys are still trying to get used to calling teachers "aunty," as they are more used to the traditional formality and distance between teacher and student, men and women.

Appendix A

1. This note has been adapted from National Council of Educational Research and Training (NCERT), *Indian Society: Textbook in Sociology for Class XII* (New Delhi: NCERT, 2014).

2. Ramachandra Guha, *India After Gandhi: The History of the World's Largest Democracy* (New Delhi: Pan Macmillan, 2011).

3. Census of India, "Population Enumeration Data (Final Population)," 2011 (www .censusindian.gov.in/2011census/population_enumeration.html). Also see Navsarjan Trust, "Who are Dalits?," 2009 (http://navsarjantrust.org/who-are-dalits/).

4. Ibid.

5. Ibid.

6. A. K. Vakil, *Reservation Policy and Scheduled Castes in India* (New Delhi: APH Publishing, 1985); Prakash Narayan Pimpley, *Profile of Scheduled Castes Students, The Case of Punjab.* Vol. 2. Dept. of Sociology, Panjab University, 1980.

Appendix C

1. Plan International, *Because I am a Girl*, 2012, p. 18.

2. UN Women, "Convention on the Elimination of All Forms of Discrimination against Women," 1979 (www.un.org/womenwatch/daw/cedaw).

3. UNICEF, "Convention on the Rights of the Child," 1989 (www.unicef.org/crc/index _30160.html).

4. UNESCO, "World Conference on EFA, Jomtien, 1990," 1990 (www.unesco.org/new /en/education/themes/leading-the-international-agenda/education-for-all/the-efa-movement /jomtien-1990).

5. UN Women, *Beijing Declaration and Platform for Action* (New York: United Nations, 1995).

6. UNESCO, *The Dakar Framework for Action* (Paris: UNESCO, 2000).

7. Center for Universal Education at Brookings, *A Global Compact on Learning* (Washington: Brookings Institution, 2011), p. 2.

8. Ila Patel, "The Contemporary Women's Movement and Women's Education in India," *International Review of Education*, vol. 44, issue 2–3 (1998), p. 156.

9. International Dalit Solidarity Network, "India: Official Dalit Population Exceeds 200 Million," 2013 (http://idsn.org/india-official-dalit-population-exceeds-200-million).

10. Navsarjan Trust, "Who are Dalits?," 2009 (http://navsarjantrust.org/who-are-dalits/).

11. Patel, "The Contemporary Women's Movement," p. 156.

12. Nandita Gandhi and Nandita Shah, *The Issues at Stake: Theory and Practice in the Contemporary Women's Movement in India* (Delhi: Kali for Women, 1992); Maitrayee Chaudhuri, editor, *Feminism in India* (London: Zed Books, 2005).

13. Balaji Pandey, "Post-Independence Educational Development among Women in India," Centre for Women's Development Studies, University of Hyderabad, March 1987.

14. Vina Mazumdar and Lotika Sarkar, *Towards Equality: Report of the Committee on the Status of Women in India* (New Delhi: Government of India, Ministry of Education & Social Welfare, 1974).

15. Patel, "The Contemporary Women's Movement," p. 161.

16. Government of India, Ministry of Human Resource Development, *Selected Educational Statistics 2004–05* (New Delhi: Government of India, Ministry of Human Resource Development, 2004), p. xiii.

17. Sarva Shiksha Abhiyan (SSA) is Government of India's flagship program for achievement of universalization of elementary education in a time-bound manner, as mandated by the 86th Amendment to the Constitution of India, making free and compulsory education to the children of six to 14 years age group a fundamental right.

18. The *Kasturba Gandhi Balika Vidyalaya* (KGBV) scheme of residential upper primary schools for girls was launched in 2004 to reach out to girls from extremely marginalized social groups. The goal is to provide access to girls living in remote areas and to free them from domestic labor so they may wholeheartedly devote themselves to their education. The KGBV

program specifically targets adolescent girls who are unable to go to regular schools, out-of-school girls in the 10+age group who are unable to complete primary school, and younger girls of migratory populations in difficult areas of scattered habitations. There are now over 3500 KGBVs in the country providing access to nearly 350,000 girls.

19. Government of India, *Revised Guidelines for Implementation of the "National Programme for Education of Girls at Elementary Level (NPEGEL)" as a Component of the Scheme of Sarva Shiksha Abhiyan (SSA)* (New Delhi: Government of India, no date).

20. Government of India, *Selected Educational Statistics 2004–05*, p. xiii.

Index